LUXURY
HOME DESIGNS
6th Edition

A collection of 300 of our most luxurious residential designs, culled from the portfolios of award-winning architects and designers across the country.

Cover Plan 60136 p.4

Photography Courtesy of Frank Betz Associates, Inc.

the Garlinghouse company

Luxury Home Designs, 6th Edition

James D. McNair III, *CEO & Publisher*
Steve Culpepper, *Editorial Director*
Christopher Berrien, *Art Director*
Debra Novitch, *Art Production Manager*
Debbie Cochran, *Managing Editor*
Gia C. Manalio, *Associate Editor*
Andrew Russell and Melani Gonzalez, *Production Artists*

Covers and 4/C interior layouts designed by Debra Novitch.

Submit all Canadian plan orders
to the following address:
Garlinghouse Company, 102 Ellis Street, Penticton, BC V2A 4L5

Library of Congress: 98-75667
ISBN: 1-893536-06-8

Photography Courtesy of Ahmann Design, Inc.

Cover Plan 97315 p.22

Table of Contents

Space for Every Purpose

Photography Courtesy of
Frank Betz Associates, Inc.

ABOVE: Elegant and impressive, this home provides all the necessary elements that give it the name "The Hermitage": luxurious space to retreat from the busy world.

OPPOSITE: From the front door, the foyer and entry hall look straight through the house to the backyard and pool. To the right is the staircase and to the left is the dining room.

Named after Andrew Jackson's famous Nashville home, this modern-day Hermitage lives up to its namesake. As a private retreat from the busy world, "The Hermitage" has few peers.

The design is well-zoned with clearly defined public and private spaces. The dramatic foyer sets the tone for this magnificent home with it's balconied overlook and sweeping views.

From that entry point, the road leads many ways: to the master suite; to the upstairs bedrooms and bonus room; to the dining room, home office, breakfast area; or to the two-story library. You can even go straight, right out through French doors onto one of the home's three covered porches — this one overlooks the pool.

This dark wood-paneled library offers the promise of perfect relaxation. The two-story room includes a central fireplace flanked by bookshelves and a shelf-lined balcony set off by a wrought-iron railing.

design 60136

Price Code	L
Total Finished	4,418 sq. ft.
First Finished	3,197 sq. ft.
Second Finished	1,221 sq. ft.
Bonus Unfinished	656 sq. ft.
Basement Unfinished	3,197 sq. ft.
Garage Unfinished	537 sq. ft.
Dimensions	76'x73'10"
Foundation	Basement
	Crawlspace
Bedrooms	4
Full Baths	3
Half Baths	1
First Ceiling	10'4"
Second Ceiling	9'
Max Ridge Height	38'4"
Roof Framing	Stick
Exterior Walls	2x4

SECOND FLOOR

Bedroom 3
13⁰ x 11⁸

Covered Porch

W.i.c.

LINEN

FRENCH DOOR

RADIUS WINDOW

FRENCH DOOR

Bath

Bedroom 4
13³ x 13⁰

Foyer Below

OVERLOOK

LINEN

Bonus Room
17⁹ x 40⁰

Upper W.i.c.

SHIP'S LADDER

W.i.c.

LINEN

Bath

OVERLOOK

STAIRS DN

STAIRS DN

Bedroom 2
13⁰ x 12⁰

Foyer Below

SHELVES

Library Below

OVERLOOK

SHELVES

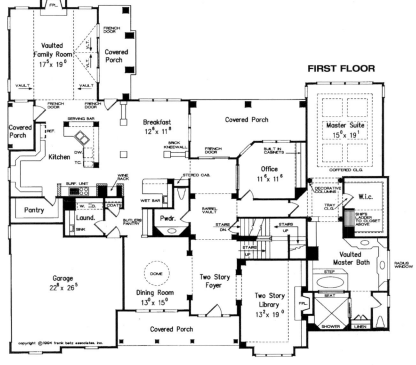

FIRST FLOOR

FPL.

Vaulted Family Room
17⁵ x 19⁰

FRENCH DOOR

Covered Porch

VLT.

VAULT

VAULT

FRENCH DOOR

FRENCH DOOR

Breakfast
12⁸ x 11⁸

Covered Porch

Master Suite
15⁰ x 19¹

COFFERED CLG.

Covered Porch

PREF.

SERVING BAR

Kitchen

DW.

T.C.

BRICK KNEEWALL

FRENCH DOOR

BUILT IN CABINETS

Office
11⁶ x 11⁶

DECORATIVE COLUMNS

W.i.c.

TRAY CLG.

WINE RACK

STEREO CAB.

SHIP'S LADDER TO CLOSET ABOVE

SURF. UNIT

Pantry

W. D.

COATS

WET BAR

BARREL VAULT.

STAIRS DN.

STAIRS UP

Laund.

SINK

BUTLER'S PANTRY

Pwdr.

STAIRS UP

Vaulted Master Bath

RADIUS WINDOW

Garage
22⁸ x 26⁵

DOME

Dining Room
13⁰ x 15⁰

Two Story Foyer

Two Story Library
13² x 19⁰

STEP

SEAT

FPL.

SHOWER

LINEN

Covered Porch

copyright ©1994 frank betz associates, inc.

Country Opulence

Photography Courtesy of
Studer Residential Design, Inc.

Curb appeal is a term that gets tossed around a great deal. However, what curb appeal actually boils down to is this: good design. And from the very curb in front of this grand home, the appeal is obviously the result of first-rate design work and careful attention to all the details. Let's start our brief tour at the entrance.

A striking double stair curves up each side of the porch to meet at the delicately colonnaded entryway. Above it, a classic standing-seam copper Mansard roof shelters the porch for visitors. Similar standing-seam copper roofs shield the two front bays, each opened to the outside through a bank of tall windows topped off by transom lites.

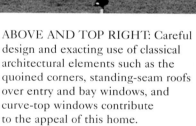

ABOVE AND TOP RIGHT: Careful design and exacting use of classical architectural elements such as the quoined corners, standing-seam roofs over entry and bay windows, and curve-top windows contribute to the appeal of this home.

CENTER RIGHT: Inside the spacious foyer, light streams in through the leaded-glass doorway with arch-top transom window. Visible off the foyer is the formal dining room.

BOTTOM RIGHT: A large gourmet kitchen with substantial island workspace shares its space with a breakfast area and a hearth room. Lots of built-ins make the kitchen suitable for even the most demanding of cooks.

LEFT: Curving off behind the large soaking tub is a secluded private shower (not shown) surrounded by marble tiles. In the distance is the dressing room and past that, one of the entries to the walk-in closet.

BELOW: A private fireplace, tall ceiling, and deep crown molding make the spacious master bedroom seem even more elegant. Through the door next to the mantle is the master bath.

RIGHT: Luxury and comfort are the watchwords in this private home library, here given over to a desk and personal collections of objets d'art. Natural light streams in through the deep bay window.

Price Code	L
Total Finished	4,589 sq. ft.
First Finished	3,392 sq. ft.
Second Finished	1,197 sq. ft.
Basement Unfinished	3,392 sq. ft.
Dimensions	87'x82'
Foundation	Basement
Bedrooms	4
Full Baths	3
Half Baths	2
Max Ridge Height	37'6"
Roof Framing	Truss
Exterior Walls	2x4, 2x6

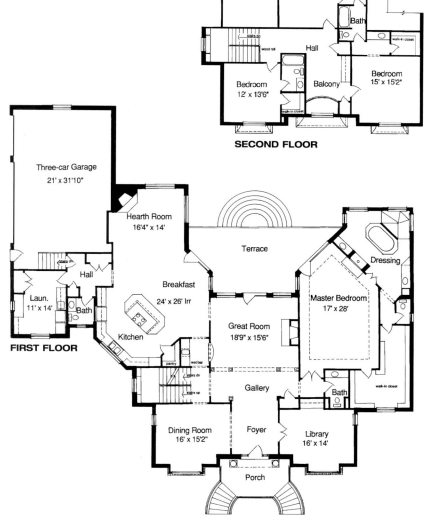

Every Room a View

Photography Courtesy of
Sater Design Collection

There's a problem with this home. And the problem is, the house looks just as good as the view. So which way do you look? In or out?

Well, we should all have such problems. This home was crafted carefully and exactingly to allow views from just about any room in the home, which, in turn, creates an extraordinary relationship between the home its, immediate site, and the greater world around it.

ABOVE: Great lines define this home, with a facade that centers on the inviting entry portico. This entry leads not into the house proper but through the courtyard, within the colonnade or lanai, to the real entrance of the home.

ABOVE LEFT: A trio of arched windows look out from the study onto the courtyard. In the distance to the right is the guest house; to the left you can make out the optional outdoor fireplace.

ABOVE CENTER: A two-story colonnade leads past the courtyard and pool to the home's main entry, shielding homeowner and guests from the sun and rain.

ABOVE RIGHT : With her vanity on one side and his on the other, we look toward the prow of the master bath, with its large step-up soaking tub firmly planted in the apex of a full corner window that reaches from floor to ceiling.

Looking over the pool through the courtyard of this magnificently conceived design, we see the leisure room to the left, the guest house to the right, and the portico entry in the center.

TOP: The shape of the grand salon, accented by high, arched windows, creates a room as uniquely beautiful as it's view.

LEFT: Wake up to this view, in this master bedroom, and you could swear you've awakened to paradise. A dramatic 14-foot stepped ceiling forms a canopy of light and shadow.

OPPOSITE: A large island defines the broad functionality of this gourmet kitchen, serving as a handy area for quick meals.

design 94246

Price Code	K
Total Finished	3,792 sq. ft.
First Finished	2,853 sq. ft.
Second Finished	627 sq. ft.
Lower Finished	312 sq. ft.
Garage Unfinished	777 sq. ft.
Porch Unfinished	326 sq. ft.
Dimensions	80'x96'
Foundation	Slab*
Bedrooms	4
Full Baths	3
Half Baths	1
First Ceiling	10'
Second Ceiling	9'4"
Vaulted Ceiling	17'8"
Max Ridge Height	31'
Roof Framing	Truss
Exterior Walls	8" concrete block construction

* Alternate foundation options available at an additional charge. Please call 1-800-235-5700 for more information.

FIRST FLOOR

SECOND FLOOR

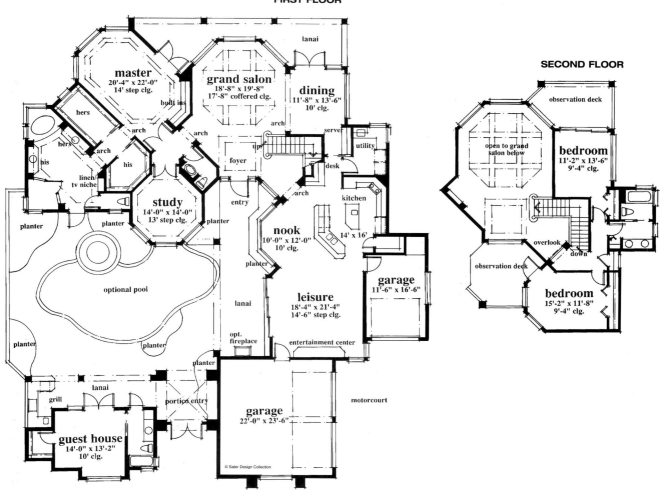

© Sater Design Collection

An Epic Home

Photography Courtesy of
Frank Betz Associates, Inc.

ABOVE: The octagonal tower
dominates the facade of the
European-style home. Upstairs
in the tower is a private sitting
room off the master suite;
downstairs is the formal
dining room.

Like a European mansion, this thoughtfully designed
home comes with its own set of architectural ancestors,
each of which finds expression here and there, throughout
the house.

From the exterior, an obvious outstanding feature of this
home is its octagonal tower, which holds the formal dining
room on the first floor and a sitting room off the master suite
on the second floor. The rest of the house is built around
the tower, just as would have been the case centuries ago
as the local lord added living accommodations to his
castle tower.

design 97298

Price Code	K
Total Finished	3,877 sq. ft.
First Finished	2,060 sq. ft.
Second Finished	1,817 sq. ft.
Basement Unfinished	2,060 sq. ft.
Dimensions	54'x78'4"
Foundation	Basement Crawlspace
Bedrooms	5
Full Baths	4
Half Baths	I
Max Ridge Height	31'9"
Roof Framing	Stick
Exterior Walls	2x4

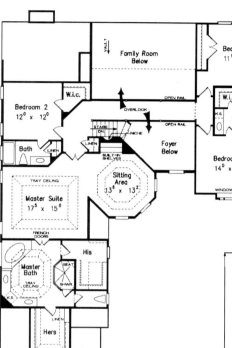

SECOND FLOOR

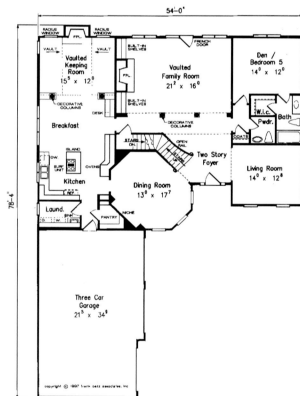

FIRST FLOOR

LEFT: The keeping room, so named because historically it's the room of the house where everything was kept, has its own fireplace, all sheltered beneath a cozy vaulted ceiling with exposed box-beam rafters.

Luxury Home Designs 19

Colonial Update

Photography Courtesy of
Donna & Ron Kolb, Exposures Unlimited

ABOVE: With an impressive enough facade to grace any neighborhood, this Colonial update exudes fresh, welcoming appeal.

What a difference a couple of centuries make. Here we are, 200 years after our forefathers built these classic, symmetrical homes for their families in what was then a brand-new country. Life expectancy was short and life itself was hard.

Sure we work just as hard as they did, in fact we probably put in more hours. And it's likely we have much less time for rest and relaxation than they did. So our hectic schedules make it that much more important that we have a real home to retreat to at the end of the day.

This is such a home. It offers the classic lines and traditional charm of the homes our forefathers built. But what a difference. Comfortable, cozy and warm in the winter; cooled in the summer. Ample room for all our modern pursuits. Spacious enough so that families aren't jammed together in one small den watching television. Here such space exists.

design 92671

Price Code	I
Total Finished	3,445 sq. ft.
First Finished	1,666 sq. ft.
Second Finished	1,036 sq. ft.
Lower Finished	743 sq. ft.
Basement Unfinished	1,612 sq. ft.
Garage Unfinished	740 sq. ft.
Porch Unfinished	203 sq. ft.
Dimensions	71'8"×38'10"
Foundation	Basement
Bedrooms	4
Full Baths	3
Half Baths	I
First Ceiling	9'
Second Ceiling	9'
Vaulted Ceiling	12'8"
Tray Ceiling	8'
Max Ridge Height	36'
Roof Framing	Stick/Truss
Exterior Walls	2×4, 2×6

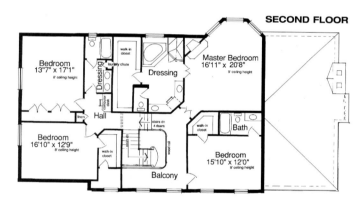

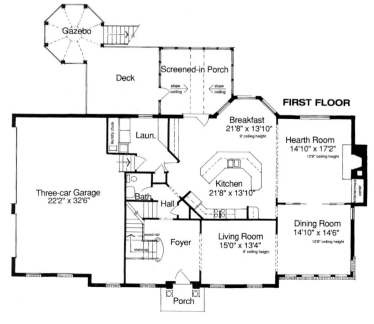

TOP: With its own private fireplace and large bay window wall, the master bedroom will become a beloved retreat for the owners of this home.

CENTER: The hearth room, so named because of its dominant feature the fireplace, could easily become one of the family's cherished places.

BOTTOM: All the right stuff: the formal dining room, which leads into the hearth room to the right, provides an elegant setting for quiet, intimate dinner parties.

Creating a Lifestyle

Photography Courtesy of
Ahmann Design, Inc.

If you've ever been to the Mediterranean coast (or seen movies where it's featured), the first thing you noticed was the unique lifestyle of the people and the homes where they live.

Comfort is the keyword on the Mediterranean. Life moves slowly. People take their time. Lunch can last two or three hours.

And their homes reflect this ease and comfort. Long, rambling, low homes with elements from the architectural classics: columns, arches, pediments — great views, too.

ABOVE: The long, low lines of the Mediterranean are clearly visible in this photo of the front elevation taken at dusk.

TOP LEFT: Standing behind the table in the breakfast nook, we look out over the spacious kitchen with its handy central island that makes a great place for feeding the kids or for laying out an informal buffet.

TOP CENTER: Built on a hilly site, this home really opens up onto the backyard, where raised decks and a screened porch allow you to really enjoy the out-of-doors.

TOP RIGHT: The hearth room (fireplace not seen) is open to the living room and the informal dining nook. The doorway to the left leads to a screened porch and the doorway to the right of the built-in niche leads to the home office.

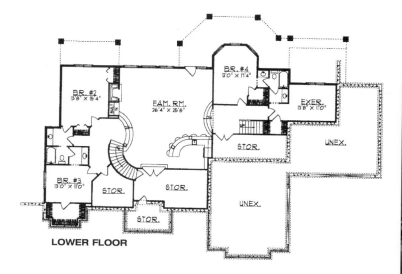

MAIN FLOOR

WD. DECK

NK
10'-1 1/8" CEILING
12'2" x 12'4"

SCRN. PRCH.
15'6" x 12'8"

WD. DECK

M.B.R.
10'-1 1/8" CEILING
15'6" x 17'10"

LIV. RM.
10'-1 1/8" CEILING
11'4" x 20'2"

HRTH. RM.
10'-1 1/8" CEILING
14'0" x 14'6"

OFF.
10'-1 1/8" CEILING
11'4" x 11'6"

1 CAR GARAGE
25'6" x 26'4"

PAN.

DEN
14'-1 1/8" CEILING
13'8" x 11'0"

E.

DIN. RM.
14'-1 1/8" CEILING
13'0" x 11'0"

2 CAR GARAGE
21'8" x 21'8"

Price Code	L
Total Finished	5,639 sq. ft.
Main Finished	2,812 sq. ft.
Lower Finished	2,827 sq. ft.
Garage Unfinished	1,136 sq. ft.
Porch Unfinished	182 sq. ft.
Dimensions	95'x62'
Foundation	Basement
Bedrooms	4
Full Baths	3
Half Baths	1
Main Ceiling	10' 1 1/8''
Roof Framing	Truss
Exterior Walls	2x6

LOWER FLOOR

BR. #2
13'8" x 15'4"

FAM. RM.
26'4" x 25'8"

BR. #4
17'0" x 11'4"

EXER.
13'8" x 11'0"

STOR.

UNEX.

BR. #3
13'0" x 11'0"

STOR.

STOR.

UNEX.

STOR.

RIGHT AND ABOVE: On the main floor is the master suite with its tremendous walk-in closet and capacious master bath with step-up tub and discrete shower and water closet.

Large Rooms **and Big Views**

Photography Courtesy of
Ahmann Design, Inc.

The entrance gives it away. Right off the bat, you know this isn't your run-of-the-mill home.

Actually, this home's assembly of gables, curves, and angles constitute an extraordinary design, which only begins with the exterior and speaks of the promise to come once inside.

Guests arrive through the tall, curved archway that opens into the gabled portico. Outdoor light streams through the arch-top transom above the front door and floods the two-story foyer.

Inside the foyer, visitors can look into the living room or enjoy the skyway that connects one side of the upstairs with the other.

design **97156**

Price Code	J
Total Finished	3,707 sq. ft.
First Finished	2,731 sq. ft.
Second Finished	976 sq. ft.
Basement Unfinished	2,731 sq. ft.
Garage Unfinished	903 sq. ft.
Dimensions	102'8"x48'10"
Foundation	Basement
Bedrooms	4
Full Baths	3
Half Baths	1
Max Ridge Height	33'4"
Roof Framing	Truss
Exterior Walls	2x4, 2x6

ABOVE: Just off the kitchen and dining area is the family room. A cozy fireplace, beautifully crafted built-ins and mantel surround, and a decorative ceiling create a pleasurable place for family to gather.

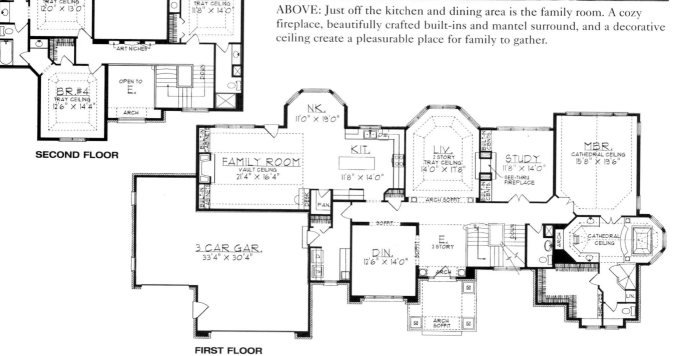

SECOND FLOOR

FIRST FLOOR

A water home doesn't have to be a tiny cottage on the sand. Offering terrific views from all rooms and a stately facade, this home is fantastic year round.

At Home on the Water

Photography By
John Ehrenclou

It takes a special kind of house to be at home on the water. But the ones that do, well, somehow they just seem to fit there; by the sea, on the lake or pond, or overlooking the river or stream. A home on the water has to do several things. It must take full advantage of views, otherwise it might as well be built in the city. It has to provide indoor and outdoor spaces that catch the cool air off the water. And, it has to be designed to withstand the unique weather conditions of life near water — rain, wind and, if the water is the sea, salt spray.

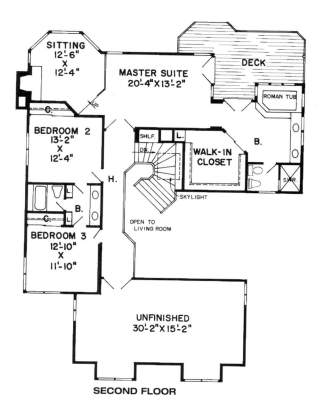

SECOND FLOOR

SITTING
12'-6" X 12'-4"

MASTER SUITE
20'-4" X 13'-2"

DECK

ROMAN TUB

BEDROOM 2
13'-2" X 12'-4"

SHLF.
WALK-IN CLOSET

B.

SKYLIGHT

OPEN TO LIVING ROOM

BEDROOM 3
12'-10" X 11'-10"

UNFINISHED
30'-2" X 15'-2"

ABOVE: A three-sided bay window nudges the breakfast nook nearly outdoors. The large extent of glass brings light and views deep into the home. The breakfast nook adjoins the kitchen, which also enjoys a broad ocean view thanks to its own bay window.

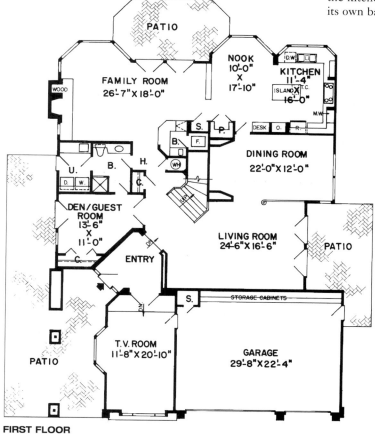

FIRST FLOOR

PATIO

FAMILY ROOM
26'-7" X 18'-0"

WOOD

NOOK
10'-0" X 17'-10"

KITCHEN
11'-4"

D.W.

ISLAND X 16'-0"

T.C.

M.W.

DESK O. R.

DINING ROOM
22'-0" X 12'-0"

DEN/GUEST ROOM
13'-6" X 11'-0"

ENTRY

LIVING ROOM
24'-6" X 16'-6"

PATIO

STORAGE CABINETS

PATIO

T.V. ROOM
11'-8" X 20'-10"

GARAGE
29'-8" X 22'-4"

design 10492

Price Code	L
Total Finished	4,441 sq. ft.
First Finished	2,409 sq. ft.
Second Finished	2,032 sq. ft.
Garage Unfinished	690 sq. ft.
Dimensions	52'x70'
Foundation	Slab
Bedrooms	4
Full Baths	2
3/4 Baths	1
Max Ridge Height	26'6"
Roof Framing	Stick
Exterior Walls	2x6

Everyday Opulence

Photography Courtesy of
Ahmann Design, Inc.

A home like this isn't for everyone. Ample room and plush detailing like this are, frankly, beyond the means of most people; which means that, to most people, if they can't have it now, they can't imagine ever having it and so won't ever get it.

Desire and passion, those are the keys. If you can summon the passion to really picture yourself in this house, living this lifestyle; if you're the type of person who knows what you want and then goes after it with both six-shooters blazing; if you set your goals high and climb over everything that gets in your way to achieve them — you can make this lifestyle your own.

And what a lifestyle it is.

The Great room of the home takes up nearly 500 square feet of the main level and provides a stylish and elegant venue for quiet entertaining or cozy quiet time. Notice the built-ins on both sides of the classic hearth.

Beautiful built-ins, alluring angles, and a pleasing shape surround the very functional gourmet kitchen, which includes this gorgeous kitchen island topped by a jutting counter that offers room for a whole battalion of snacking kids.

The bumped-out center-wall hearth in the family room includes space for a wide-screen television and home stereo speakers. To either side of the hearth are tall built-ins topped by long, deep windows for non-distracting light.

design 97322

Price Code	H
Total Finished	3,012 sq. ft.
Main Finished	3,012 sq. ft.
Lower Finished	2,067 sq. ft.
Basement Unfinished	945 sq. ft.
Garage Unfinished	930 sq. ft.
Dimensions	88'1"x77'3"
Foundation	Basement
Bedrooms	5
Full Baths	3
Half Baths	1
3/4 Baths	1
Main Ceiling	9'
Roof Framing	Truss
Exterior Walls	2x6

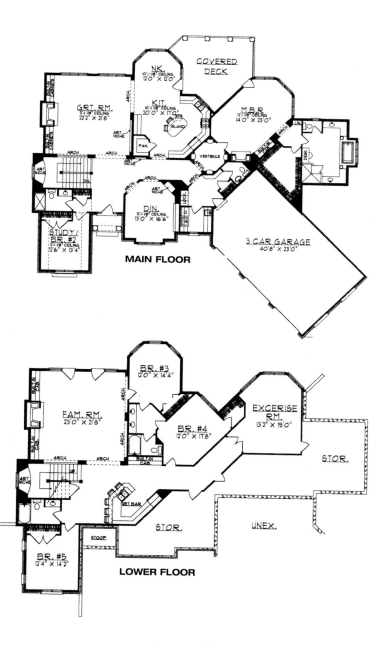

MAIN FLOOR

LOWER FLOOR

The Quality of Life

Photography Courtesy of
Sater Design Collection

The quality of light in a home, the way it enters a room, the way the room takes in the light and spreads the light throughout the space; the way the house is designed and angled just so to capture this light — these are large measures of a great home.

Light isn't the only measure. What the light shows off is also critical. A great floor plan, with views available throughout, even in the home's center; a careful flowing of one space into another — these also are marks of first-class design.

BELOW: This amazing corner window seems to bring the world and the pleasing views into the large luxurious living room. This marvel of modern design and engineering seems to support one corner of the home all with glass.

ABOVE: Pleasing and warm, subtle and gracious, the front elevation provides a welcoming tall arched portico to all visitors.
BELOW: A small pool outside the lanai and below the second-floor observation deck offers a cool retreat on hot summer days.

design **94245**

Price Code	I
Total Finished	3,462 sq. ft.
First Finished	2,894 sq. ft.
Second Finished	568 sq. ft.
Garage Unfinished	598 sq. ft.
Dimensions	67'x102'
Foundation	Slab*
Bedrooms	3
Full Baths	3
Half Baths	I
Max Ridge Height	33'
Roof Framing	Truss

* Alternate foundation options available at an additional charge. Please call 1-800-235-5700 for more information.

ABOVE: The wide-open kitchen/leisure room/eating nook forms the heart of this home's casual family space.

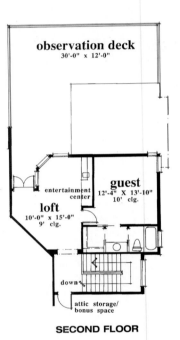

SECOND FLOOR

FIRST FLOOR

© The Sater Group, Inc.

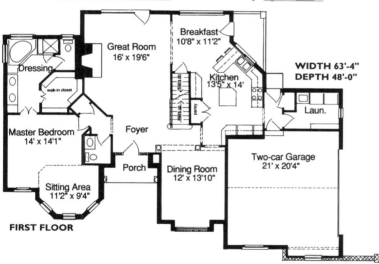

Breakfast 10'8" x 11'2"

Great Room 16' x 19'6"

Dressing

walk-in closet

Kitchen 13'5" x 14'

pantry

WIDTH 63'-4"
DEPTH 48'-0"

Laun.

Master Bedroom 14' x 14'1"

Foyer

Two-car Garage 21' x 20'4"

Porch

Dining Room 12' x 13'10"

Sitting Area 11'2" x 9'4"

FIRST FLOOR

high glass

Bath

Bedroom 11'4" x 12'6"

Great Room Below

high ceiling

Hall

plant shelf

linen

Bedroom 10' x 13'10"

Bath

SECOND FLOOR

walk-in closet

Bedroom 12' x 10'6"

slope ceiling

Dynamic Two-Story

Price Code: E

■ This plan features:

— Four bedrooms

— Three full and one half baths

■ Sheltered Entry surrounded by glass leads into open Foyer and Great Room with high ceiling, hearth fireplace, and Atrium door to backyard

■ Columns frame entrance to conveniently located Dining Room

■ Efficient Kitchen, with built-in Pantry, work island, and bright Breakfast Area, accesses Laundry, backyard, and Garage

■ Master Bedroom wing with Sitting Area and private Bath with corner window tub

■ This home is designed with basement and slab foundation options

FIRST FLOOR — 1,710 SQ. FT.
SECOND FLOOR — 693 SQ. FT.
BASEMENT — 1,620 SQ. FT.
GARAGE — 467 SQ. FT.

TOTAL LIVING AREA:
2,403 SQ. FT.

To order your Blueprints, call 1-800-235-5700

Impressive Two–Story

Price Code: G

■ This plan features:

— Four bedrooms

— Two full and one half baths

■ Two-story Foyer highlighted by lovely angled staircase and decorative window

■ Bay windows enhance Dining and Living Rooms

■ Efficient Kitchen with work island and an open Breakfast Area with backyard access

■ Spacious, yet cozy Family Room with a fireplace and future Sunroom access

■ This home is designed with basement, slab and crawlspace foundation options

FIRST FLOOR — 1,497 SQ. FT.
SECOND FLOOR — 1,460 SQ. FT.
FUTURE SUNROOM — 210 SQ. FT.
GARAGE — 680 SQ. FT.

TOTAL LIVING AREA:
2,957 SQ. FT.

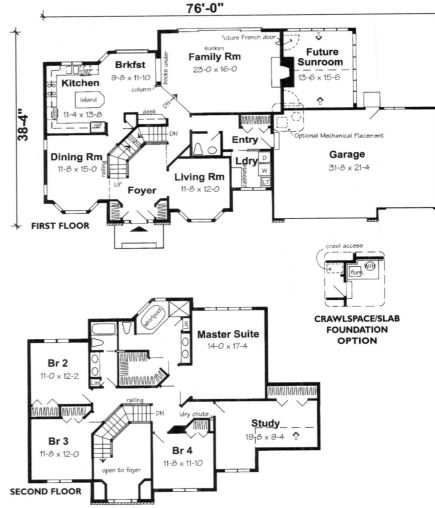

SECOND FLOOR

Br. 4
12⁰x15⁵

Br. 2
13⁰x17⁷

Br. 3
14⁰x13⁰

Fam. rm.
16⁰x18⁰

Bfst.
12⁰x12⁰

Kit.
12⁰x17⁰

Gar.
24⁰x21³

Liv. rm.
20⁰x17⁴

Mbr.
17⁸x14⁰

Gar.
24⁰x21⁰

Din.
14⁰x16⁶

Den
12⁰x14⁰

© Design Basics, Inc.

FIRST FLOOR

73'-4"

83'-5"

Spectacular Voluminous Entry

Price Code: J

- This plan features:

— Four bedrooms

— Two full, two three-quarter, and one half baths

- Dramatic Kitchen is equipped with a large snack bar, Pantry, and desk

- Double doors introduce the Master Suite with private back Patio door, oval whirlpool, and large walk-in closet

- Beautiful arched windows in each secondary Bedroom add natural light and elegance

- This home is designed with a basement foundation

- Alternate foundation options available at an additional charge. Please call 1-800-235-5700 for more information.

FIRST FLOOR — 2,617 SQ. FT.
SECOND FLOOR — 1,072 SQ. FT.

TOTAL LIVING AREA:
3,689 SQ. FT.

A Home of Distinction

Price Code: F

■ This plan features:

— Four bedrooms

— Three full and one half baths

■ The Dining Room and the Study are to either side of the Entry

■ The Study entrance is at an angle with a double door Entry

■ The two-story Family Room includes a fireplace and a windowed rear wall

■ The Breakfast Room is open to the Kitchen

■ The first floor Master Bath includes a whirlpool tub

■ This home is designed with a slab foundation

■ Alternate foundation options available at an additional charge. Please call 1-800-235-5700 for more information.

FIRST FLOOR — 1,844 SQ. FT.
SECOND FLOOR — 794 SQ. FT.

TOTAL LIVING AREA:
2,638 SQ. FT.

FIRST FLOOR

SECOND FLOOR

To order your Blueprints, call 1-800-235-5700

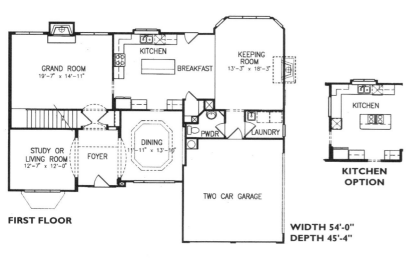

FIRST FLOOR

GRAND ROOM
19'-7" x 14'-11"

KITCHEN

BREAKFAST

KEEPING ROOM
13'-3" x 18'-3"

STUDY OR LIVING ROOM
12'-7" x 12'-0"

FOYER

DINING
11'-11" x 13'-10"

PWDR

LAUNDRY

TWO CAR GARAGE

KITCHEN

KITCHEN OPTION

WIDTH 54'-0"
DEPTH 45'-4"

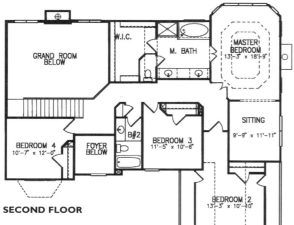

SECOND FLOOR

GRAND ROOM BELOW

W.I.C.

M. BATH

MASTER BEDROOM
13'-3" x 18'-9"

BEDROOM 4
10'-7" x 12'-0"

FOYER BELOW

B#2

BEDROOM 3
11'-5" x 10'-6"

SITTING
9'-9" x 11'-11"

BEDROOM 2
13'-3" x 10'-10"

Ideal Family Home
Price Code: G

■ This plan features:
— Four bedrooms
— Two full and one half baths

■ From the two-story Foyer, enter either the Living Room or the Dining Room

■ In the rear of the home there are the Grand and Keeping Rooms, each with a fireplace

■ The L-shaped Kitchen has a center island and is open to the Breakfast Nook

■ Upstairs, the Master Bedroom has a decorative ceiling and a huge walk-in closet

■ This home is designed with basement and slab foundation options

FIRST FLOOR — 1,535 SQ. FT.
SECOND FLOOR — 1,236 SQ. FT.
GARAGE — 418 SQ. FT.

TOTAL LIVING AREA:
2,771 SQ. FT.

Distinguished Dwelling

Price Code: F

■ This plan features:

— Four bedrooms

— Two full and one half baths

■ Grand two-story Entry into Foyer

■ Formal Living Room with a decorative window and a vaulted ceiling extending into Family Room with cozy fireplace

■ Convenient Kitchen with cooktop work island, Pantry, octagon Dining Area, and nearby Study, Laundry and Garage Entry

■ Luxurious Master Bedroom offers a glass alcove, walk-in closet and pampering Bath with a corner tub

■ This home is designed with a basement foundation

FIRST FLOOR — 1,514 SQ. FT.
SECOND FLOOR — 1,219 SQ. FT.
BASEMENT — 1,465 SQ. FT.
GARAGE — 596 SQ. FT.

TOTAL LIVING AREA:
2,733 SQ. FT.

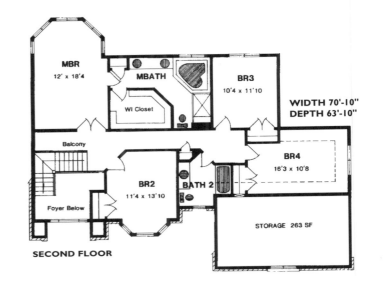

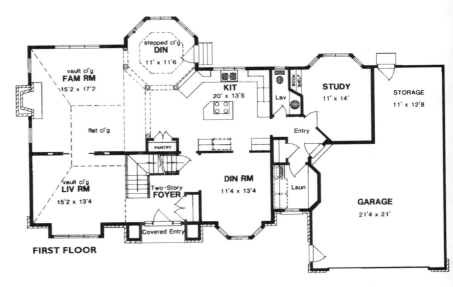

BEDROOM #4
14'-10" X 13'-4"

LIV. ROOM BELOW

OPEN RAIL

DN

FOYER
BELOW

BEDROOM #2
14'-0" X 11'-0"

BEDROOM #3
14'-2" X 11'-4"

43'-4"

36'-0"

SECOND FLOOR

PRIVATE
COURT

HOT TUB

PATIO

MASTER BEDROOM #1
20'-2" X 14'-0"

LIVING ROOM
27'-4" X 17'-4"

SUN PORCH
15'-0" X 9'-8"

DINING ROOM
14'-10" X 13'-4"

UP DN

LINEN CHINA DESK

BAR
WINE

B.

H.

FOYER

MORNING
ROOM
11'-0" X 13'-4"

REF.

SINK

BR

CLO.

LAUND.

LIBRARY-STUDY
20'-0" X 11'-4"

COVERED PORCH

LANDSCAPED
COURT

GARAGE
23'-4" X 23'-8"

60'-4"

W.

DRIVE

73'-4"

FIRST FLOOR

Private Court with Hot Tub

Price Code: I

■ This plan features:

— Four bedrooms

— Three full and one half baths

■ A Private Court, with hot tub, joins the Master Suite

■ A cozy Library which opens onto the two-story Foyer through French doors

■ A Morning Room with built-ins, a Bar with wine storage, and a Sun Porch

■ This home is designed with basement, slab, and crawlspace foundation options

FIRST FLOOR — 2,486 SQ. FT.
SECOND FLOOR — 954 SQ. FT.
BASEMENT — 2,486 SQ. FT.
GARAGE — 576 SQ. FT.

TOTAL LIVING AREA:
3,440 SQ. FT.

Stately Presence

Price Code: H

■ This plan features:

— Four bedrooms

— Three full and one half baths

■ The Patio and Covered Patio expand living space to the outdoors

■ The cathedral ceiling in the Living Room gives added volume to the room

■ The future Playroom on the second floor is a perfect location for kids to play, keeping peace and quiet downstairs

■ This home is designed with basement, slab, and crawlspace foundation options

FIRST FLOOR — 2,115 SQ. FT.
SECOND FLOOR — 947 SQ. FT.
BONUS ROOM — 195 SQ. FT.
GARAGE — 635 SQ. FT.

TOTAL LIVING AREA:
3,062 SQ. FT.

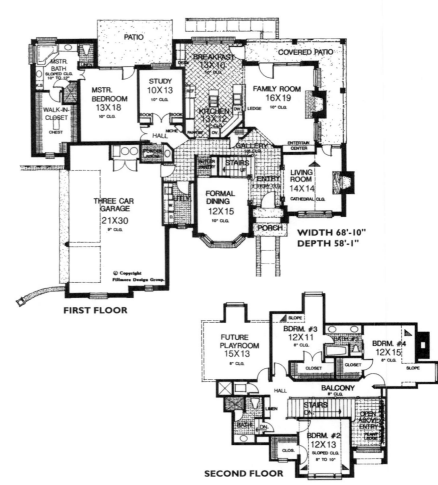

To order your Blueprints, call 1-800-235-5700

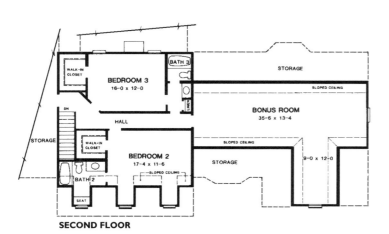

SCREENED PORCH
22-0 x 12-0

MASTER BATH

WALK-IN
CLOSET

PWDR.
RM.

HEARTH

FAMILY ROOM
23-8 x 15-6

KITCHEN
14-0 x 12-6

BREAKFAST
11-0 x 11-6

UTILITY
10-0 x 9-6

SINK

S. UNIT

BAR

DW

OVEN

PANTRY

WASH DRY

FREEZ

DESK

REFG.

MASTER
BEDROOM
15-0 x 18-0

TREY CEILING

UP

ENTRY

COATS

NICHE

LIVING ROOM
16-0 x 11-6

DINING ROOM
14-0 x 12-6

GARAGE
22-0 x 22-0

FIRST FLOOR

PORCH
28-0 x 6-0

WIDTH 79'-4"
DEPTH 46'-0"

9' CEILING HT.

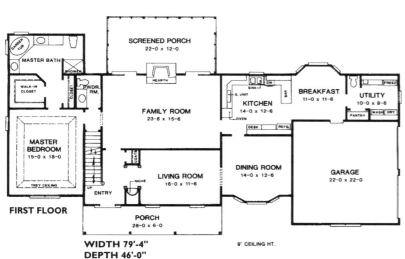

WALK-IN
CLOSET

BATH 3

BEDROOM 3
16-0 x 12-0

STORAGE

SLOPED CEILING

DN

STORAGE

HALL

BONUS ROOM
35-6 x 13-4

WALK-IN
CLOSET

BEDROOM 2
17-4 x 11-6

SLOPED CEILING

BATH 2

SLOPED CEILING

STORAGE

9-0 x 12-0

SEAT

SECOND FLOOR

Traditional that has it All

Price Code: G

■ This plan features:

— Three bedrooms

— Three full and two half baths

■ A Master Suite with two closets and a private Bath with separate shower, corner tub and dual vanity

■ A large Dining Room with a bay window, adjacent to the Kitchen

■ A formal Living Room for entertaining and a cozy Family Room with fireplace for informal relaxation

■ A Bonus Room to allow the house to grow with your needs

■ This home is designed with basement, slab and crawlspace foundation options

FIRST FLOOR — 1,927 SQ. FT.
SECOND FLOOR — 832 SQ. FT.
BONUS ROOM — 624 SQ. FT.
BASEMENT — 1,674 SQ. FT.

TOTAL LIVING AREA:
2,759 SQ. FT.

Dignified Family Home

Price Code: F

- This plan features:
  - — Three bedrooms
  - — Two full and one half baths
- The Living Room adjoins the formal Dining Room
- A U-shaped Kitchen equipped with a built-in Pantry
- A large Family Room flows from the Kitchen
- A second floor Master Suite topped by a decorative ceiling
- A Bonus Room for future needs
- This home is designed with basement, slab and crawlspace foundation options

FIRST FLOOR — 1,245 SQ. FT.
SECOND FLOOR — 1,333 SQ. FT.
BONUS ROOM — 192 SQ. FT.
GARAGE — 614 SQ. FT.

TOTAL LIVING AREA:
2,578 SQ. FT.

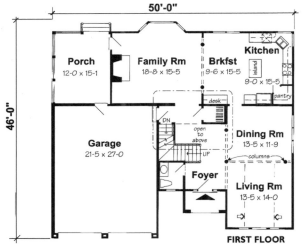

50'-0"
46'-0"

Porch
12-0 x 15-1

Family Rm
18-8 x 15-5

Brkfst
9-6 x 15-5

Kitchen
island
9-0 x 15-5
pantry

DN
open to above
desk
UP

Garage
21-5 x 27-0

Dining Rm
13-5 x 11-9
columns

Foyer

Living Rm
13-5 x 14-0

FIRST FLOOR

crawl access   w/h
fur.

CRAWLSPACE/SLAB FOUNDATION OPTION

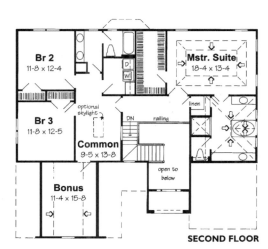

Br 2
11-8 x 12-4

D
W

Mstr. Suite
18-4 x 13-4

linen

optional skylight

Br 3
11-8 x 12-5

DN   railing

Common
9-5 x 13-8

open to below

Bonus
11-4 x 15-8

SECOND FLOOR

To order your Blueprints, call 1-800-235-5700

Superior Comfort and Privacy

Price Code: F

■ This plan features:
— Four bedrooms
— Three full baths

■ A natural stone exterior with slate floors in the Foyer leading to the private Patio off the Master Bedroom

■ A two-way fireplace between the Living Room and Family Room

■ A Breakfast Nook with a large bow window facing the terrace and pool

■ Four Bedrooms grouped in one wing for privacy

■ This home is designed with a basement foundation

MAIN FLOOR — 2,679 SQ. FT.
BASEMENT — 2,679 SQ. FT.
GARAGE — 541 SQ. FT.

TOTAL LIVING AREA:
2,679 SQ. FT.

REAR ELEVATION

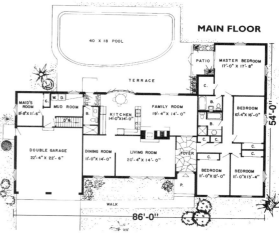

MAIN FLOOR

Foyer Welcomes Guests

Price Code: I

■ This plan features:
— Four bedrooms
— Two full, one three-quarter, and one half baths

■ A massive welcoming foyer which steps right into the Great Room

■ A Great Room enlarged by a wraparound deck and highlighted by a fireplace, built-in bookcases, and a wetbar

■ A Kitchen with a built-in desk, an octagonal morning room, and a central island

■ This home is designed with a basement foundation

FIRST FLOOR — 2,419 SQ. FT.
SECOND FLOOR — 926 SQ. FT.
BASEMENT — 2,419 SQ. FT.
GARAGE — 615 SQ. FT.

TOTAL LIVING AREA:
3,345 SQ. FT.

FIRST FLOOR

SECOND FLOOR

To order your Blueprints, call 1-800-235-5700

Magnificent Stature

Price Code: L

- This plan features:
- — Four bedrooms
- — Three full and one half baths

- A two-story cathedral ceiling crowns the Living Room of this manor-styled home

- The first floor Master Suite features a private octagonal Study

- The second floor includes a Media Area and a Bonus Space

- The expansive Family Room opens on to the Covered Patio

- This home is designed with basement, slab and crawlspace foundation options

FIRST FLOOR — 3,168 SQ. FT.
SECOND FLOOR — 998 SQ. FT.
BONUS — 320 SQ. FT.
GARAGE — 810 SQ. FT.

TOTAL LIVING AREA:
4,166 SQ. FT.

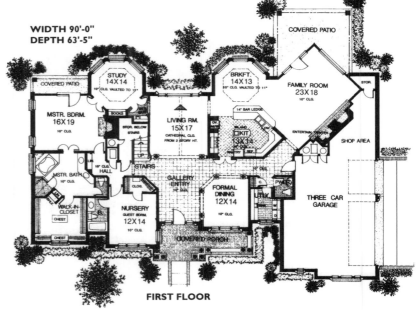

WIDTH 90'-0"
DEPTH 63'-5"

FIRST FLOOR

SECOND FLOOR

To order your Blueprints, call 1-800-235-5700

Rustic Formal Ranch

Price Code: J

■ This plan features:
— Three bedrooms
— Three full baths
- The stone exterior is complemented by large windows with arched transoms
- The Kitchen has plenty of work and storage space with its central island eating bar
- The Great Room features high ceilings a central fireplace, large windows to the rear, built-in cabinetry, and a wetbar
- The luxurious Master Bedroom has a tray ceiling, his and her walk-in closets, a private Master Bath featuring a large whirlpool, a cathedral ceiling, two vanities, and a free standing shower
- This home is designed with a basement foundation

MAIN FLOOR — 2,443 SQ. FT.
LOWER FLOOR — 1,135 SQ. FT.
BASEMENT —1,308 SQ. FT.

TOTAL LIVING AREA:
3,578 SQ. FT.

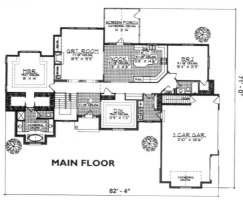

PLAN NO. 93154

Unusual Tile Roof

Price Code: H

- This plan features:
— Four bedrooms
— Three full baths
- Stone arched Porch accesses tiled Entry with sloped ceiling and Parlor through French doors
- Spacious Living Room with sloped ceiling, tiled hearth fireplace, and access to brick Patio
- Convenient Dining Room enhanced by arches and a double window
- Hub Kitchen with large Pantry, a Breakfast Bar, and glass eating Nook
- Comfortable Family Room offers another fireplace with wood storage, a wetbar, and access to Laundry and Garage
- Den/Guest Room provides many options
- Expansive Master Bedroom with a bay window, Patio access, walk-in closet, Dressing Area, and private Bath
- Two additional Bedrooms with private access to a full Bath
- This home is designed with a slab foundation

MAIN FLOOR — 3,025 SQ. FT.
GARAGE — 722 SQ. FT.

TOTAL LIVING AREA:
3,025 SQ. FT.

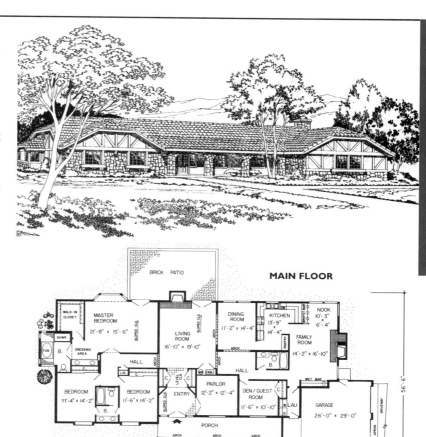

PLAN NO. 10601

Elegant Living
Price Code: F

■ This plan features:

— Three bedrooms

— Two full and one half baths

■ The spacious Great Room has a two-story ceiling, a fireplace and naturally illuminating rear windows

■ The Den features built-in cabinetry located immediately off the Great Room

■ The formal Dining Room located at the front of the house provides a quiet place for entertaining

■ The Master Bedroom with generous windows to the rear, also has a private Bath

■ This home is designed with a basement foundation

FIRST FLOOR — 1,408 sq. ft.
SECOND FLOOR — 1,184 sq. ft.
BASEMENT — 1,408 sq. ft.

TOTAL LIVING AREA:
2,592 sq. ft.

WIDTH 64'-0"
DEPTH 45'-0"

DEN 13'4" X 13'0"

GR.RM. 2 STORY 16'0" X 17'0"

NK. 13'0" X 11'4"

BUILT-IN CABINETS

KIT. 13'0" X 13'8"

ARCH SOFFIT

3 CAR GAR. 34'0" X 31'8"

E. 2 STORY

DIN. 13'0" X 11'8"

FIRST FLOOR

MBR. 13'4" X 16'10"

OPEN TO GR.RM.

BR.#2 13'0" X 14'6"

LINEN

OPEN TO E.

BR.#3 13'0" X 14'0"

BRICK ARCH

SECOND FLOOR

To order your Blueprints, call 1-800-235-5700

Photography supplied by The Meredith Corporation

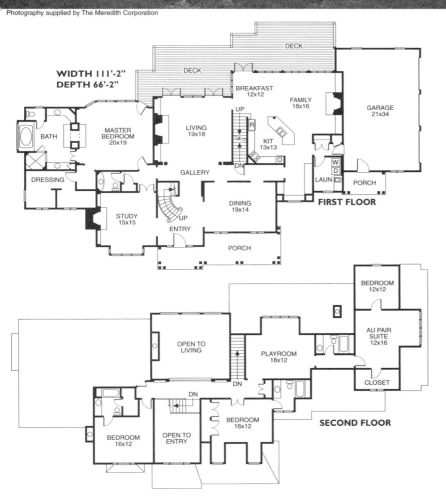

WIDTH 111'-2"
DEPTH 66'-2"

DECK

DECK

BREAKFAST
12x12

FAMILY
18x16

GARAGE
21x34

BATH

MASTER
BEDROOM
20x19

LIVING
19x18

UP

R

KIT
13x13

DRESSING

GALLERY

DN

W
D

LAUN

PORCH

STUDY
15x15

DINING
19x14

UP

FIRST FLOOR

ENTRY

PORCH

BEDROOM
12x12

OPEN TO
LIVING

PLAYROOM
18x12

AU PAIR
SUITE
12x16

DN

CLOSET

DN

BEDROOM
16x12

BEDROOM
16x12

SECOND FLOOR

OPEN TO
ENTRY

Country Manor

Price Code: L

■ This plan features:

— Four Bedrooms

— Four full and one half baths

■ Combined with the Study, Master Suite occupies entire wing of the first floor

■ Living Room and Dining Room with adjacent locations for ease in entertaining

■ Kitchen, Breakfast Nook and Family Room create large informal area

■ Three Bedrooms, Au Pair Suite, three Baths and Playroom complete the second floor

■ Second floor balcony connects the Bedroom wings and overlooks Living Room above Foyer

■ This home is designed with a basement foundation

FIRST FLOOR — 3,322 SQ. FT.
SECOND FLOOR — 1,966 SQ. FT.

TOTAL LIVING AREA:
5,288 SQ. FT.

Lasting Impression

Price Code: G

- ■ This plan features:
- — Four bedrooms
- — Three full and one half baths
- ■ The two-story Foyer is enhanced by a cascading staircase with an open rail
- ■ The Living Room is topped by a 12-foot 8-inch tray ceiling
- ■ The Master Suite includes a Sitting Area and a five-piece Bath
- ■ Three additional Bedrooms have access to full Baths
- ■ This home is designed with basement, slab, and crawlspace foundation options

FIRST FLOOR — 2,044 SQ. FT.
SECOND FLOOR — 896 SQ. FT.
BONUS ROOM — 197 SQ. FT.
BASEMENT — 2,044 SQ. FT.
GARAGE — 544 SQ. FT.

TOTAL LIVING AREA:
2,940 SQ. FT.

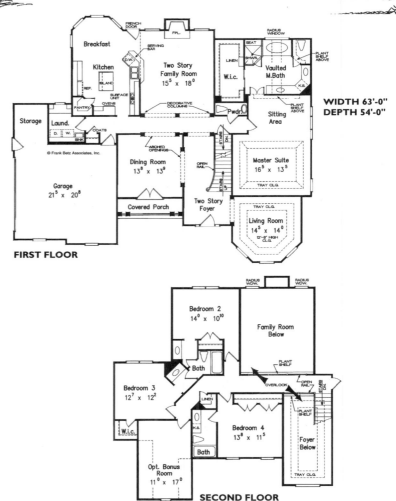

WIDTH 63'-0"
DEPTH 54'-0"

FIRST FLOOR

SECOND FLOOR

Arches Dominate Facade

Price Code: L

- This plan features:
- — Five bedrooms
- — Three full and one half baths
- A window wall and French doors link the Living Room to the in-ground pool
- A wetbar with wine storage and built-in bookcases near the Family Room
- A Library on the second floor has space for the largest book collections
- Dressing rooms and adjoining Baths in all the Bedrooms
- This home is designed with basement, slab, and crawlspace foundation options

FIRST FLOOR — 3,625 SQ. FT.
SECOND FLOOR — 937 SQ. FT.
GARAGE — 636 SQ. FT.

TOTAL LIVING AREA:
4,562 SQ. FT.

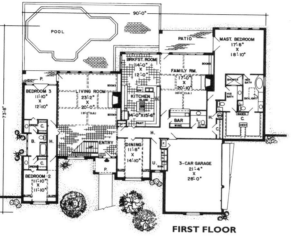

FIRST FLOOR

SECOND FLOOR

Energy–Saving Sunroom Warms Classic Tudor

Price Code: L

- This plan features:
- — Four bedrooms
- — Three full and two half baths
- Upstairs Bedrooms with adjoining Baths and a Loft with built-in bookshelves
- A Master Bedroom with a Study and a Bath equipped with a hot tub
- An island Kitchen open to the Family Room which accesses the Sunroom
- This home is designed with a basement foundation

FIRST FLOOR — 3,332 SQ. FT.
SECOND FLOOR — 1,218 SQ. FT.
BASEMENT — 3,672 SQ. FT.
GARAGE — 1,137 SQ. FT.

TOTAL LIVING AREA:
4,890 SQ. FT.

FIRST FLOOR

SECOND FLOOR

To order your Blueprints, call 1-800-235-5700

49

A Splendid Porch

Price Code: E

■ This plan features:

— Four bedrooms

— Two full and one half baths

■ A stylish front Porch enhances this attractive home

■ Dual closets and an attractive staircase greet you upon entering

■ There is a room devoted to a Home Office or a Media Center

■ The Great Room is open to the Kitchen and they share a serving bar

■ The Breakfast Nook overlooks the rear Deck

■ This home is designed with basement, slab and crawlspace foundation options

FIRST FLOOR — 1,305 SQ. FT.
SECOND FLOOR — 1,121 SQ. FT.
BASEMENT — 1,194 SQ. FT.
GARAGE — 576 SQ. FT.

TOTAL LIVING AREA:
2,426 SQ. FT.

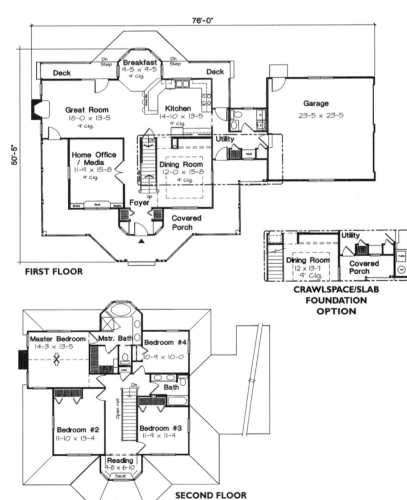

FIRST FLOOR

CRAWLSPACE/SLAB
FOUNDATION
OPTION

SECOND FLOOR

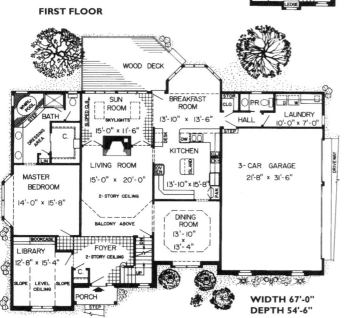

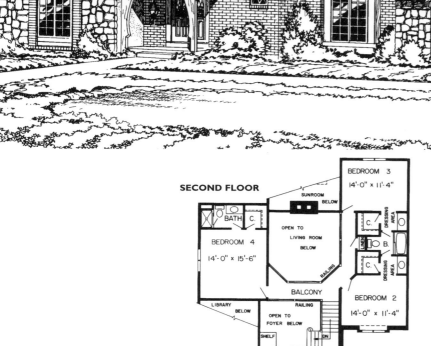

SECOND FLOOR

BEDROOM 3
14'-0" x 11'-4"

SUNROOM
BELOW

BATH C.

BEDROOM 4
14'-0" x 15'-6"

OPEN TO
LIVING ROOM
BELOW

C.
DRESSING AREA

LINEN B.

C.
DRESSING AREA

RAILING

BALCONY

LIBRARY
BELOW

RAILING
OPEN TO
FOYER BELOW

BEDROOM 2
14'-0" x 11'-4"

SHELF

LEDGE DN

FIRST FLOOR

WOOD DECK

WHIRL. POOL

BATH

SUN ROOM
SKYLIGHTS
15'-0" x 11'-6"

BREAKFAST ROOM
13'-10" x 13'-6"

SLOPED CLG.

DRESSING AREA

C.

LIN.

DESK

STOR. CLO.

HALL

PR.

DW

LAUNDRY
10'-0" x 7'-0"

LIVING ROOM
15'-0" x 20'-0"
2-STORY CEILING

KITCHEN
13'-10" x 15'-8"

ISLAND

OVEN

STEP

PAN.

3- CAR GARAGE
21'-8" x 31'-6"

DRIVEWAY

MASTER BEDROOM
14'-0" x 15'-8"

BALCONY ABOVE

DINING ROOM
13'-10" x 13'-4"

BOOKCASE

LIBRARY
12'-8" x 15'-4"

FOYER
2-STORY CEILING

C.
UP

SLOPE LEVEL CEILING SLOPE

PORCH

STEP

WIDTH 67'-0"
DEPTH 54'-6"

Traditional Energy Saver
Price Code: H

■ This plan features:

— Four bedrooms

— Two full, one three-quarter, and one half baths

■ A heat storing floor in the Sunroom which joins the Living and Breakfast Rooms

■ A Living Room with French doors and a massive fireplace

■ A balcony overlooking the soaring two-story Foyer and Living Room

■ An island Kitchen centrally located between the formal and informal Dining Rooms

■ This home is designed with a basement foundation

FIRST FLOOR — 2,186 SQ. FT.
SECOND FLOOR — 983 SQ. FT.
BASEMENT — 2,186 SQ. FT.
GARAGE — 704 SQ. FT.

TOTAL LIVING AREA:
3,169 SQ. FT.

Impressive Brick

Price Code: F

- ■ This plan features:
- — Four bedrooms
- — Two full and one half baths
- ■ Decorative facade of brick and windows
- ■ A covered entrance leading into a two-story raised Foyer with a curved staircase
- ■ A Family Room with a unique fireplace and built-in entertainment center opens to the Breakfast/Kitchen Area
- ■ A Master Suite with a walk-in closet, plush Bath with a corner window tub, two vanities, and an oversized shower
- ■ This home is designed with a basement foundation

FIRST FLOOR — 1,433 SQ. FT.
SECOND FLOOR — 1,283 SQ. FT.
BASEMENT — 1,433 SQ. FT.
GARAGE — 923 SQ. FT.

TOTAL LIVING AREA: 2,716 SQ. FT.

FIRST FLOOR

74'-8"
42'-4"

Family 15 x 18-4
Brkfst 12 x 13
Kitchen 11-6 x 11
Util.
Garage 33-8 x 33-4
Dining 13 x 13
Foyer
Living 13 x 14
ent. center
see-thru
fireplace
bench
pan.
desk

SECOND FLOOR

M Br 15 x 16
Br 2 13 x 11-1
Br 3 12 x 11-1
Br 4 13 x 11
whirlpool
ledge
railing
open to below
shelves

Classic and Classy Design

Price Code: F

- ■ This plan features:
- — Four bedrooms
- — Two full and one half baths
- ■ A gracious entrance into a bright Foyer with a landing staircase and convenient closet
- ■ Formal Living and Dining rooms highlighted by bay windows
- ■ A comfortable Family Room offers a fireplace and lots of windows
- ■ An efficient Kitchen with a work island/snackbar, Pantry and adjacent Utility room that accesses the Garage
- ■ A private Master Bedroom suite offers a decorative window below a sloped ceiling, a large walk-in closet, and plush Bath with whirlpool tub
- ■ Two additional Bedrooms and an Office have ample closets and share a double-vanity bath
- ■ This home is designed with basement, slab, and crawlspace foundation options

FIRST FLOOR — 1,377 SQ. FT.
SECOND FLOOR — 1,264 SQ. FT.
BASEMENT — 1,316 SQ. FT.
GARAGE — 673 SQ. FT.

TOTAL LIVING AREA: 2,641 SQ. FT.

FIRST FLOOR

70'-0"
40'-0"

Deck 14 x 12
Brkfst 11 x 13-6
Family 13 x 17
Kitchen 10-6 x 15-6
Util.
Living 13 x 13-8
Dining 11 x 15
Foyer
Garage 31-8 x 21-8
pantry

SECOND FLOOR

Br 2 12 x 11-2
Office 11 x 12-6
Mstr Br 13 x 16
Br 3 11-6 x 13-8
Open

To order your Blueprints, call 1-800-235-5700

Grandeur Within

Price Code: K

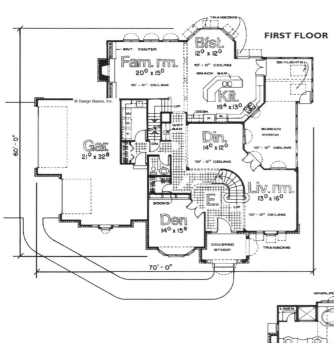

FIRST FLOOR

- ENT. CENTER
- Fam. rm. 20⁰ x 15⁰ — 10' - 0" CEILING
- Bfst. 12⁰ x 12⁰ — 10' - 0" CEILING
- SNACK BAR
- SKYLIGHTS
- Kit. 19⁴ x 13⁰
- Gar. 21⁰ x 32⁸
- DESK
- WET BAR
- Din. 14⁰ x 12⁰ — 10' - 0" CEILING
- SCREEN PORCH — 10' - 0" CEILING
- Liv. rm. 13⁰ x 16⁰ — 10' - 0" CEILING
- BOOKS
- Den 14⁰ x 15⁸
- COVERED STOOP
- TRANSOMS
- © Design Basics, Inc.
- 60' - 0"
- 70' - 0"

SECOND FLOOR

- WHIRLPOOL
- LINEN
- St. 12⁰ x 12⁰
- DRESSER
- ENT. CENTER
- Mbr. 16⁰ x 16⁸
- Br. 4 13⁴ x 12⁶
- SEAT
- DRESSERS
- Br. 2 13⁴ x 15⁰
- Br. 3 14⁰ x 14⁰ — 10' - 0" CLG.
- OPEN TO BELOW

■ This plan features:

— Four bedrooms

— Two full one three-quarter and one half baths

■ The Living and Dining Rooms both have 10-foot ceilings and access a Screen Porch

■ The Family Room, Nook and Kitchen contain all of the amenities that you expect

■ The upstairs Master Suite has built-ins, a Sitting Area and a wonderful Bath

■ This home is designed with a basement foundation

■ Alternate foundation options available at an additional charge. Please call 1-800-235-5700 for more information.

FIRST FLOOR — 1,923 SQ. FT.
SECOND FLOOR — 1,852 SQ. FT.
BASEMENT — 1,923 SQ. FT.
GARAGE — 726 SQ. FT.

TOTAL LIVING AREA:
3,775 SQ. FT.

Photography by John Erenclou

Reaching for the Skies

Price Code: J

■ This plan features:

— Four bedrooms

— Three full and one half baths

■ A unique vaulted ceiling towers above the luxurious Living Room

■ The Master Bedroom straddles the corner beneath a special tray ceiling

■ A functional and attractive island and snack bar graces the center of an ultra-modern Kitchen

■ The raised Deck, open to the Kitchen, makes a perfect spot for outdoor celebrations

■ This home is designed with basement, slab, and crawlspace foundation options

FIRST FLOOR — 2, 054 SQ. FT.
SECOND FLOOR — 1,472 SQ. FT.
BASEMENT — 2,054 SQ. FT.
GARAGE — 745 SQ. FT.

TOTAL LIVING AREA:
3,526 SQ. FT.

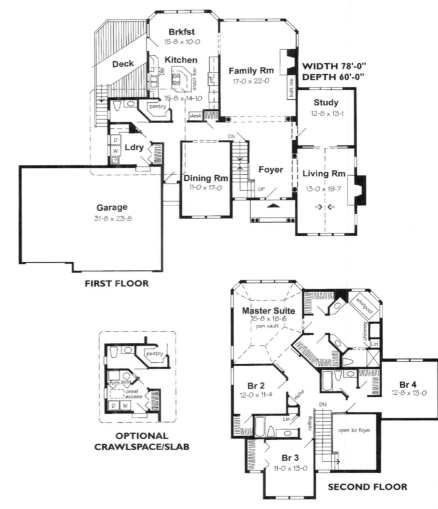

To order your Blueprints, call 1-800-235-5700

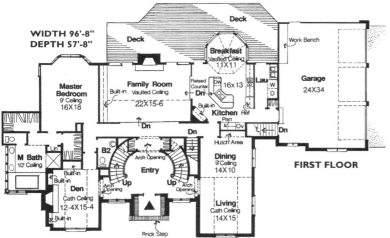

WIDTH 96'-8"
DEPTH 57'-8"

Master Bedroom
9' Ceiling
16X18

Family Room
Vaulted Ceiling
22X15-6

Built-in

Deck

Deck

Breakfast
Vaulted Ceiling
11X11

Raised Counter

Work Bench

Garage
24X34

Lau

W
D

DW

16x13

Kitchen
Pan
Ref
Ov

Built-in

Dn

Dn

Dn

Dn

Dn

M Bath
10' Ceiling

Lin

Built-in
Built-in

B2

Arch Opening

Entry

Up   Up

Arch Opening   Arch Opening

Hutch Area

Dining
9' Ceiling
14X10

FIRST FLOOR

Den
Cath Ceiling
12-4X15-4

Built-in

Arch Opening

Living
Cath Ceiling
14X15

Brick Step

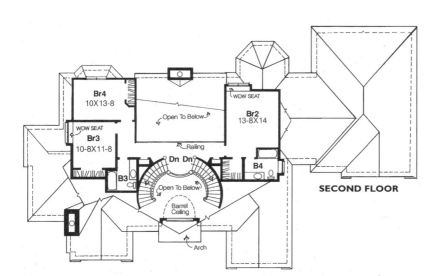

Br4
10X13-8

WDW SEAT

Open To Below

WDW SEAT

Br2
13-8X14

Railing

Br3
10-8X11-8

WDW SEAT

Dn Dn

B4

B3

Open To Below

Barrel Ceiling

Arch

SECOND FLOOR

Unusual and Dramatic

Price Code: I

■ This plan features:

— Four bedrooms

— Three full and one half baths

■ Elegant Entry with arched openings and a double curved staircase

■ Cathedral ceilings crown arched windows in the Den and Living Room

■ Spacious Family Room with a vaulted ceiling and a large fireplace

■ Hub Kitchen with a work island/serving counter and Breakfast Alcove

■ Secluded Master Suite with a lovely bay window, two walk-in closets, and a plush Bath

■ This home is designed with a basement foundation

FIRST FLOOR — 2,646 SQ. FT.
SECOND FLOOR — 854 SQ. FT.
BASEMENT — 2,656 SQ. FT.

TOTAL LIVING AREA:
3,500 SQ. FT.

Luxurious Master Suite

Price Code: G

- This plan features:
  — Four bedrooms
  — Three full and one half baths
- Fireplace in the formal Living Room and one in the Family Room
- Optional Sunroom expanding living space
- Kitchen located between the Breakfast Area and the formal Dining Room
- A plush Bath with a whirlpool tub, vaulted ceiling over the Bath and a tray ceiling over the Bedroom highlighting the Master Suite
- Three additional Bedrooms, each with private access to a full Bath
- Bonus Room available for future expansion
- This home is designed with basement, slab, and crawlspace foundation options

FIRST FLOOR — 1,523 SQ. FT.
SECOND FLOOR — 1,370 SQ. FT.
BASEMENT — 1,722 SQ. FT.
GARAGE — 484 SQ. FT.

TOTAL LIVING AREA: 2,893 SQ. FT.

OPTIONAL CRAWLSPACE/SLAB

Photography supplied by The Meredith Corporation

Forest Cottage

Price Code: L

- This plan features:
  — Four Bedrooms
  — Four full and one half baths
- The Kitchen, with its island and built-in Pantry, has an easy flow into the Breakfast Room and the Great Room
- The Great Room is highlighted by a fireplace and access to the Screened Porch
- The Library/Den with a double door entrance is located off the main Entry hall
- The upper floor Master Bedroom has two walk-in closets and is pampered by a five-piece Bath
- The lower floor contains a Media Room, a Play Room, and a Guest Suite
- This home is designed with a basement foundation

MAIN FLOOR — 1,642 SQ. FT.
UPPER FLOOR — 1,411 SQ. FT.
LOWER FLOOR — 1,230 SQ. FT.
BASEMENT — 412 SQ. FT.

TOTAL LIVING AREA: 4,283 SQ. FT.

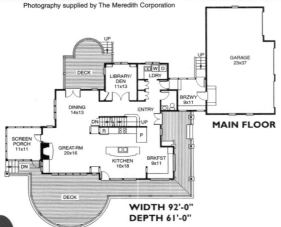

To order your Blueprints, call 1-800-235-5700

Tropical Dreams

Price Code: L

- This plan features:
— Four bedrooms
— Three full one three-quarter and one half baths
- Spacious Gardens surround the outer walls
- An inviting Foyer runs the entire length of the ground floor
- The Living Room comes equipped with a special corner wetbar
- A Library with built-in shelving sits directly across from the Dining Room
- The large Pool and nearby Lanai connect to the Living Room, Family Room and Breakfast Nook
- This home is designed with a slab foundation

MAIN FLOOR - 4,346 SQ. FT.

TOTAL LIVING AREA:
4,346 SQ. FT.

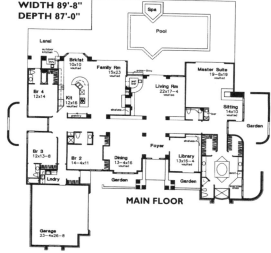

WIDTH 89'-8"
DEPTH 87'-0"

MAIN FLOOR

Cottage Appeal

Price Code: H

- This plan features:
— Four bedrooms
— Two full, two three-quarter, and one half baths
- A curving staircase accents the formal Entry with gracious elegance
- Enhanced by a fireplace and a bay window, the Living Room is a welcoming spot
- The Great Room has a fireplace and access to the rear Patio
- Each Bedroom has private access to a Bath
- Three-car Garage offers additional Storage Space and an easy entrance into the home
- This home is designed with basement and slab foundation options

FIRST FLOOR — 2,337 SQ. FT.
SECOND FLOOR — 882 SQ. FT.
BONUS ROOM — 357 SQ. FT.
GARAGE — 640 SQ. FT.

TOTAL LIVING AREA:
3,219 SQ. FT.

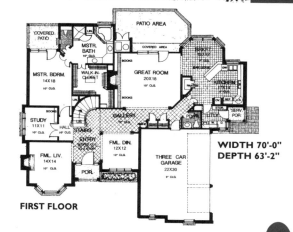

SECOND FLOOR

WIDTH 70'-0"
DEPTH 63'-2"

FIRST FLOOR

To order your Blueprints, call 1-800-235-5700

Sitting Rooms Fills Two-Story Bay

Price Code: H

■ This plan features:
— Five bedrooms
— Four full and one half baths
■ Triple arches and a dramatic roofline comprise this home's facade
■ Bay windows illuminate Master Suite Sitting Room
■ An older child or live-in relative will appreciate the privacy of the lone first floor Bedroom
■ French doors in the Living Room open onto the covered front Porch
■ This home is designed with a basement foundation

FIRST FLOOR — 1,645 SQ. FT.
SECOND FLOOR — 1,645 SQ. FT.
BASEMENT — 1,645 SQ. FT.
GARAGE — 473 SQ. FT.

TOTAL LIVING AREA:
3,027 SQ. FT.

WIDTH 57'-0"
DEPTH 57'-6"

FIRST FLOOR

SECOND FLOOR

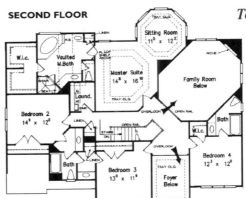

All Bedrooms Secluded on Second Floor

Price Code: H

■ This plan features:
— Four bedrooms
— Three full and one half baths
■ A strategic pass-through between the Family Room and the Kitchen unites the spaces
■ The angled Family Room with a corner fireplace simplifies furniture layout
■ This home is designed with basement and crawlspace foundation options

FIRST FLOOR — 1,415 SQ. FT.
SECOND FLOOR — 1,632 SQ. FT.
BASEMENT — 1,415 SQ. FT.
GARAGE — 766 SQ. FT.

TOTAL LIVING AREA:
3,047 SQ. FT.

FIRST FLOOR

SECOND FLOOR

To order your Blueprints, call 1-800-235-5700

FIRST FLOOR

WIDTH 68'-0"
DEPTH 45'-4"

Garage 12⁹ x 19⁵

Study/Bedroom 5 14⁸ x 11⁰

W.i.c.

Bath

COATS

Kitchen

OVENS

SURFACE UNIT

SERVING BAR

Breakfast

FRENCH DOOR

DW

DECORATIVE COLUMNS

FPL

Two Story Family Room 16¹⁰ x 19¹⁰

REF.

BUTLER'S PANTRY

PANTRY

DESK

STAIRS DN

OPEN RAIL

COATS

Pwdr.

Garage 20⁸ x 20⁸

Dining Room 13⁰ x 15⁶

Two Story Foyer

Living Room 12⁰ x 13⁰

Covered Entry

copyright © 1997 frank betz associates, inc.

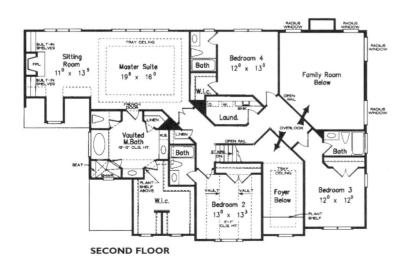

SECOND FLOOR

BUILT-IN SHELVES

FPL

Sitting Room 11⁸ x 13⁵

BUILT-IN SHELVES

TRAY CEILING

Master Suite 19⁸ x 16⁰

FRENCH DOOR

Bath

W.i.c.

LINEN

Laund.

D. W. SINK

RADIUS WINDOW

RADIUS WINDOW

Bedroom 4 12⁰ x 13⁰

RADIUS WINDOW

OPEN RAIL

Family Room Below

RADIUS WINDOW

Vaulted M.Bath 13'-0" CLG. HT.

SEAT

SHWR

LINEN

K.S.

Bath

PLANT SHELF ABOVE

W.i.c.

STAIRS DN

OPEN RAIL

OVERLOOK

VAULT

VAULT

Bedroom 2 13⁰ x 13³ 11'-7" CLG. HT.

TRAY CEILING

Foyer Below

PLANT SHELF

Bath

Bedroom 3 12⁰ x 12⁰

A Glamorous Estate
Price Code: J

■ This plan features:
— Five bedrooms
— Five full and one half baths

■ Decorative columns grace the two-story Family Room, which is open to the Breakfast Nook

■ The Kitchen is equipped with a center island, a large walk in Pantry and plenty of counter space

■ The Master Suite has built-in bookshelves, a fireplace and a spacious Bath with large walk in closet

■ All the Bedrooms have private Baths and ample closet space

■ A Study or optional Bedroom is privately located on the first floor

■ This home is designed with basement and crawlspace foundation options

FIRST FLOOR — 1,802 SQ. FT.
SECOND FLOOR — 1,896 SQ. FT.

TOTAL LIVING AREA:
3,698 SQ. FT.

Low-Maintenence Facade

Price Code: K

■ This plan features:
— Three bedrooms
— Three full and two half baths

■ This home accommodates a sloping lot with the option of a finished basement

■ The Great Room and Hearth Room easily access the Kitchen

■ The home is designed with crawlspace, slab, and basement foundation options

MAIN FLOOR — 2,777 SQ. FT.
UPPER FLOOR — 1,170 SQ. FT.
BASEMENT — 1,616 SQ. FT.
GARAGE — 794 SQ. FT.
PORCH — 704 SQ. FT.

TOTAL LIVING AREA:
3,947 SQ. FT.

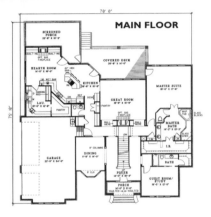

MAIN FLOOR

UPPER FLOOR

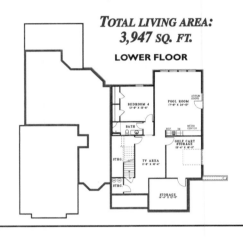

LOWER FLOOR

A Wealth of Living Space and More

Price Code: J

■ This plan features:
— Five bedrooms
— Five full baths

■ Fabulous exterior accents give a mere hint of the exquisite interior plan

■ Unusual shapes define the Living, Family, and Dining Rooms

■ A Covered Patio extends over a great portion of the rear of the home, perfect for entertaining

■ Guests will want to stay in the Guest Room with its walk-in closet and full Bath

■ A volume ceiling, Sitting Area, double walk-in closets, and luxurious Bath make an impressive Master Suite

■ Second floor bonus space allows for future expansion

■ This home is designed with a slab foundation

MAIN FLOOR — 3,723 SQ. FT.
BONUS — 390 SQ. FT.
GARAGE — 850 SQ. FT.

TOTAL LIVING AREA:
3,732 SQ. FT.

WIDTH 82'-4"
DEPTH 89'-0"

MAIN FLOOR

BONUS

To order your Blueprints, call 1-800-235-5700

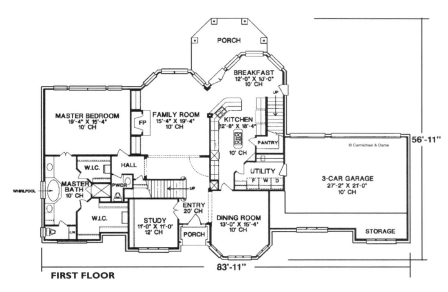

FIRST FLOOR

83'-11"

56'-11"

PORCH

BREAKFAST
12'-0" X 10'-0"
10' CH

MASTER BEDROOM
19'-4" X 15'-4"
10' CH

FAMILY ROOM
15'-4" X 19'-4"
10' CH

FP

KITCHEN
12'-8" X 18'-4"

PANTRY
10' CH

© Carmichael & Dame

UTILITY

3-CAR GARAGE
27'-2" X 21'-0"
10' CH

W.I.C.

HALL

MASTER
BATH
10' CH

WHIRLPOOL

PWDR

UP

W.I.C.

STUDY
11'-0" X 11'-0"
12' CH

ENTRY
20' CH

PORCH

DINING ROOM
13'-0" X 15'-4"
10' CH

STORAGE

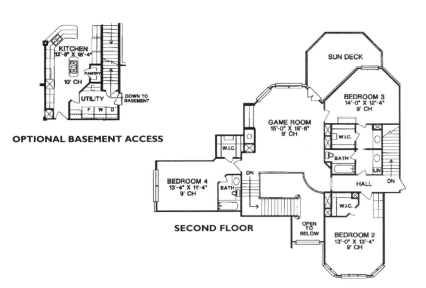

OPTIONAL BASEMENT ACCESS

KITCHEN
12'-8" X 18'-4"
10' CH

PANTRY

UTILITY

DOWN TO BASEMENT

F W D

SECOND FLOOR

SUN DECK

BEDROOM 3
14'-0" X 12'-4"
9' CH

GAME ROOM
15'-0" X 19'-8"
9' CH

W.I.C.

BATH

LIN

W.I.C.

HALL

DN

DN

BEDROOM 4
13'-4" X 11'-4"
9' CH

BATH

OPEN TO BELOW

W.I.C.

BEDROOM 2
13'-0" X 13'-4"
9' CH

Eye Catching Tower
Price Code: I

- This plan features:
- — Four bedrooms
- — Three full and one half baths
- Study with high ceiling and windows
- Family Room with fireplace is open to the Breakfast Bay and gourmet Kitchen
- First floor Master Bedroom spans the width of the home and contains every luxury imaginable
- This plan has a three-car Garage with Storage Space
- This home is designed with basement and slab foundation options
- Alternate foundation options available at an additional charge. Please call 1-800-235-5700 for more information.

FIRST FLOOR — 2,117 SQ. FT.
SECOND FLOOR — 1,206 SQ. FT.
GARAGE — 685 SQ. FT.

TOTAL LIVING AREA:
3,323 SQ. FT

Conveniant and Compact

Price Code: K

■ This plan features:

— Five bedrooms

— Three full and one half bath

■ A full-front Entry features columns and four windows to brighten up the front rooms

■ Just off the Foyer, a central hallway connects the Dining Room to the spacious Family Room and compact Kitchen

■ If you're running late and don't have time to use the grand Dining Room, the Nook located just off the Kitchen is perfect for quick breakfasts and late-night snack

■ A large second floor Bonus Room has potential for anything from a game room to a study to an attic with a view

■ This home is designed with a slab foundation

FIRST FLOOR — 3,097 SQ. FT.
SECOND FLOOR — 813 SQ. FT.
GARAGE — 481 SQ. FT.

TOTAL LIVING AREA:
3,097 SQ. FT.

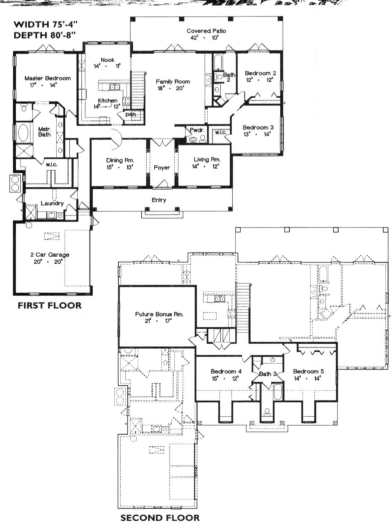

WIDTH 75'-4"
DEPTH 80'-8"

FIRST FLOOR

SECOND FLOOR

To order your Blueprints, call 1-800-235-5700

Photography supplied by The Meredith Corporation

WIDTH 64'-0"
DEPTH 65'-0"

PORCH

PLAYROOM
14x12

BRKFST
9x9

PORCH

UP   MUDRM

FAMILY
21x15

KITCHEN
14x11

R

MECH

GARAGE
21x26

P

UP

LIVING
14x15

ENTRY

DINING
14x16

PORCH

FIRST FLOOR

DRESSING

MASTER
BEDROOM
16x21

BATH

BEDROOM
12x12

CLOS CLOS

BATH

DN

HALL

DN

LDRY
W
D

BEDROOM
12x12

BEDROOM
14x13

BEDROOM
14x13

BATH

SECOND FLOOR

Luxurious Country

Price Code: L

- ■ This plan features:
- — Five bedrooms
- — Four full and one half baths
- ■ A welcoming front Porch adds style to this luxurious Country home
- ■ The Living Room and the Dining Room are located in the front of the home
- ■ The Family Room in the rear has a fireplace and doors to the rear Porch
- ■ A Playroom for the kids is located behind the Garage
- ■ Upstairs find the Master Bedroom, which comprises half of the space
- ■ This home is designed with a crawlspace foundation

FIRST FLOOR — 1,928 SQ. FT.
SECOND FLOOR — 2,364 SQ. FT.
GARAGE — 578 SQ. FT.

TOTAL LIVING AREA:
4,292 SQ. FT.

Touch of Country

Price Code: F

- This plan features:
— Three bedrooms
— Two full and one three-quarter baths

- A Study/Guest Room with convenient access to a full, hall Bath

- An elegant Dining Room topped by a decorative ceiling treatment

- An expansive Family Room equipped with a massive fireplace and built-in bookshelves

- An informal Breakfast Room conveniently enhanced by a built-in planning desk

- This home is designed with basement, slab and crawlspace foundation options

FIRST FLOOR — 1,378 SQ. FT.
SECOND FLOOR — 1,269 SQ. FT.
BASEMENT — 1,378 SQ. FT.
GARAGE — 717 SQ. FT.

TOTAL LIVING AREA:
2,647 SQ. FT.

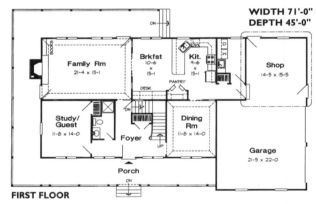

WIDTH 71'-0"
DEPTH 45'-0"

FIRST FLOOR

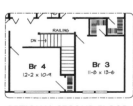

OPTIONAL SECOND FLOOR

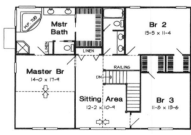

SECOND FLOOR

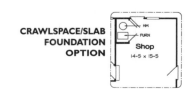

CRAWLSPACE/SLAB FOUNDATION OPTION

To order your Blueprints, call 1-800-235-5700

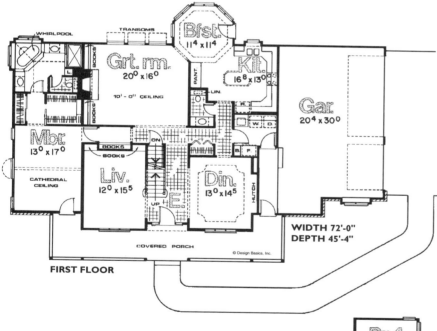

WHIRLPOOL

TRANSOMS

Bfst.
11⁴ x 11⁴

Grt. rm.
20⁰ x 16⁰

BOOKS

10'-0" CEILING

Kit.
16⁸ x 13⁰

PANT.

LIN.

Gar
20⁴ x 30⁰

Mbr.
13⁰ x 17⁰

BOOKS

BOOKS

DN

W. D.

CATHEDRAL
CEILING

Liv.
12⁰ x 15⁵

UP

E.

Din.
13⁰ x 14⁵

HUTCH

B. F.

WIDTH 72'-0"
DEPTH 45'-4"

COVERED PORCH

© Design Basics, Inc.

FIRST FLOOR

SECOND FLOOR

Br. 4
12⁰ x 13⁰

LIN.

GALLERY

DN

Br. 2
12⁰ x 13⁰

OPEN
TO
BELOW

Br. 3
12⁰ x 13⁰

PLANT SHELF

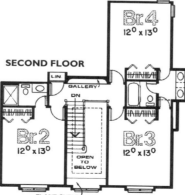

Fashionable Country-Style

Price Code: F

■ This plan features:

— Four bedrooms

— Two full, one three-quarter and one half baths

■ The large Covered Porch adds old-fashioned appeal to this modern floor plan

■ The Kitchen has a center island and is adjacent to the Gazebo-shaped Breakfast Area

■ This home is designed with basement and slab foundation options

■ Alternate foundation options available at an additional charge. Please call 1-800-235-5700 for more information.

FIRST FLOOR — 1,881 SQ. FT.
SECOND FLOOR — 814 SQ. FT.
BASEMENT — 1,881 SQ. FT.
GARAGE — 534 SQ. FT.

TOTAL LIVING AREA:
2,695 SQ. FT.

© HOME DESIGN SERVICES, INC.

Mexican–Style Facade

Price Code: H

- ■ This plan features:
  - — Four bedrooms
  - — Three full and one three-quarter baths

- ■ With a traditional Mexican-style exterior and a truly contemporary indoors, this house offers the best of both worlds: stylish aesthetics and convenient design

- ■ Upon entering the French doors in the front, you've got three options: forward to the large Living Room, left toward the Den or right into the Dining Room

- ■ A Family Room with a cozy corner fireplace literally reaches for the sky with its volume ceiling stretching up into the second floor

- ■ This home is designed with a slab foundation

FIRST FLOOR — 2,624 SQ. FT.
SECOND FLOOR — 540 SQ. FT.
GARAGE — 802 SQ. FT.
PORCH — 355 SQ. FT

TOTAL LIVING AREA:
3,164 SQ. FT.

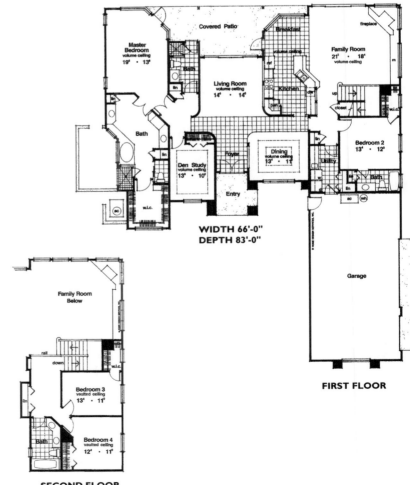

WIDTH 66'-0"
DEPTH 83'-0"

FIRST FLOOR

SECOND FLOOR

To order your Blueprints, call 1-800-235-5700

Master Suite Fireplace

Price Code: I

■ This plan features:
— Four bedrooms
— Two full and one half baths

■ The Living Room has views to the front and side and opens onto a rear Patio

■ The Kitchen, featuring an island and a Pantry, is open to the Breakfast Nook and Family Room

■ This home is designed with a slab foundation

FIRST FLOOR — 1,971 SQ. FT.
SECOND FLOOR — 1,482 SQ. FT.
GARAGE — 610 SQ. FT.

TOTAL LIVING AREA:
3,453 SQ. FT.

WIDTH 73'-0"
DEPTH 62'-0"

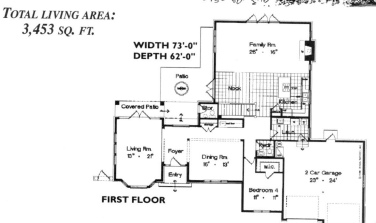

FIRST FLOOR

SECOND FLOOR

Home Theater

Price Code: K

■ This plan features:
— Three bedrooms
— Two full and two half baths

■ A pair of turrets house two secondary Bedrooms on the second floor

■ Windows and doors flood the Family Room with light

■ This home is designed with a slab foundation

FIRST FLOOR — 2,553 SQ. FT.
SECOND FLOOR — 1,370 SQ. FT.
BONUS — 760 SQ. FT.
GARAGE — 1,153 SQ. FT.

TOTAL LIVING AREA:
3,923 SQ. FT.

WIDTH 74'-0"
DEPTH 99'-4"

FIRST FLOOR

SECOND FLOOR

Corner Family Room Fireplace

Price Code: H

■ This plan features:
— Four bedrooms
— Three full and two three quarter baths
■ One of the main floor Baths is accessible from the rear Patio—ideal for location near a pool
■ The spacious Master Bath with walk-in closet provides plenty of room to circulate
■ This home is designed with a slab foundation

MAIN FLOOR — 2,624 SQ. FT.
UPPER FLOOR — 540 SQ. FT.
GARAGE — 802 SQ. FT.

TOTAL LIVING AREA:
3,164 SQ. FT.

WIDTH 66'-0"
DEPTH 83'-0"

MAIN FLOOR

UPPER FLOOR

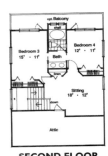

Secondary Bedroom Balcony

Price Code: H

■ This plan features:
— Four bedrooms
— Three full and two half baths
■ Curved walls of glass featured in the Dining Room and the Master Bedroom
■ A separate Bath accessible from the backyard is convenient if near a Pool
■ This home is designed with a slab foundation

FIRST FLOOR — 2,531 SQ. FT.
SECOND FLOOR — 669 SQ. FT.
GARAGE — 656 SQ. FT.

TOTAL LIVING AREA:
3,200 SQ. FT.

WIDTH 70'-0"
DEPTH 82'-4"

FIRST FLOOR

SECOND FLOOR

To order your Blueprints, call 1-800-235-5700

Family
& Kitch"

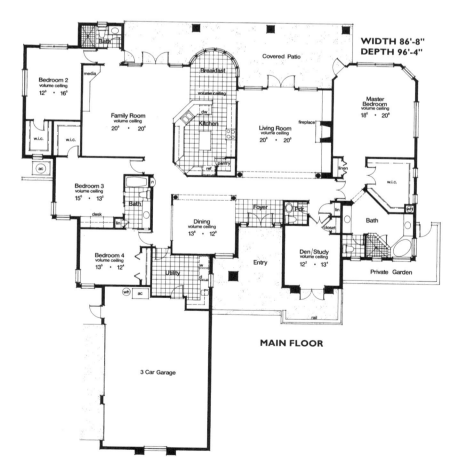

WIDTH 86'-8"
DEPTH 96'-4"

Covered Patio

Breakfast
volume ceiling

Bedroom 2
volume ceiling
12⁹ · 16⁹

media

Family Room
volume ceiling
20⁰ · 20⁴

Kitchen
dw

pantry

ref

Living Room
volume ceiling
20⁸ · 20⁰

fireplace

Master
Bedroom
volume ceiling
18⁰ · 20⁰

linen

w.i.c.

w.i.c.

w.i.c.

ac

Bedroom 3
volume ceiling
15⁰ · 13⁰

Bath

desk

lin

Dining
volume ceiling
13⁰ · 12⁰

Foyer

Pdr

lin

closet

Bath

Bedroom 4
volume ceiling
13⁰ · 12⁴

Utility

Entry

Den/Study
volume ceiling
12² · 13⁴

Private Garden

wh

ac

rail

MAIN FLOOR

3 Car Garage

Bay Master Bedroom

Price Code: K

■ This plan features:

— Four bedrooms

— Three full and one half baths

■ Curved windows define the shape of the Breakfast Area

■ French doors in the Den open to a paved front Patio

■ The Bath next to the Covered Patio is convenient for a backyard pool

■ This home is designed with a slab foundation

MAIN FLOOR — 3,891 SQ. FT.
GARAGE — 813 SQ. FT.

TOTAL LIVING AREA:
3,891 SQ. FT.

Art Niches in Foyer

Price Code: L

- **This plan features:**
- — Five bedrooms
- — Three full, two three-quarter, and two half baths
- **The living areas and Master Bedroom access the rear Patio, which features a half Bath and outdoor Kitchen**
- **The Kitchen includes an island with cooktop and a walk-in Pantry**
- **This home is designed with a slab foundation**

FIRST FLOOR — 3,739 SQ. FT.
SECOND FLOOR — 778 SQ. FT.
GARAGE — 844 SQ. FT.

TOTAL LIVING AREA:
4,517 SQ. FT.

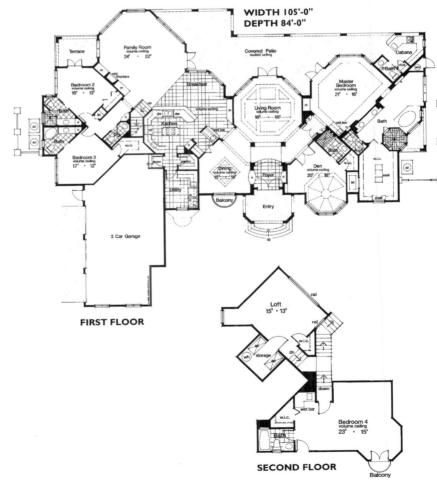

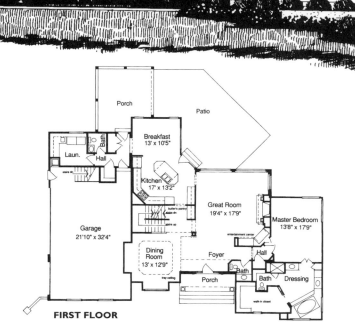

FIRST FLOOR

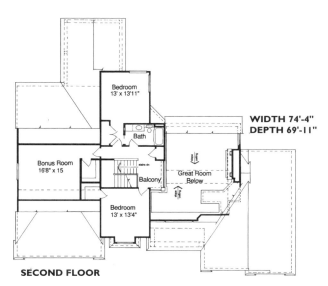

WIDTH 74'-4"
DEPTH 69'-11"

SECOND FLOOR

European Classic

Price Code: G

- ■ This plan features:
- — Three bedrooms
- — Two full and two half baths
- ■ A classic design with decorative stucco, keystone arches and boxed windows surrounding a broad pillar entrance into a spacious Foyer and two-story Great Room beyond
- ■ Island Kitchen opens to the Patio and a spacious Breakfast Room
- ■ A private wing featuring the Master Bedroom with a luxurious Bath, an over-sized walk-in closet, two vanities and a raised corner window tub
- ■ This home is designed with a basement foundation

FIRST FLOOR — 2,192 SQ. FT.
SECOND FLOOR — 654 SQ. FT.
BONUS ROOM — 325 SQ. FT.

TOTAL LIVING AREA:
2,846 SQ. FT.

Elegant Estate

Price Code: L

- This plan features:
— Four bedrooms
— Three full and three three-quarter baths
- The Master Bath has curved vanities, a corner soaking tub with views of the private garden and a shower with double doors
- Bedroom 4, which accesses a Bath and balcony and is close to the other secondary Bedrooms, is well-suited for a nanny's suite
- This home is designed with a slab foundation

MAIN FLOOR — 4,222 SQ. FT.
GARAGE — 869 SQ. FT.

TOTAL LIVING AREA:
4,812 SQ. FT.

WIDTH 83'-10"
DEPTH 112'-0"

MAIN FLOOR

BONUS

Morning Kitchen in Master Suite

Price Code: K

- This plan features:
— Three bedrooms
— Two full and one half baths
- Angled windows in the Leisure Room and Nook maximize natural light
- The Powder Room is set off from the traffic flow, allowing guests privacy
- This home is designed with a crawlspace foundation
- Alternate foundation options available at an additional charge. Please call 1-800-235-5700 for more information.

FIRST FLOOR — 1,664 SQ. FT.
SECOND FLOOR — 1,463 SQ. FT.
GARAGE — 599 SQ. FT.

TOTAL LIVING AREA:
3,127 SQ. FT.

WIDTH 59'-10"
DEPTH 62'-0"

FIRST FLOOR

SECOND FLOOR

To order your Blueprints, call 1-800-235-5700

Fluid Definition

Price Code: K

- This plan features:
  — Four Bedrooms
  — Two full, one three-quarter and one half baths
- A circular front Porch and an abundance of arched windows accent this home
- The Entry leads into a grand Foyer, where a radius staircase leads gracefully up to the second floor
- The Master Suite connects to a deluxe Bath with a whirlpool tub
- The Study has a window seat and built-in cabinetry
- The Leisure Room sports a built-in entertainment center and two sets of double doors to the wraparound Porch
- This home is designed with a crawlspace foundation
- Alternative foundation options are available at an additional cost. Please call 800-235-570 for more information.

MAIN FLOOR — 2,083 SQ. FT.
SECOND FLOOR — 1,013 SQ. FT.

TOTAL LIVING AREA:
3,096 SQ. FT.

WIDTH 74'-0"
DEPTH 88'-6"

FIRST FLOOR

SECOND FLOOR

A Grand Entrance

Price Code: F

- This plan features:
  — Five bedrooms
  — Three full baths
- The arched window above the front door provides a grand entrance
- Inside the two-story Foyer find the first of two open rail staircases in this home
- The formal Living and Dining Rooms are only separated by a set of boxed columns
- The U-shaped Kitchen has a walk-in Pantry and a wall oven
- A serving bar services the Breakfast Nook
- The Family Room has a fireplace as well as a vaulted ceiling
- Rounding out the first floor is a Den/Bedroom with a Bath located off of it
- Upstairs find the family sleeping quarters and Baths
- This home is designed with basement and crawlspace foundation options

FIRST FLOOR — 1,424 SQ. FT.
SECOND FLOOR — 1,256 SQ. FT.
BASEMENT — 1,424 SQ. FT.
GARAGE — 494 SQ. FT.

TOTAL LIVING AREA:
2,680 SQ. FT.

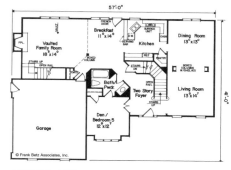

FIRST FLOOR

SECOND FLOOR

Volume Ceiling
Price Code: K

■ This plan features:
— Four bedrooms
— One full, two three-quarter, and one half bath
■ Triple French doors open the Great Room to the rear Porch
■ A curved balcony connects two Bedroom Suites featuring three-quarter Baths and walk-in closets
■ This home is designed with a crawlspace foundation
■ Alternate foundation options available at an additional charge. Please call 1-800-235-5700 for more information.

FIRST FLOOR — 2,138 SQ. FT.
SECOND FLOOR — 944 SQ. FT.
BONUS ROOM — 427 SQ. FT.

TOTAL LIVING AREA:
3,082 SQ. FT.

SECOND FLOOR

WIDTH 77'-2"
DEPTH 64'-0"

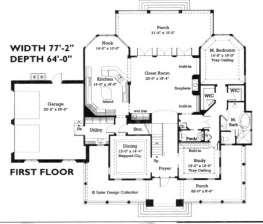

FIRST FLOOR

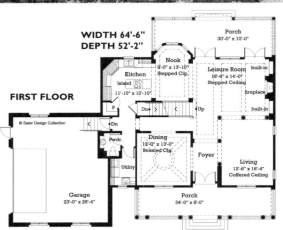

Two-Story Columns
Price Code: K

■ This plan features:
— Three bedrooms
— Two full and one half baths
■ The loft extends the columns of the Living Room to the two-story coffered ceiling
■ An island cooktop, corner Pantry, built-in refrigerator, and a bay window Nook highlight the Kitchen
■ This home is designed with a crawlspace foundation
■ Alternate foundation options available at an additional charge. Please call 1-800-235-5700 for more information.

FIRST FLOOR — 1,373 SQ. FT.
SECOND FLOOR — 1,581 SQ. FT.

TOTAL LIVING AREA:
2,954 SQ. FT.

WIDTH 64'-6"
DEPTH 52'-2"

FIRST FLOOR

SECOND FLOOR

To order your Blueprints, call 1-800-235-5700

Second Floor Decks

Price Code: L

■ This plan features:
— Five bedrooms
— Three full and one half baths
■ A curved staircase in the Foyer greets visitors
■ There are built-in desks in the Kitchen and Master Bedroom
■ This home is designed with a basement foundation

FIRST FLOOR — 2,482 SQ. FT.
SECOND FLOOR — 1,722 SQ. FT.
GARAGE — 792 SQ. FT.

TOTAL LIVING AREA: 4,204 SQ. FT.

FIRST FLOOR

SECOND FLOOR

Elegant Victorian

Price Code: E

■ This plan features:
— Three bedrooms
— Two full and one half baths
■ Sit and relax on the front Porch at the end of the day with family and friends
■ Serve guests dinner in the bayed Dining Room and then gather in the Living Room which features a cathedral ceiling
■ There is plenty of space for activities in the Family Room which is accented by a fireplace
■ The Master Bedroom has a Sitting Area, walk-in closet, and a private Bath
■ Two additional Bedrooms share a full Bath, and there is a Bonus Room upstairs for future expansion
■ This plan features a three-car Garage with space for storage
■ This home is designed with basement and slab foundation options

FIRST FLOOR — 1,447 SQ. FT.
SECOND FLOOR — 1,008 SQ. FT.
GARAGE — 756 SQ. FT.

TOTAL LIVING AREA: 2,455 SQ. FT.

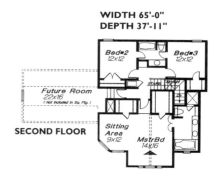

FIRST FLOOR

WIDTH 65'-0"
DEPTH 37'-11"

SECOND FLOOR

Desks and Shelves in Upstairs Bedrooms

Price Code: L

■ This plan features:

— Four bedrooms

— Five full and one half baths

■ The Garage includes workbenches, a bay for a golf cart, and extra storage space

■ The Den, Family Room and Master Bedroom all feature fireplaces

■ This home is designed with a crawlspace foundation

FIRST FLOOR — 3,465 SQ. FT.
SECOND FLOOR — 975 SQ. FT.
BONUS ROOM — 440 SQ. FT.
GARAGE — 808 SQ. FT.

TOTAL LIVING AREA:
4,440 SQ. FT.

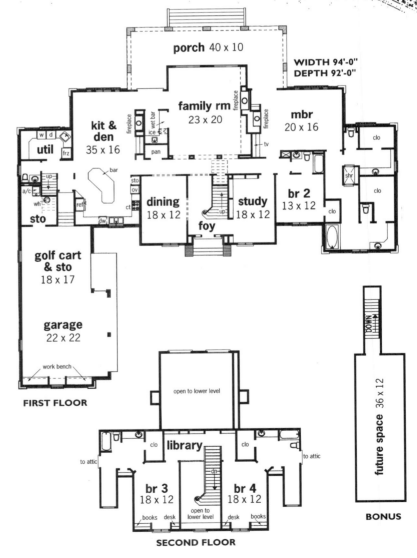

Floor Plan Labels

FIRST FLOOR

- PATIO
- FAMILY ROOM — VAULTED CEILING — 24'-2"x14'-10"
- FIREPLACE
- NOOK — 10'-0"x11'-6"
- KITCHEN — 10'-6"x12'-6"
- OVEN
- DW
- REF
- PANTRY
- STUDY/BEDROOM — 10'-0"x13'-0"
- BATH
- DINING ROOM — 11'-6"x11'-8"
- SHELF
- LNDRY.
- D W
- DN
- UP
- LIVING ROOM — 11'-6" CEILING — 15'-4"x12'-10"
- OPTIONAL WORKBENCH
- OPTIONAL DOOR
- 2-CAR GARAGE — OPTIONAL 3-CAR GARAGE
- FOYER — 10'-6" CEILING
- PORCH
- 45'-0"
- 52'-4"

SECOND FLOOR

- OPEN TO BELOW
- BEDROOM — 11'-8"x12'-0"
- LIN
- BATH
- OPTIONAL FIREPLACE
- MASTER BEDROOM — VAULTED CEILING — 17'-0"x16'-0"
- DN
- OPEN TO BELOW
- BEDROOM — 11'-6"x15'-0"
- HIS
- LINEN
- MASTER BATH
- HERS

Comfortable Living

Price Code: F

- ■ This plan features:
- — Four bedrooms
- — Three full baths

- ■ Easy access between Living Room and Dining Room for ease in entertaining

- ■ Modern Kitchen with double sink, built-in Pantry and peninsula counter

- ■ Vaulted ceiling in the Family Room, which also features a fireplace

- ■ A Master Suite with vaulted ceiling, optional fireplace, his and her walk-in closets and lavish Master Bath

- ■ This home is designed with basement, slab and crawlspace foundation options

FIRST FLOOR — 1,574 SQ. FT.
SECOND FLOOR — 1,098 SQ. FT.

TOTAL LIVING AREA: 2,672 SQ. FT.

Opulence and Grandeur

Price Code: K

- This plan features:

— Four bedrooms

— Three full and one half baths

- Dramatic two-story glass Entry with a curved staircase

- Both Living and Family Rooms offer high ceilings, decorative windows and large fireplaces

- Large but efficient Kitchen with a cooktop serving island, walk-in Pantry, bright Breakfast Area and Patio access

- Lavish Master Bedroom with a cathedral ceiling, two walk-in closets and Bath

- This home is designed with basement and slab foundation options

FIRST FLOOR — 2,506 SQ. FT.
SECOND FLOOR — 1,415 SQ. FT.
GARAGE — 660 SQ. FT.

TOTAL LIVING AREA:
3,921 SQ. FT.

WIDTH 80'-5"
DEPTH 50'-4.5"

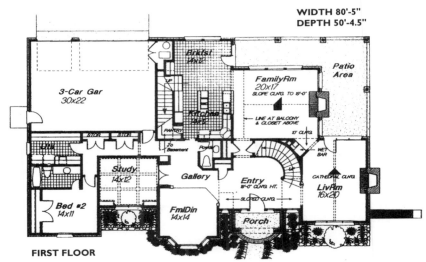

FIRST FLOOR

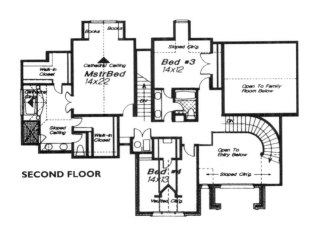

SECOND FLOOR

To order your Blueprints, call 1-800-235-5700

Master Bedroom Opens to a Private Covered Patio

Price Code: H

This plan features:

- Four bedrooms
- Two full, one three-quarter, and one half baths
- Each Bedroom has a large closet and an adjacent Bathroom
- Access from the Garage is through a hall, which houses the Utility Room and a Pantry
- The Master Bedroom opens to a private covered Patio for those who need a peaceful getaway
- This home is designed with a slab foundation

FIRST FLOOR — 2,169 SQ. FT.
SECOND FLOOR — 833 SQ. FT.
BONUS — 272 SQ. FT.
GARAGE — 675 SQ. FT.

TOTAL LIVING AREA:
3,002 SQ. FT.

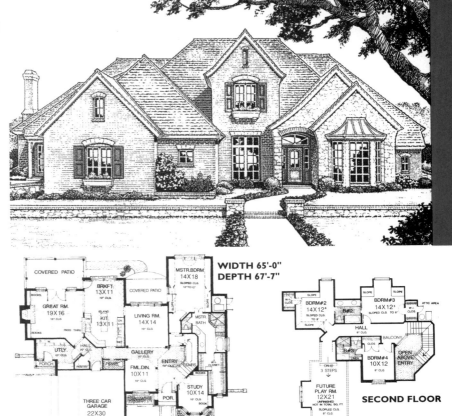

Country Elegance

Price Code: J

This plan features:

- Four bedrooms
- Three full and one half bath
- An inviting Covered Porch adds a touch of elegance
- The combination Bedroom/Study and Formal Dining Room flank a grand Foyer
- A Master Bedroom with a window-lined Sitting Area is connected to a generous walk-in closet by a large Master Bath
- The Family Room comes complete with a fireplace and entertainment center
- This home is designed with basement, slab, and crawlspace foundation options

FIRST FLOOR — 3,578 SQ. FT.
BONUS — 460 SQ. FT.
GARAGE — 864 SQ. FT

TOTAL LIVING AREA:
3,578 SQ. FT.

To order your Blueprints, call 1-800-235-5700

79

PLAN NO. 66014

Symphony in Brick
Price Code: J

■ This plan features:
— Four bedrooms
— Three full and one half baths
■ The entrance opens onto a Gallery with wood flooring
■ A Main Hall leads straight past a Study connected to a special Private Lanai
■ The Family Living Room sits just off the Great Room, complete with bookshelves and an Entertainment Center
■ A large Playroom rests above a spacious three-car Garage
■ An impressive Kitchen island and bayed Breakfast Area accentuate the Kitchen
■ This home is designed with slab and crawlspace foundation options

FIRST FLOOR — 2,498 SQ. FT.
SECOND FLOOR — 1,012 SQ. FT.
BONUS — 340 SQ. FT.
GARAGE — 810 SQ. FT.

TOTAL LIVING AREA:
3,510 SQ. FT.

WIDTH 72'-0"
DEPTH 62'-0"

FIRST FLOOR

SECOND FLOOR

PLAN NO. 98419

Stucco & Stone
Price Code: E

■ This plan features:
— Three bedrooms
— Two full and one half baths
■ Vaulted Great Room unfolds directly beyond the Entry and is highlighted by a fireplace and French doors to the rear yard
■ Decorative columns define the Dining Room
■ A built-in Pantry and a radius window above the double sink in the Kitchen add style
■ The Breakfast Bay is crowned by a vaulted ceiling
■ There is a tray ceiling over the Master Bedroom and Sitting Area, while a vaulted ceiling crowns the Master Bath
■ Two additional Bedrooms, each with a walk-in closet, share the full double-vanity Bath in the hall
■ This home is designed with basement, slab, and crawlspace foundation options

FIRST FLOOR — 1,796 SQ. FT.
SECOND FLOOR — 629 SQ. FT.
BONUS ROOM — 208 SQ. FT.
BASEMENT — 1,796 SQ. FT.
GARAGE — 588 SQ. FT.

TOTAL LIVING AREA:
2,425 SQ. FT.

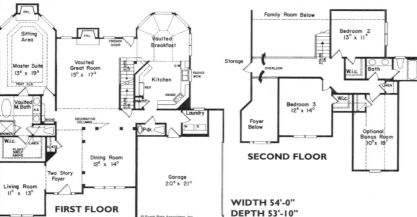

FIRST FLOOR
SECOND FLOOR

WIDTH 54'-0"
DEPTH 53'-10"

© Frank Betz Associates, Inc.

WIDTH 107'-10"
DEPTH 92'-8"

DOUBLE GARAGE

BRKFST ROOM

UTILITY

COVERED PATIO

MASTER BEDRM. 19 X 16

MASTER BATH

KITCHEN

WALK-IN CLOSET

FAMILY ROOM 23 X 18

STUDY

PANTRY

FORMAL DINING 15 X 14

FORMAL LIVING 14 X 19

BEDRM. TWO 13 X 15

BATH TWO

PORTE-COCHERE

COVERED PORCH

SINGLE GARAGE

FIRST FLOOR

ATTIC SPACE

FUTURE BONUS RM. 427 SQ. FT. NOT INCLUDED IN OVERALL SQ. FTGE.

STOR.

BEDRM. THREE 13 X 14

BATH THREE

BEDRM. THREE 13 X 16

HALL

STAIRS

BALCONY

ATTIC SPACE

BATH FOUR

BEDRM. FIVE 13 X 14

SITTING ROOM

OPEN TO ENTRY BELOW

OPEN TO COVD PORCH

SECOND FLOOR

French Chateau

Price Code: L

■ This plan features:

— Five bedrooms

— Four full and one half baths

■ A two-story Foyer with a dramatic circular staircase defines the elegant style of this home

■ Fireplaces flanked by built-ins are featured in the formal Living Room and Family Room

■ The gourmet Kitchen has a wetbar with wine cooler and a huge walk-in Pantry

■ This home is designed with basement and slab foundation options

FIRST FLOOR — 3,920 SQ. FT.
SECOND FLOOR — 1,434 SQ. FT.
BONUS ROOM — 427 SQ. FT.
GARAGE — 740 SQ. FT.

TOTAL LIVING AREA:
5,354 SQ. FT.

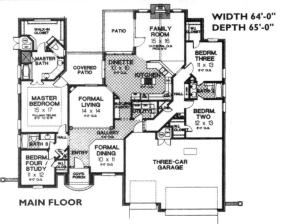

European Character

Price Code: F

- This plan features:
- — Four bedrooms
- — Three full and one half baths
- The columned Formal Living Room greets you as you enter the home
- A Butler's Pantry off the Kitchen serves the formal Dining Room
- An angled hallway links the Family Room to the gallery
- This home is designed with a slab foundation

MAIN FLOOR — 2,526 SQ. FT.
GARAGE — 664 SQ. FT.

TOTAL LIVING AREA:
2,526 SQ. FT.

WIDTH 64'-0"
DEPTH 65'-0"

MAIN FLOOR

PLAN NO. 66026

Magnificent Manor

Price Code: L

- This plan features:
- — Five bedrooms
- — Four full and two half baths
- The high ceilings on the first and second floors give this home palatial proportions
- A spectacular Master Bedroom includes an octagonal Library with French door access to the Living Room and wetbar
- This home is designed with a slab foundation

FIRST FLOOR — 3,746 SQ. FT.
SECOND FLOOR — 1,643 SQ. FT.
GARAGE — 920 SQ. FT.

TOTAL LIVING AREA:
5,389 SQ. FT.

WIDTH 100'-0"
DEPTH 70'-1"

FIRST FLOOR

SECOND FLOOR

To order your Blueprints, call 1-800-235-5700

Especially Unique

Price Code: F

■ This plan features:
 – Four bedrooms
 – Three full and one half baths
■ An arch covered Entry and arched windows add a unique flair to the home
■ From the 11-foot Entry turn left in to the Study/Media Room
■ The formal Dining Room is open to the Gallery, and the Living Room beyond
■ The Family Room has a built-in entertainment center, fireplace and access to the rear Patio
■ The isolated Master Bedroom has a fireplace, a private Bath and a walk-in closet
■ Three additional Bedrooms on the opposite side of the home share two full Baths
■ This home is designed with a slab foundation

MAIN FLOOR — 2,748 SQ. FT.
GARAGE — 660 SQ. FT.

TOTAL LIVING AREA:
2,748 SQ. FT.

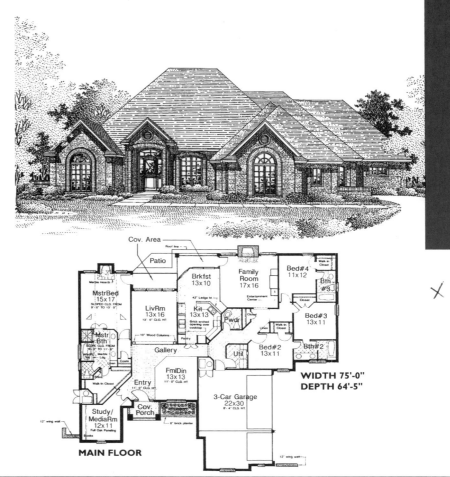

WIDTH 75'-0"
DEPTH 64'-5"

MAIN FLOOR

Side Entry

Price Code: F

■ This plan features:
 — Four bedrooms
 — Three full and one half baths
■ Durable tile flooring in high traffic areas makes cleaning a snap
■ A raised ledge in the Kitchen offers meal-prep privacy in the Kitchen while letting the cook enjoy views into the Great Room
■ This home is designed with a slab foundation

MAIN FLOOR — 2,701 SQ. FT.
BONUS ROOM — 473 SQ. FT.
GARAGE — 662 SQ. FT.

TOTAL LIVING AREA:
2,701 SQ. FT.

BONUS OPTION

WIDTH 73'-6"
DEPTH 67'-4"

MAIN FLOOR

Arched Stone Entry

Price Code: F

- This plan features:
  — Four bedrooms
  — Three full and one half baths
- A window wall in the Great Room overlooks the Covered Patio and rear yard
- Expansion and customization options are found in the Study and Bonus Room
- This home is designed with a slab foundation

MAIN FLOOR — 2,625 SQ. FT.
BONUS ROOM — 350 SQ. FT.
GARAGE — 702 SQ. FT.

TOTAL LIVING AREA:
2,625 SQ. FT.

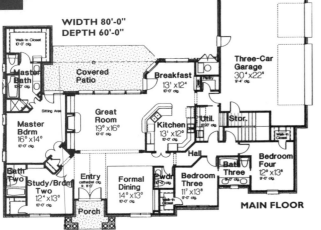

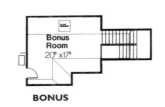

Stunning Entry

Price Code: I

- This plan features:
  — Four bedrooms
  — Three full and one half baths
- A curving staircase and views through the house highlight the Entry
- The focal point fireplace in the Great Room is surrounded by glass, filling the room with natural light
- This home is designed with a slab foundation

FIRST FLOOR — 2,326 SQ. FT.
SECOND FLOOR — 1,013 SQ. FT.
BONUS ROOM — 256 SQ. FT.
GARAGE — 704 SQ. FT.

TOTAL LIVING AREA:
3,339 SQ. FT.

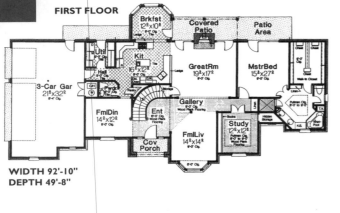

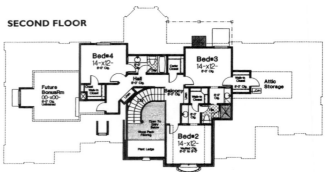

To order your Blueprints, call 1-800-235-5700

BOOKS

Br.4
12⁰ x 13⁰

LIN.

Br.2
12⁰ x 14⁰

10' - 0"
CEILING

Br.3
12⁰ x 14⁰

SECOND FLOOR

WHIRLPOOL

COVERED VERANDA

SKYLIGHTS

Grt. rm.
18⁰ x 18⁰

Hrth.
12⁷ x 15³

Bfst.
11³ x 11³

11' - 8" CEILING

ENT. CENTER

SNACK BAR

Mbr.
16³ x 14⁰

10' - 0" CEILING

UP

P

Kit.
12⁹ x 12⁸

DN

E.

Den
13³ x 14⁰

10' - 4"
CLG.

Din.
12⁰ x 15⁰

Gar.
21³ x 31³

COVERED
STOOP

TRANSOMS

60' - 0"

FIRST FLOOR

© Design Basics, Inc.

68' - 8"

Stucco, Brick and Elegant Details

Price Code: G

■ This plan features:

— Four bedrooms

— Three full and one half baths

■ Majestic Entry opens to Den and Dining Room

■ Expansive Great Room shares a see-thru fireplace with the Hearth Room

■ Lovely Hearth Room enhanced by three skylights above triple arched windows

■ Sumptuous Master Bedroom Suite with corner windows and two closets

■ This home is designed with basement and slab foundation options

■ Alternate foundation options available at an additional charge. Please call 1-800-235-5700 for more information.

FIRST FLOOR — 2,084 SQ. FT.
SECOND FLOOR — 848 SQ. FT.
BASEMENT — 2,084 SQ. FT.
GARAGE — 682 SQ. FT.

TOTAL LIVING AREA:
2,932 SQ. FT.

Entertaining Options

Price Code: J

- This plan features:
— Three bedrooms
— Two full, one three-quarter, and one half baths
- The Formal Dining Room enjoys magnificent views of the circular staircase in the Foyer
- In the Study, a built-in desk is hidden behind double doors
- This home is designed with a slab foundation

FIRST FLOOR — 2,862 SQ. FT.
SECOND FLOOR — 675 SQ. FT.
BONUS ROOM — 416 SQ. FT.
GARAGE — 702 SQ. FT.

TOTAL LIVING AREA:
3,537 SQ. FT.

WIDTH 78'-9"
DEPTH 72'-3"

FIRST FLOOR

SECOND FLOOR

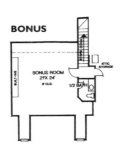

Extra Storage

Price Code: E

- This plan features:
— Four bedrooms
— Two full and one half baths
- Views of the front and rear yard from the Kitchen allow the cook to oversee all outdoor activity
- Keeping toys and clutter out of sight is easy in the Bonus Room with built-ins and half Bath
- This home is designed with a slab foundation

MAIN FLOOR — 2,543 SQ. FT.
BONUS ROOM — 504 SQ. FT.
GARAGE — 704 SQ. FT.

TOTAL LIVING AREA:
2,543 SQ. FT.

MAIN FLOOR

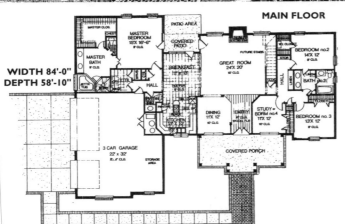

WIDTH 84'-0"
DEPTH 58'-10"

BONUS

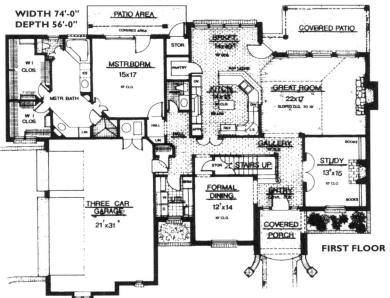

WIDTH 74'-0"
DEPTH 56'-0"

PATIO AREA
COVERED AREA

STOR.

W.I. CLOS.

KS

MSTR.BDRM.
15x17
10' CLG.

MSTR. BATH

W.I. CLOS.

LIN.

HALL

LIN.

PANTRY

OV

KITCH.
14x15

BRKFT.
14x9

COVERED PATIO

GREAT ROOM
22x17
SLOPED CLG. TO 19'

REF.

GALLERY

STAIRS UP

STOR.

BOOKS

STUDY
13'x15
10' CLG.

BOOKS

THREE CAR GARAGE
21'x31'

FORMAL DINING
12'x14
10' CLG.

ENTRY

COVERED PORCH

FIRST FLOOR

DORMER

SLOPE

BDRM.4
15'x11
8' CLG.

DORMER

SLOPE

BDRM.3
13'x11
8' CLG.

SLOPE

OPEN TO FAMILY ROOM BELOW
SLOPED CLG. 19'

CLOS.

LINEN

CLOS.

HALL

BALCONY

UP 3 STEPS

W.I. CLOS.

RECREATION ROOM
12x25
SLOPED CLG. 8' TO 8'

BDRM.2
12'x14

COVERED PORCH

SECOND FLOOR

SLOPE

Stone, Stucco, and Brick Siding

Price Code: J

■ This plan features:

— Three bedrooms

— Three full and one half baths

■ Beautiful and practical, the exterior of this home is almost maintenance-free

■ The cozy Study, with fireplace and built-in bookshelves, opens to the Entry through double doors

■ A curving balcony overlooks the Entry and Great Room

■ This home is designed with a slab foundation

FIRST FLOOR — 2,317 SQ. FT.
SECOND FLOOR — 1,302 SQ. FT.
GARAGE — 672 SQ. FT.

TOTAL LIVING AREA:
3,619 SQ. FT.

Luxury and Style

Price Code: G

- This plan features:
  — Three bedrooms
  — Two full and one half baths
- A two-story Foyer sets the tone for grandeur
- A two-story ceiling and two-way fireplace accent the formal Living Room and the Family Room
- The Family Room, Breakfast Nook and Kitchen designed in an open layout create a terrific flow
- A first floor Master Suite boasts a tray ceiling, enhanced by a lavish Bath and walk-in closet
- Two additional Bedrooms, one with a sloped ceiling and built-in desk, can be found on the second floor
- This home is designed with crawlspace and slab foundation options

FIRST FLOOR — 1,979 SQ. FT.
SECOND FLOOR — 948 SQ. FT.

TOTAL LIVING AREA:
2,927 SQ. FT.

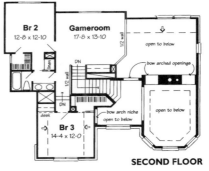

FIRST FLOOR

SECOND FLOOR

Single-Level Convenience

Price Code: I

- This plan features:
  — Four bedrooms
  — Three full and one half baths
- Enjoy the stately facade of a two-story home with the convenience of single-level living
- Mixed rooflines add to the interest of this home
- Interior columns separate the Entry, Great Room, and formal Dining Room
- This home is designed with a crawlspace foundation

MAIN FLOOR — 3,439 SQ. FT.
BONUS ROOM — 541 SQ. FT.
GARAGE — 816 SQ. FT.

TOTAL LIVING AREA:
3,439 SQ. FT.

MAIN FLOOR

BONUS OPTION

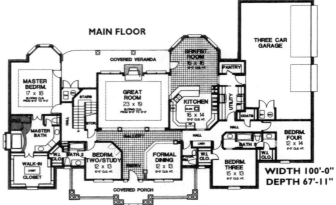

To order your Blueprints, call 1-800-235-5700

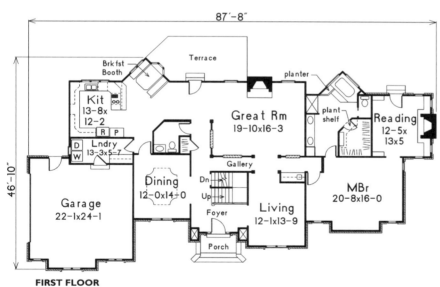

FIRST FLOOR

87'-8"

46'-10"

Brkfst Booth

Terrace

Kit 13-8x 12-2

R P

D W

Lndry 13-3x5-7

Garage 22-1x24-1

Dining 12-0x14-0

Great Rm 19-10x16-3

Gallery

Dn Up

Foyer

Porch

Living 12-1x13-9

planter

plant shelf

Reading 12-5x 13x5

MBr 20-8x16-0

SECOND FLOOR

Br 2 12-11x12-7

open to below

Br 3 12-0x13-3

Dn

open to below

Br 4 12-1x12-4

Walk-in Bedroom Closets

Price Code: H

■ This plan features:

— Four bedrooms

— Three full and one half baths

■ The Master Bedroom has a separate reading room complete with a fireplace and bookshelves

■ A banquette in the Breakfast Area features a bay window

■ This home is designed with basement, slab, and crawlspace foundation options

FIRST FLOOR — 2,273 SQ. FT.
SECOND FLOOR — 961 SQ. FT.

TOTAL LIVING AREA: 3,234 SQ. FT.

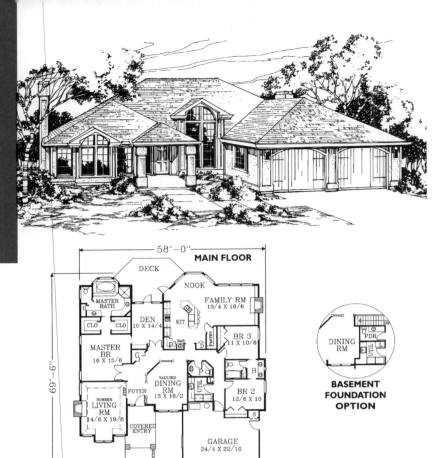

Accent on Privacy
Price Code: F

■ This plan features:
— Three bedrooms
— Two full and one half baths
■ Stucco exterior and arched windows create a feeling of grandeur
■ Sunken Living Room has a fireplace and elegant decorative ceiling
■ Sweeping views of the backyard and direct access to the rear Deck from the Den, Kitchen and Breakfast Nook
■ Gourmet Kitchen with two Pantries, full-height shelving, and a large island snack bar
■ Master Bedroom enjoys its privacy on the opposite side of the home from the other Bedrooms
■ Fabulous Master Bath with recessed tub and corner shower
■ Continental Bath connecting the two secondary Bedrooms
■ This home is designed with basement, slab, and crawlspace foundation options

MAIN FLOOR — 2,591 SQ. FT.
BASEMENT — 2,591 SQ. FT.

TOTAL LIVING AREA:
2,591 SQ. FT.

Finished Lower Floor
Price Code: L

■ This plan features:
— Four bedrooms
— Three full and one half baths
■ A staircase in the Great Room leads down a two-story Atrium window wall to a lower floor Home Theater
■ Gardeners will appreciate the Lawn-and-Garden Room that opens to a Patio
■ This home is designed with a basement foundation

MAIN FLOOR — 3,050 SQ. FT.
LOWER FLOOR — 1,776 SQ. FT.

TOTAL LIVING AREA:
4,826 SQ. FT.

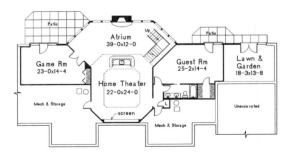

To order your Blueprints, call 1-800-235-5700

Sloped Gable End

Price Code: J

■ This plan features:
— Four bedrooms
— Three full and one half baths
■ A sloped gable, window boxes, and shutters add to the curb appeal of this cottage
■ A gently curving balcony has a sweeping view of the two-story Living Room
■ This home is designed with basement, slab, and crawlspace foundation options

MAIN FLOOR — 2,518 SQ. FT.
SECOND FLOOR — 1,013 SQ. FT.
BONUS ROOM — 792 SQ. FT.
GARAGE — 793 SQ. FT.

TOTAL LIVING AREA:
3,531 SQ. FT.

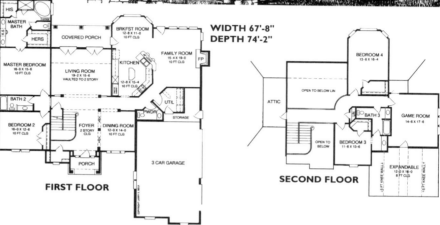

WIDTH 67'-8"
DEPTH 74'-2"

FIRST FLOOR

SECOND FLOOR

Grand Estate

Price Code: J

■ This plan features:
— Three bedrooms
— Three full and one half baths
■ The Foyer leads straight into a gigantic Great Room featuring built-in shelves
■ The rear is graced by a long and elegant Veranda
■ A Mud Room and unheated Shop connect with a huge three-car Garage
■ Ample storage space can be found on the second floor, where a Bonus Room connects with two Bedrooms and a large attic
■ This home is designed with slab and crawlspace foundation options

FIRST FLOOR — 2,698 SQ. FT.
SECOND FLOOR — 819 SQ. FT.
BONUS — 370 SQ. FT.

TOTAL LIVING AREA:
3,517 SQ. FT.

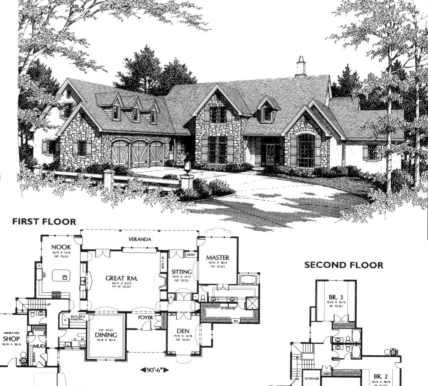

FIRST FLOOR

SECOND FLOOR

Amazing Stories
Price Code: L

- This plan features:
  - Four bedrooms
  - Two full, one half and one three-quarter baths
- A bayed Den with built-in shelving sits just off the main entrance
- The circular staircase connects both floors, allowing for a generous two-story Living Room and Family Room
- The Master Bedroom is conveniently connected to the Linen Closet and a large Master Bathroom, featuring a spa tub
- A Butler's Pantry, Kitchen Island and Desk complement the Kitchen Nook
- The Bonus Space above the Garage offers great potential
- This home is designed with a crawlspace foundation

FIRST FLOOR — 3,098 SQ. FT.
SECOND FLOOR — 1,113 SQ. FT.
BONUS — 567 SQ. FT.
GARAGE — 1,050 SQ. FT.

TOTAL LIVING AREA: 4,211 SQ. FT.

SECOND FLOOR

FIRST FLOOR

Classic Home
Price Code: L

- This plan features:
  - Four bedrooms
  - Three full and one half baths
- Space and light connect the Entry, Gallery, Dining Room and Living Room
- A Butler's Pantry connects the Kitchen to the Dining Room
- The Master Suite encompasses a whole wing on the first floor
- Up the curved staircase find three Bedrooms, all with walk-in closets
- Also upstairs is a Game Room with built-in cabinets
- A three-car Garage completes this home
- This home is designed with basement and slab foundation options
- Alternate foundation options available at an additional charge. Please call 1-800-235-5700 for more information.

FIRST FLOOR — 2,688 SQ. FT.
SECOND FLOOR — 1,540 SQ. FT.
BASEMENT — 2,688 SQ. FT.
GARAGE — 635 SQ. FT.

TOTAL LIVING AREA: 4,228 SQ. FT.

WIDTH 84'-3"
DEPTH 81'-0"

SECOND FLOOR

FIRST FLOOR

OPTIONAL BASEMENT STAIR LOCATION

Rural and Regal
Price Code: I

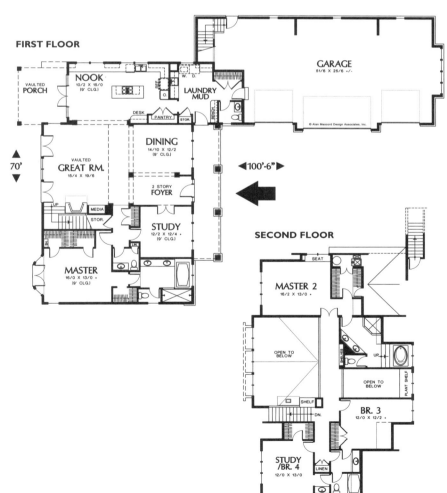

FIRST FLOOR

GARAGE
51/6 X 25/6 +/-

VAULTED PORCH

NOOK
10/2 X 15/0
(9' CLG.)

LAUNDRY
MUD

DESK
PANTRY
STOR.

DINING
14/10 X 12/2
(9' CLG.)

70'

VAULTED
GREAT RM.
15/4 X 19/6

◄100'-6"►

2 STORY
FOYER

UP
MEDIA
STOR

STUDY
12/2 X 12/4
(9' CLG.)

MASTER
16/0 X 13/0 +
(9' CLG.)

© Alan Mascord Design Associates, Inc.

SECOND FLOOR

SEAT

MASTER 2
16/2 X 13/0 +

OPEN TO
BELOW

UP

OPEN TO
BELOW

PLANT SHELF

SHELF

BR. 3
12/0 X 12/2

DN.

STUDY
/BR. 4
12/0 X 13/0

LINEN

■ This plan features:

— Four bedrooms

— Three full and two half bathrooms

■ A charming Front Porch and a
Vaulted Porch in the back offer the
great outdoors

■ The two-story Foyer connects the
Vaulted Great Room and Spacious
Dining Room, with a Kitchen Nook
just off the main hall

■ A plant shelf in the Foyer has potential
to be an indoor greenhouse

■ The combination Mud Room and
Laundry links the house to a
three-car Garage

■ This home is designed with a
crawlspace foundation

FIRST FLOOR — 2,222 SQ. FT.
SECOND FLOOR — 1,235 SQ. FT.
GARAGE — 1,388 SQ. FT.

TOTAL LIVING AREA:
3,457 SQ. FT.

Dual Porch Bays

Price Code: J

■ This plan features:

— Three bedrooms

— Three full and two half baths

■ The second floor Game Room, with computer center and balcony access, is a kid's haven

■ Walk-in closets in every Bedroom provide storage for all seasons

■ This home is designed with basement, slab, and crawlspace foundation options

FIRST FLOOR — 1,583 SQ. FT.
SECOND FLOOR — 1,973 SQ. FT.
GARAGE — 2,139 SQ. FT.

TOTAL LIVING AREA:
3,556 SQ. FT.

FIRST FLOOR

68' 2"

61' 0"

COVERED PORCH 18'-6" X 10'-0"
FRENCH DOORS
STORAGE 8'-2" X 14'-6"
BREAKFAST ROOM 12'-2" X 11'-0"
FIREPLACE
3-CAR GARAGE 28'-0" X 33'-2"
GREAT ROOM 18'-6" X 21'-0"
LAU. ROOM 8'-0" X 8'-6"
M.W. OVEN
KITCHEN 12'-2" X 16'-4"
REF
DW
PAN
8" COLUMNS
DINING ROOM 13'-10" X 11'-8"
FOYER 8'-0" X 18'-4"
FORMAL LIVING 13'-10" X 14'-6"
8" COLUMNS
9' COVERD PORCH
12" COLUMNS
20" COLUMNS

SECOND FLOOR

BALCONY 18'-6" X 10'-0"
FRENCH DOORS
WINDOW SEAT
WHP TUB
M.BATH 14'-4" X 13'-6"
BEDROOM 3 12'-8" X 12'-10"
MASTER SUITE 16'-0" X 14'-8"
LIN
ATTIC STORAGE
GLASS SHWR
LIN
M.CLOSET 13'-0" X 6'-8"
BUILT-INS
COMPUTER CENTER
BEDROOM 2 14'-4" X 11'-8"
GAME ROOM 22'-8" X 22'-8"
10' BALCONY

Southern Style

Price Code: L

- This plan features:
  — Four bedrooms
  — Three full and two half baths
- The stately Portico boasts four two-story columns
- A railed staircase connects both floors of a stunning receiving hall
- The Study and Breakfast Room each connect to a spacious one-story Terrace
- An elegant Gathering Room is the first floor's central point
- Beneath a covered Porch, an old-fashioned Service Entrance leads to the Laundry and Kitchen
- This home is designed with a basement foundation

FIRST FLOOR — 2,529 SQ. FT.
SECOND FLOOR — 1,872 SQ. FT.

TOTAL LIVING AREA:
4,401 SQ. FT.

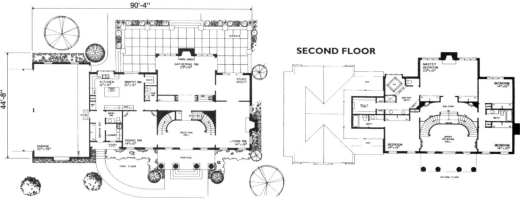

FIRST FLOOR

SECOND FLOOR

Maintenance Free Brick Exterior

Price Code: H

- This plan features:
  — Four bedrooms
  — Four full baths
- This traditional style brick home has a wraparound Porch
- Upon entering the two-story Foyer, an open rail staircase comes into view
- On either side of the Foyer are the identically sized Living and Dining Rooms
- In the rear, find the Great Room which offers a fireplace and built-in cabinets
- The U-shaped Kitchen with a center island is located adjacent to the Nook
- The Study is located in a quiet rear corner of the home
- Upstairs are the sleeping quarters, all with ample closet space
- This home is designed with basement and crawlspace foundation options

FIRST FLOOR — 1,609 SQ. FT.
SECOND FLOOR — 1,445 SQ. FT.
BASEMENT — 1,609 SQ. FT.
GARAGE — 527 SQ. FT.

TOTAL LIVING AREA:
3,054 SQ. FT.

FIRST FLOOR

SECOND FLOOR

Country French Design

Price Code: F

■ This plan features:

— Three bedrooms

— Two full and one half baths

■ Open Foyer receives light from the dormer above

■ Formal Living and Dining Rooms are in traditional location on either side of the Foyer

■ Great Room features rear wall hearth fireplace and a built-in media center

■ Breakfast Bay is open into the fully equipped U-shaped Kitchen

■ This home is designed with basement and crawlspace foundation options

FIRST FLOOR — 1,997 SQ. FT.
SECOND FLOOR — 717 SQ. FT.
BONUS ROOM — 541 SQ. FT.
GARAGE — 575 SQ. FT.

TOTAL LIVING AREA:
2,714 SQ. FT.

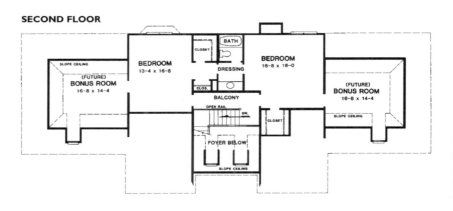

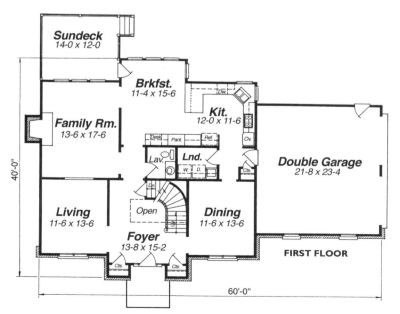

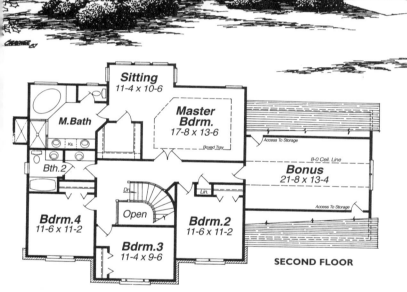

Sitting
11-4 x 10-6

Master Bdrm.
17-8 x 13-6

Boxed Tray

Access To Storage

8-0 Ceil. Line

Bonus
21-8 x 13-4

Access To Storage

M.Bath

Bth.2

Bdrm.4
11-6 x 11-2

Open

Dn.

Bdrm.2
11-6 x 11-2

Lin.

Bdrm.3
11-4 x 9-6

SECOND FLOOR

Sundeck
14-0 x 12-0

Brkfst.
11-4 x 15-6

Kit.
12-0 x 11-6

Family Rm.
13-6 x 17-6

Desk | Pant. | Ref.

Ov.

Lav. | **Lnd.**

W. | D.

Double Garage
21-8 x 23-4

Living
11-6 x 13-6

Open

Dn.

Dining
11-6 x 13-6

Foyer
13-8 x 15-2

40'-0"

60'-0"

FIRST FLOOR

Elegant Master Suite

Price Code: F

- This plan features:
  - Four bedrooms
  - Two full and one half baths
- Comfortable Family Room with a fireplace
- Efficient Kitchen with built-in Pantry and serving counter
- Master Suite with decorative ceiling, Sitting Room, and a plush Bath
- This home is designed with basement, slab and crawlspace foundation options

FIRST FLOOR — 1,307 SQ. FT.
SECOND FLOOR — 1,333 SQ. FT.
BONUS — 308 SQ. FT.
BASEMENT — 1,307 SQ. FT.
GARAGE — 528 SQ. FT.

TOTAL LIVING AREA: 2,640 SQ. FT.

Vaulted Sunken Living Room

Price Code: F

■ This plan features:

— Four bedrooms

— Two full and one three-quarter baths

■ A dramatic, sunken Living Room with a vaulted ceiling, fireplace, and glass walls to enjoy the view

■ A well-appointed, Kitchen with a peninsula counter and direct access to the Family Room, Dining Room, or Sun Deck

■ A Master Suite with a walk-in closet and a private Bath

■ A Family Room with direct access to the rear Sun Deck

■ This home is designed with a slab foundation

MAIN FLOOR — 1,464 SQ. FT.
LOWER FLOOR— 1,187 SQ. FT.
GARAGE — 418 SQ. FT.

TOTAL LIVING AREA:
2,651 SQ. FT.

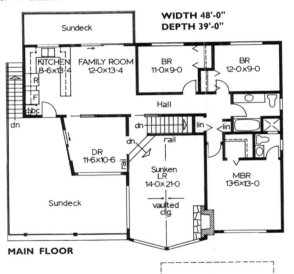

WIDTH 48'-0"
DEPTH 39'-0"

Sundeck

KITCHEN 8-6x13-4

FAMILY ROOM 12-0x13-4

BR 11-0x9-0

BR 12-0x9-0

Hall

dn

DR 11-6x10-6

Sunken LR 14-0x21-0

MBR 13-6x13-0

Sundeck

vaulted clg.

MAIN FLOOR

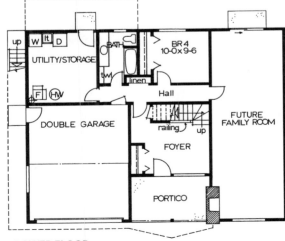

up   W   D

BATH

BR 4 10-0x9-6

UTILITY/STORAGE

linen

F   HW

Hall

DOUBLE GARAGE

railing   up

FUTURE FAMILY ROOM

FOYER

PORTICO

LOWER FLOOR

Grand Entrance

Price Code: H

■ This plan features:
— Four bedrooms
— Two full and one half baths

■ Dramatic roof lines and a seven-foot tall arched transom above front door

■ Columns, arches, angled stairs, a high ceiling and a large plant ledge in the Foyer

■ High vaulted ceilings and an abundance of windows in the Sunroom, Breakfast Nook and Great Room

■ The Master Bedroom has a lavish whirlpool Bath and a large walk-in closet

■ Each additional Bedroom features large closets and easy access to a full Bath

■ This home is designed with a slab foundation

FIRST FLOOR — 2,123 SQ. FT.
SECOND FLOOR — 911 SQ. FT.
GARAGE & STORAGE — 565 SQ. FT.

TOTAL LIVING AREA:
3,034 SQ. FT.

Eye-Catching Glass Turrets

Price Code: F

■ This plan features:
— Three bedrooms
— Three full baths

■ Two-story Foyer with a curved staircase, opens to a unique Living Room with an alcove of windows and inviting fireplace

■ Alcove of glass and a vaulted ceiling in the open Dining Area

■ Kitchen with built-in Pantry and desk, cooktop island/snack bar and a Nook with double door

■ Comfortable Family Room highlighted by another fireplace and wonderful outdoor views

■ Vaulted Master Suite offers a plush Dressing Area with walk-in closet and Spa tub

■ Two additional Bedrooms, one with a glass alcove, share a double vanity Bath

■ This home is designed with a crawlspace foundation

FIRST FLOOR — 1,592 SQ. FT.
SECOND FLOOR — 958 SQ. FT.
BONUS ROOM — 194 SQ. FT.
GARAGE — 956 SQ. FT.

TOTAL LIVING AREA:
2,550 SQ. FT.

Nothing Short of Luxury

Price Code: F

■ This plan features:
— Five bedrooms
— Two full and one half baths
■ There are arched entrances to the Dining and Great rooms, adding sophistication
■ The Study has French doors and a vaulted ceiling
■ Connected to the Breakfast Area and the snack bar off the Kitchen, the Great Room has an open, warm feel
■ The Master Suite is set off from the rest of the house, and has a tray ceiling
■ On the second floor, there are four additional Bedrooms and a Rec Room that overlooks the Entry
■ This home is designed with a slab foundation

FIRST FLOOR — 1,823 SQ. FT.
SECOND FLOOR — 1,256 SQ. FT.
GARAGE & STORAGE — 479 SQ. FT.

TOTAL LIVING AREA:
3,079 SQ. FT.

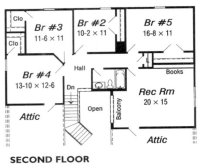

FIRST FLOOR

SECOND FLOOR

All Seasons

Price Code: H

■ This plan features:
— Three bedrooms
— One full and two three-quarter baths
■ A wall of windows taking full advantage of the front view
■ An open stairway to the upstairs Study and Master Bedroom
■ A Master Bedroom with a private Master Bath and a walk-in wardrobe
■ An efficient Kitchen including a Breakfast Bar that opens into the Dining Area
■ A formal Living Room with a vaulted ceiling and a stone fireplace
■ This home is designed with a basement foundation

MAIN FLOOR — 1,306 SQ. FT.
UPPER FLOOR — 598 SQ. FT.
LOWER FLOOR — 1,288 SQ. FT.

TOTAL LIVING AREA:
3,192 SQ. FT.

MAIN FLOOR

UPPER FLOOR

LOWER FLOOR

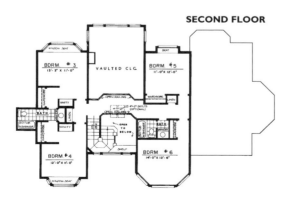

FIRST FLOOR

WIDTH 112'-0"
DEPTH 49'-0"

SECOND FLOOR

Expansive Decks

Price Code: J

■ This plan features:

— Six bedrooms

— Four full and one half baths

■ The first floor Master Suite offers a Sitting Area with a bay window

■ All secondary Bedrooms feature bay windows or window seats

■ This home is designed with basement and crawlspace foundation options

FIRST FLOOR — 2,498 SQ. FT.
SECOND FLOOR — 1,190 SQ. FT.
BONUS — 133 SQ. FT.
BASEMENT — 1,464 SQ. FT.

TOTAL LIVING AREA:
3,688 SQ. FT.

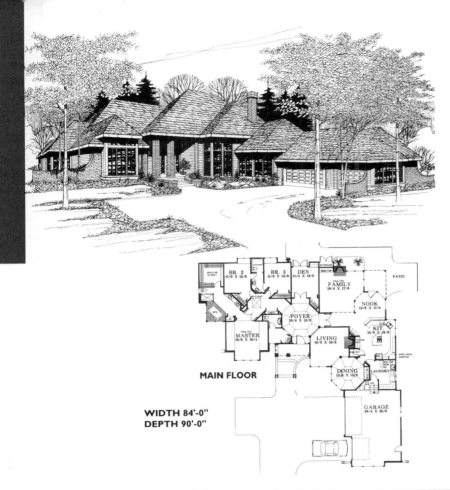

Sprawling Sun-Catcher
Price Code: H

- This plan features:
  — Three bedrooms
  — Two full and one half baths
- A central Foyer opening to every area of the house
- A fabulous Master Suite with a garden Spa, double vanity and a room-size walk-in closet
- A cozy Den with French doors to the rear Patio
- Columns separating the Living Room with fireplace from the octagonal vaulted-ceiling Dining Room
- An island Kitchen with twin ovens and a peninsula counter
- An eating Nook area open to the Kitchen
- An informal Family Room with a cozy fireplace
- This home is designed with a crawlspace foundation

MAIN FLOOR — 3,160 SQ. FT.

TOTAL LIVING AREA:
3,160 SQ. FT.

MAIN FLOOR

WIDTH 84'-0"
DEPTH 90'-0"

Beautiful See-Through Fireplace
Price Code: E

- This plan features:
  — Four bedrooms
  — Two full and one half baths
- Large repeating windows to the rear of the Great Room illuminate naturally
- The Great Room and the cozy Hearth Room share a beautiful see-through fireplace
- The bayed Breakfast Area is a bright and cheery way to start your day
- The gourmet Kitchen includes a Pantry, work island, ample counter space and a corner sink
- Secluded Master bedroom has a skylight in the Dressing Area and a large walk-in closet
- The secondary Bedrooms share a generous, compartmented Bathroom
- This home is designed with a basement foundation
- Alternate foundation options available at an additional charge. Please call 1-800-235-5700 for more information.

FIRST FLOOR — 1,733 SQ. FT.
SECOND FLOOR — 672 SQ. FT.
BASEMENT — 1,733 SQ. FT.
GARAGE — 613 SQ. FT.

TOTAL LIVING AREA:
2,405 SQ. FT.

FIRST FLOOR

SECOND FLOOR

WIDTH 62'-4"
DEPTH 54'-6"

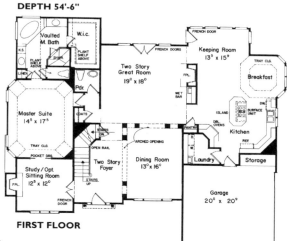

FIRST FLOOR

© Frank Betz Associates, Inc.

SECOND FLOOR

Stately Stone and Stucco

Price Code: H

- This plan features:
  - Four bedrooms
  - Three full and one half baths
- Two-story Foyer with angled staircase
- Expansive two-story Great Room enhanced by a fireplace
- Convenient Kitchen with a cooktop island
- Open Keeping Room accented by a wall of windows and backyard access
- Master Suite wing offers a tray ceiling, a plush Bath and roomy walk-in closet
- This home is designed with basement, slab, and crawlspace foundation options

FIRST FLOOR — 2,130 SQ. FT.
SECOND FLOOR — 897 SQ. FT.
BASEMENT — 2,130 SQ. FT.
GARAGE — 494 SQ. FT.

TOTAL LIVING AREA:
3,027 SQ. FT.

A Traditional Home with Modern Features

Price Code: F

- This plan features:
  — Three bedrooms
  — Two full and one half baths
- A beautiful bay window and built in shelves in the private first floor Den
- A decorative ceiling, picture window and lovely fireplace in the roomy formal Living Room
- An elegant formal Dining Room enhanced by a decorative ceiling treatment and conveniently located by the Living Room and next to the Kitchen
- A relaxing atmosphere provided by the cozy fireplace in the Family Room
- A second floor Master Suite equipped with a compartmented Bath and huge walk-in closet
- This home is designed with a crawlspace foundation

FIRST FLOOR — 1,465 SQ. FT.
SECOND FLOOR — 1,103
BONUS ROOM — 303 SQ. FT.

TOTAL LIVING AREA: 2,568 SQ. FT.

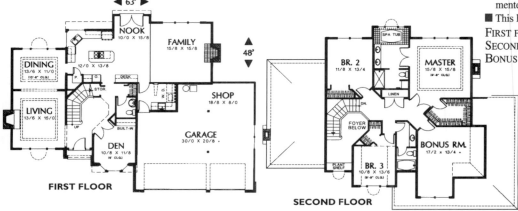

Deceptively Complex

Price Code: G

- This plan features:
  — Four bedrooms
  — Two full and one half baths
- A two-story Foyer leads straight to a large Kitchen Nook
- The Dining Area is connected to both the Parlor and the Kitchen Nook
- A large Family Room features a media center in the corner
- All of the Bedrooms on the second floor feature ample built-in closet space
- A Bonus Room atop the Garage offers endless potential
- This home is designed with a crawlspace foundation

FIRST FLOOR — 1,509 SQ. FT.
SECOND FLOOR — 1,286 SQ. FT.
BONUS — 538 SQ. FT.

TOTAL LIVING AREA: 2,795 SQ. FT.

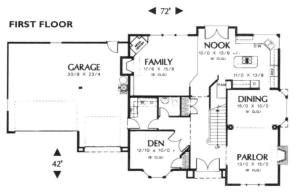

To order your Blueprints, call 1-800-235-5700

Beautiful Balconies

Price Code: I

■ This plan features:
— Three bedrooms
— Two full and one half baths
■ Cascading steps lead up to gracious entrance into formal Dining and Living Rooms defined by columns
■ Spacious and convenient Kitchen has a cooktop island/snack bar, corner Pantry and eating Nook with outdoor access
■ Corner Master Bedroom offers a private balcony, decorative ceiling and deluxe Dressing Area with a roomy walk-in closet and garden tub
■ This home is designed with a crawlspace foundation

FIRST FLOOR — 1,989 SQ. FT.
SECOND FLOOR — 1,349 SQ. FT.
LOWER FLOOR — 105 SQ. FT.
BONUS ROOM — 487 SQ. FT.

TOTAL LIVING AREA:
3,443 SQ. FT.

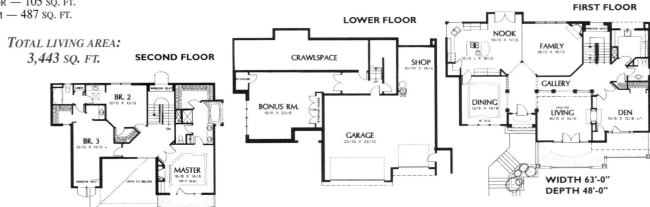

SECOND FLOOR
LOWER FLOOR
FIRST FLOOR

BR. 2 12/0 X 13/0
BR. 3 12/0 X 11/0
MASTER 16/6 X 14/8

CRAWLSPACE
SHOP 10/10 X 16/4
BONUS RM. 19/6 X 20/6
GARAGE 32/10 X 25/10

NOOK 10/0 X 17/0
FAMILY 18/0 X 16/0
DINING 13/6 X 14/8
GALLERY
LIVING 16/0 X 15/0
DEN 15/4 X 12/8

WIDTH 63'-0"
DEPTH 48'-0"

Let the Sun Shine In

Price Code: G

■ This plan features:
— Four bedrooms
— Two full and one three-quarter baths
■ Two-story entry features a second floor window
■ Den has windows on two sides including a corner window
■ Family Room, Nook and Kitchen open to each other for a spacious feeling
■ Cooktop island/snack bar, built-in desk and Pantry highlight the efficient Kitchen
■ Family Room enhanced by a second fireplace
■ Lavish Master Suite with a decorative ceiling in the Bedroom and a private, plush Bath
■ This home is designed with a crawlspace foundation

FIRST FLOOR — 1,575 SQ. FT.
SECOND FLOOR — 1,338 SQ. FT.
GARAGE — 864 SQ. FT.

TOTAL LIVING AREA:
2,913 SQ. FT.

◄ 66' ►
48'

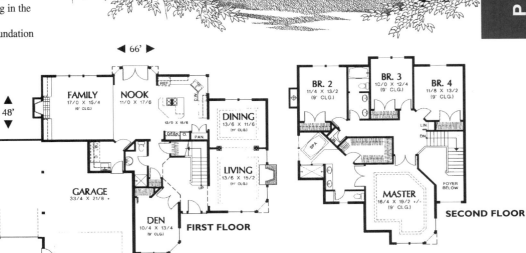

FAMILY 17/0 X 15/4
NOOK 11/0 X 17/6
DINING 13/6 X 11/6
LIVING 13/6 X 15/2
GARAGE 33/4 X 21/8
DEN 10/4 X 13/4
FIRST FLOOR

BR. 2 11/4 X 13/2
BR. 3 10/0 X 12/4
BR. 4 11/8 X 13/2
MASTER 16/4 X 19/2
SECOND FLOOR

Wide Open Spaces
Price Code: L

- This plan features:
  — Four bedrooms
  — Four full and one half baths
- The Great Room has a two-story ceiling and a fireplace
- A second fireplace and built-in bookcases enhance the Study
- The Dining Room has elegant columns and a built-in area for the hutch
- The Kitchen includes a peninsula counter/snack bar and an island
- The Nook accesses the Sunroom and the rear Porch
- The Master Suite is topped by a vaulted ceiling and includes a spacious Master Bath and a private Deck
- The Guest Room has access to a private Bath, as do the secondary Bedrooms
- This home is designed with a crawlspace foundation

FIRST FLOOR — 2,597 SQ. FT.
SECOND FLOOR — 2,171 SQ. FT.

TOTAL LIVING AREA:
4,768 SQ. FT.

WIDTH 76'-6"
DEPTH 68'-6"

SECOND FLOOR

FIRST FLOOR

French Country Styling
Price Code: I

- This plan features:
  — Four bedrooms
  — Two full and one three-quarter and one half baths
- Brick and stone blend masterfully for an impressive French Country exterior
- Master Suite has an expansive Bath and closet
- Study contains a built-in desk and a bookcase
- Angled island Kitchen is highlighted by a walk-in Pantry
- Fantastic Family Room includes a brick fireplace and a built-in entertainment center
- Three additional Bedrooms each have private access to a full Bath
- This home is designed with a slab foundation

MAIN FLOOR — 3,352 SQ. FT.
GARAGE — 672 SQ. FT.

TOTAL LIVING AREA:
3,352 SQ. FT.

MAIN FLOOR

WIDTH 91'-0"
DEPTH 71'-9"

To order your Blueprints, call 1-800-235-5700

Country-Style For Today

Price Code: E

■ This plan features:
— Three bedrooms
— Two full and one half baths
■ A wide wraparound Porch for a farmhouse style
■ A spacious Living Room with a large front window
■ A garden window over the double sink in the huge, country Kitchen, which includes two islands, one a butcher block, and the other an eating bar
■ A corner fireplace in the Family Room enjoyed throughout the Nook and Kitchen, thanks to an open layout
■ A Master Suite with a Spa tub and a huge walk-in closet, as well as a shower and double vanities
■ This home is designed with basement and crawlspace foundation options

FIRST FLOOR — 1,785 SQ. FT.
SECOND FLOOR — 621 SQ. FT.

TOTAL LIVING AREA:
2,406 SQ. FT.

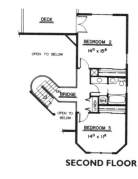

PLAN NO. 91700

WIDTH 55'-0"
DEPTH 42'-0"

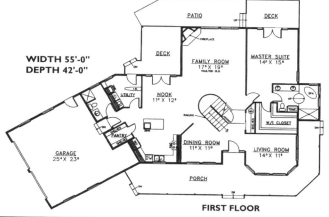

FIRST FLOOR

SECOND FLOOR

Stately Colonial Home

Price Code: G

■ This plan features:
— Four bedrooms
— Three full and one half baths
■ Stately columns and arched windows project luxury and quality that is evident throughout this home
■ The Entry is highlighted by a palladian window, a plant shelf and an angled staircase
■ The formal Living and Dining Rooms located off the Entry for ease in entertaining
■ The comfortable Great Room has an inviting fireplace and opens to the Kitchen/Breakfast Area and the Patio
■ The Master Bedroom wing offers Patio access, a luxurious Bath and a walk-in closet
■ This home is designed with crawlspace, slab and combination basement/crawlspace foundation options

FIRST FLOOR — 1,848 SQ. FT.
SECOND FLOOR — 1,111 SQ. FT.
GARAGE — 722 SQ. FT.

TOTAL LIVING AREA:
2,959 SQ. FT.

PLAN NO. 98534

WIDTH 73'-4"
DEPTH 44'-0"

SECOND FLOOR

FIRST FLOOR

Spectacular Victorian
Price Code: L

- This plan features:
  — Six bedrooms
  — Four full baths
- A multitude of Porches, Decks, balconies, and a Captain's Walk
- L-shaped Kitchen with an angled range/counter and plenty of modern amenities
- A large windowed Exercise Room and Wicker Room with a luxurious step-up Spa
- An enormous Living Room with corner window seats, a fireplace and double doors opening out to a curving Porch
- A Family Room with a woodstove, two full Baths and two large Bedrooms complete the expansive first floor
- A fireplaced Master Suite with corner window seats, a circular Sitting Room and access to the Captain's Walk grace the second floor
- A third floor Observatory tops the Sitting Room
- Three Bedrooms on the second floor, two with double doored private balconies, share a full hall Bath
- This home is designed with a crawlspace foundation

FIRST FLOOR — 3,031 SQ. FT.
SECOND FLOOR — 1,578 SQ. FT.
OBSERVATORY — 133 SQ. FT.
WORK SHOP — 133 SQ. FT.
GARAGE — 514 SQ. FT.

TOTAL LIVING AREA:
4,609 SQ. FT.

SECOND FLOOR

FIRST FLOOR

WIDTH 101'-0"
DEPTH 56'-0"

OBSERVATORY PLAN

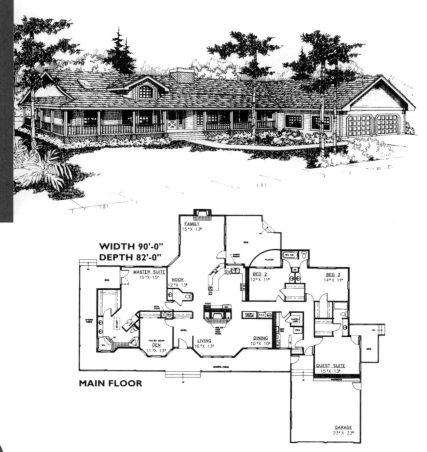

Relax on the Veranda
Price Code: H

- This plan features:
  — Four bedrooms
  — Three full and one half baths
- A wraparound Veranda
- A Master Suite with elevated custom Spa, twin basins, a walk-in closet, and an additional vanity outside the Bathroom
- A vaulted ceiling in the Den
- A fireplace in both the Family Room and the formal Living Room
- An efficient Kitchen with a peninsula counter and a double sink
- Two additional Bedrooms with walk-in closets, served by a compartmentalized Bath
- A Guest Suite with a private Bath
- This home is designed with a crawlspace foundation

MAIN FLOOR — 3,051 SQ. FT.
GARAGE — 646 SQ. FT.

TOTAL LIVING AREA:
3,051 SQ. FT.

WIDTH 90'-0"
DEPTH 82'-0"

MAIN FLOOR

Out of the English Countryside

Price Code: F

■ This plan features:

— Four bedrooms

— Three full baths

■ From the Foyer, arched entrances lead into the Dining Room and the Great Room

■ The Great Room is complimented by a 10-foot tray ceiling

■ The Master Suite is located in a secluded part of the first floor

■ The Breakfast Room shares a see-through fireplace with the Great Room

■ This home is designed with basement, slab and crawlspace foundation options

FIRST FLOOR — 2,050 SQ. FT.
SECOND FLOOR — 561 SQ. FT.
BONUS — 272 SQ. FT.
GARAGE — 599 SQ. FT.

TOTAL LIVING AREA:
2,611 SQ. FT.

SECOND FLOOR

BEDROOM 4
13-4 X 10-4

EXPANDABLE
17-4 X 18-0

LIN

BATH 3

BEDROOM 3
13-0 X 11-6

OPEN TO
FOYER
BELOW

PLANT
LEDGE

FIRST FLOOR

WIDTH 64'-10"
DEPTH 64'-0"

MASTER BEDRM
13-4 X 16-4
10 FT TRAY CLG

BRKFST RM
11-4 X 13-0
10 FT TRAY CLG

PORCH

KITCHEN
16-6 X 13-4
9 FT CLG

GREAT ROOM
17-4 X 20-4
10 FT TRAY CLG

MASTER
BATH

DESK

BATH 2

UTIL
11-4 X 6-0
9 FT CLG

STORAGE

PAN

LIN

ARCH

DINING ROOM
12-6 X 15-4
10 FT CLG

ARCH

FOYER
2 STORY CLG

BEDROOM 2
12-6 X 13-6
9 FT CLG

GARAGE

COPYRIGHT LARRY E. BELK

PORCH

To order your Blueprints, call 1-800-235-5700

Stately Two-Story
Price Code: G

■ This plan features:
— Four bedrooms
— Three full and one half baths
■ Refined colonial styling and the use of brick add a stately presence to this home
■ The Living Room has a lovely boxed bay window in the front
■ In the Dining Room find a space specifically for a china hutch
■ A railing separates the Nook from the Family Room
■ The Kitchen has an island with a raised counter on one side
■ A private Den is located in a rear corner of the home
■ The Family Room features a raised hearth fireplace with built-in cabinets on either side
■ Upstairs find the Bedrooms all with access to Baths
■ This home is designed with a basement foundation

FIRST FLOOR — 1,514 SQ. FT.
SECOND FLOOR — 1,386 SQ. FT.
BASEMENT — 1,514 SQ. FT.

TOTAL LIVING AREA:
2,900 SQ. FT.

53'-4"

44'-4"

DECK

BUILT INS
FAMILY ROOM
10'6" CEILING
21'x14'6"
HEARTH
BUILT INS

BRK'FST
10'9"x15'6"
KIT
DEN
11'6"x11'6"

RAILING
RAISED COUNTER
DESK

W.R.O. B4
LAUNDRY
DN
DN
RAILING
LANDING
UP

GARAGE
21'8"x22'
DINING
11'x12'6"
ENTRY
LIVING
12'x16'5"
PORCH

FIRST FLOOR

Br4
11'6"x12'5"
Br3
11'6"x12'10"
B2

B1
MBR
TRAY CEILING
17'6"x15'6"
RAILING
LANDING
DN

B3

SITTING
Br2
12'x11'
SHELVES

SECOND FLOOR

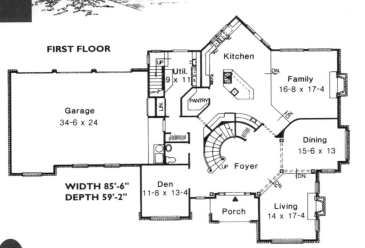

Curved Stairway
Price Code: K

■ This plan features:
— Three bedrooms
— Two full and one three-quarter and one half baths
■ The Master Bedroom offers a fireplace and plenty of natural light
■ All secondary Bedrooms feature access to a Bath
■ This home is designed with a crawlspace foundation

FIRST FLOOR — 2,108 SQP. FT.
SECOND FLOOR — 1,884 SQ. FT.

TOTAL LIVING AREA:
3,992 SQ. FT.

FIRST FLOOR

Garage
34-6 x 24

Util.
9 x 11
Kitchen

PANTRY
LIN

Family
16-8 x 17-4

UP
Foyer

Dining
15-6 x 13

Den
11-8 x 13-4

Porch

Living
14 x 17-4

WIDTH 85'-6"
DEPTH 59'-2"

SECOND FLOOR

Br #3
10 x 12-8
Master Bedroom

Game Rm.
22-6 x 15-6
DN.

Br #2
13-6 x 11-6
OPEN TO BELOW
DN.
M.Bath

SECOND FLOOR

SITTING AREA

WHIRLPOOL

Br.4
12⁰ x 15⁰

Mbr.
16⁴ x 23⁰

GLASS BLOCK

9'-0" CEILING

LIN.

LIN.

9'-0" CLG.

ON

Br.3
14⁰ x 12⁸

SEAT

Br.2
12⁴ x 14⁰

OPEN TO BELOW

10'-0" CLG.

FIRST FLOOR

Bfst.
12⁰ x 12⁰

Fam. rm.
21⁸ x 15⁰

Kit.
24⁰ x 15⁰

SNACK BAR

DESK

BOOKS

Gar.
24⁰ x 34⁰

P.

UP

Din.
14⁰ x 14⁰

11'-0" CEILING

W D

ON

E

Libr.
13⁸ x 13⁰

BOOKS

UP

Liv. rm.
17⁴ x 13⁰

14'-0" CLG.

COVERED STOOP

© Design Basics, Inc.

58'-0"

66'-0"

Stone, Stucco & Band Boards

Price Code: J

■ This plan features:

— Four bedrooms

— Two full, one three-quarter and one half baths

■ The two-story Entry reveals French doors to the Library and the formal Living Room

■ The gourmet Kitchen presents an expansive island with a triple cooktop

■ This home is built with a basement foundation

■ Alternate foundation options available at an additional charge. Please call 1-800-235-5700 for more information.

FIRST FLOOR — 1,857 SQ. FT.
SECOND FLOOR — 1,754 SQ. FT.
BASEMENT — 1,857 SQ. FT.
GARAGE — 633 SQ. FT.

TOTAL LIVING AREA:
3,611 SQ. FT.

Modern Amenities with a Classic Look

Price Code: L

- This plan features:
  — Three bedrooms
  — Two full, one three-quarter, and one half bath
- Easy access to all levels via elevator
- A fireplace exudes coziness into the Master Bedroom and its windowed Sitting Area
- A wall of rear windows lines the open design of the first floor for an airy and spacious atmosphere
- A soda fountain creates a magical centerpiece for the Kitchen, Nook, and Family Room
- A Library opens up to the Reading Gallery on the top of the tower
- Car aficionados will love the Automobile Gallery with automobile elevator, two Baths, and adjoining vault
- This home is designed with basement and slab foundation options

FIRST FLOOR — 3,162 SQ. FT.
SECOND FLOOR — 1,595 SQ. FT.
BASEMENT — 2,651 SQ. FT.
GARAGE — 708 SQ. FT.

TOTAL LIVING AREA: *4,757 SQ. FT.*

FIRST FLOOR

SECOND FLOOR

GARAGE

WIDTH 110'-2"
DEPTH 68'-11"

Impressive Foyer with Columns

Price Code: G

- This plan features:
  — Three bedrooms
  — Two full and one half baths
- Arched multi-paned windows and an elegant brick design enhance the exterior
- Impressive Foyer with columns and a sky-bridge above the Family Room
- An elegant entertaining area created by the formal Dining Room and the Parlor
- An island Kitchen, enhanced by convenience to both the Breakfast Nook and the formal Dining Room, that is well-appointed and efficient
- A first floor private Master bedroom includes a first class Bath, private Patio and a walk-in closet
- Two additional large Bedrooms located on the second floor, each with window seats, share a full Bath
- This home is designed with a crawlspace foundation

FIRST FLOOR — 2,024 SQ. FT.
SECOND FLOOR — 874 SQ. FT.
GARAGE — 648 SQ. FT.

TOTAL LIVING AREA: *2,898 SQ. FT.*

FIRST FLOOR

SECOND FLOOR

Uncommon Brickwork Enhances Facade

Price Code: H

■ This plan features:
— Four bedrooms
— Three full and one half baths
■ Sheltered Porch leads into Entry and spacious Living Room with Pool access
■ Quiet Study with focal point fireplace and open formal Dining Room
■ Expansive Kitchen with cooktop work island, efficiently serves Breakfast Nook, Patio and Dining Room
■ Master Bedroom wing offers a vaulted ceiling, two walk-in closets and a corner window tub
■ Three second floor Bedrooms share two Baths
■ This home is designed with a slab foundation

FIRST FLOOR — 2,304 SQ. FT.
SECOND FLOOR — 852 SQ. FT.
GARAGE — 690 SQ. FT.

TOTAL LIVING AREA: 3,156 SQ. FT.

SECOND FLOOR

FIRST FLOOR

This Home Has It All

Price Code: L

■ This plan features:
— Four bedrooms
— Four full and two half baths
■ Home Office, Home Theater, and Kids' Retreat options make this home everything you need in one
■ Built-in bookshelves, media center, benches, desks, and dining table add artistic practicality
■ Cooking island adorns Kitchen as plenty of workspace surrounds the room
■ Overlooking the Family Room, Lofts connect the secondary Bedrooms
■ This home is designed with a basement and crawlspace foundation options

FIRST FLOOR — 2,120 SQ. FT.
SECOND FLOOR — 1,520 SQ. FT.
BONUS ROOM — 183 SQ. FT.
BASEMENT — 377 SQ. FT.

TOTAL LIVING AREA: 3,640 SQ. FT.

SECOND FLOOR

FIRST FLOOR

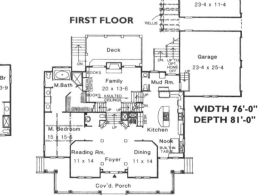

WIDTH 76'-0"
DEPTH 81'-0"

OPTIONAL HOME OFFICE

OPTIONAL HOME THEATRE

OPTIONAL KIDS RETREAT

To order your Blueprints, call 1-800-235-5700

113

Multiple Roof Lines add to Charm

Price Code: I

- This plan features:
  — Four bedrooms
  — Three full baths
- Entry opens to Gallery, formal Dining and Living Rooms, each with decorative ceilings
- Spacious Kitchen with a work island opens to Dining alcove, Family Room, and Patio beyond
- Comfortable Family Room offers vaulted ceiling above fireplace and a wetbar
- Corner Master Bedroom enhanced by a vaulted ceiling, double-vanity Bath, and huge walk-in closet
- Three additional Bedrooms with walk-in closets have access to full Baths
- This home is designed with a slab foundation

MAIN FLOOR — 3,292 SQ. FT.
GARAGE — 670 SQ. FT.

TOTAL LIVING AREA:
3,292 SQ. FT.

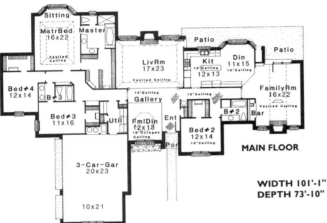

MAIN FLOOR

WIDTH 101'-1"
DEPTH 73'-10"

Tremendous Appeal

Price Code: J

- This plan features:
  — Four bedrooms
  — Three full and one half baths
- A European country exterior merges with a modern American interior
- The circular stairway highlights the Entry
- The formal Dining Room has a bay window and easy access to the Kitchen
- A private Study has a double-door Entry
- Formal Living Room has a fireplace and elegant columns
- The large Family Room boasts a brick fireplace and a built-in TV cabinet
- An angled Kitchen contains all the conveniences that the cook demands, including a built-in Pantry and ovens
- A large informal Dining Area that is adjacent to the Kitchen
- The Master Suite occupies one wing of the house with a Bath and a huge walk-in closet
- This home is designed with a slab foundation

FIRST FLOOR — 2,658 SQ. FT.
SECOND FLOOR — 854 SQ. FT.
GARAGE — 660 SQ. FT.

TOTAL LIVING AREA:
3,512 SQ. FT.

SECOND FLOOR

FIRST FLOOR

WIDTH 86'-0"
DEPTH 58'-1"

To order your Blueprints, call 1-800-235-5700

A Country Estate

Price Code: L

- This plan features:
  — Four bedrooms
  — Four full and one half baths
- A formal Living Room and Dining Room located at opposite sides of the Foyer
- A Library tucked into a corner of the house for quiet Study
- A sunken Family Room highlighted by a fireplace and built-in shelves
- A gourmet Kitchen with two built-in Pantries, a generous counter, ample storage space and an island with a vegetable sink
- This home is designed with a basement foundation

FIRST FLOOR — 3,199 SQ. FT.
SECOND FLOOR — 2,531 SQ. FT.
BASEMENT — 3,199 SQ. FT.
GARAGE — 748 SQ. FT.
BONUS — 440 SQ. FT.

**TOTAL LIVING AREA:
5,730 SQ. FT.**

SECOND FLOOR

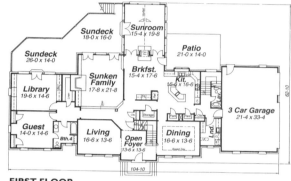

FIRST FLOOR

Three Fireplaces

Price Code: I

- This plan features:
  — Four bedrooms
  — Two full, one three-quarter, and one half baths
- Fireplaces warm the formal Dining Room, Living Room, and Family Room
- The Master Bedroom has access to a private covered Patio
- This home is designed with basement, slab, and crawlspace foundation options

FIRST FLOOR — 2,432 SQ. FT.
SECOND FLOOR — 903 SQ. FT.
BASEMENT — 2,432 SQ. FT.
GARAGE — 742 SQ. FT.

**TOTAL LIVING AREA:
3,335 SQ. FT.**

FIRST FLOOR

SECOND FLOOR

With Room for All

Price Code: F

■ This plan features:
— Four bedrooms
— Three full and one three-quarter baths
■ Corner quoins, segmented arches and shutters, a fan light above the door, and side lights flanking the door create an extremely appealing elevation
■ A formal Living Room sits directly across from the Entry
■ A Kitchen/Breakfast Bay area with ample cabinet and counter space borders the Family Room
■ A fireplace adds a cozy effect to the Family Room
■ A formal Dining Room located across the Gallery from the Kitchen includes a butler's pantry
■ Two secondary Bedrooms share a Bath with shower
■ A Master Suite at the opposite end of the house includes a large compartmented Bath and a walk-in closet
■ A third secondary Bedroom with direct access to a full Bath makes a perfect Guest Room
■ This home is designed with a slab foundation

MAIN FLOOR — 2,615 SQ. FT.
GARAGE — 713 SQ. FT.

TOTAL LIVING AREA:
2,615 SQ. FT.

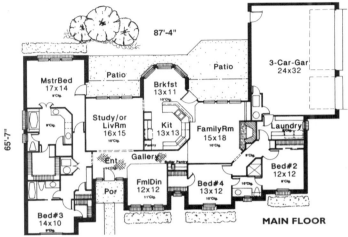

MAIN FLOOR

Attractive Roof Line

Price Code: F

■ This plan features:
— Four bedrooms
— Two full and one three-quarter baths
■ The Foyer flows easily across the tiled Galley into the formal Living Room
■ An island in the center of the U-shaped Kitchen adds to the abundance of work area
■ Tiling in the Breakfast Room adds style
■ A cathedral ceiling tops the Family Room, which includes a fireplace
■ The Master Suite is positioned for maximum privacy
■ This home is designed with crawlspace and slab foundation options

MAIN FLOOR — 2,620 SQ. FT.
GARAGE — 567 SQ. FT.

TOTAL LIVING AREA:
2,620 SQ. FT.

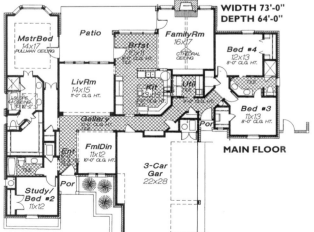

WIDTH 73'-0"
DEPTH 64'-0"

MAIN FLOOR

To order your Blueprints, call 1-800-235-5700

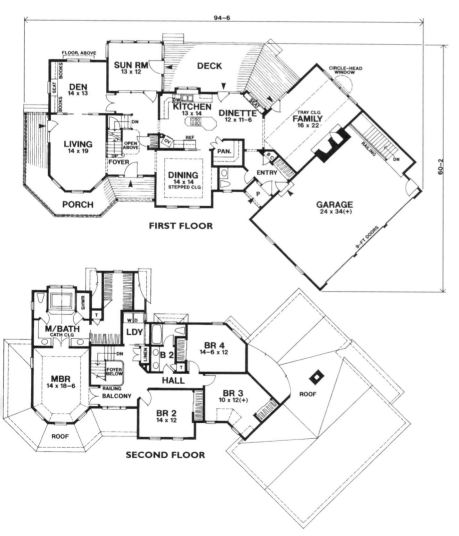

94–6

FLOOR, ABOVE

SUN RM
13 x 12

DECK

DEN
14 x 13

BOOKS
SEAT
BOOKS

CIRCLE–HEAD
WINDOW

Dw
KITCHEN
13 x 14

DINETTE
12 x 11–6

TRAY CLG
FAMILY
16 x 22

DN

LIVING
14 x 19

OPEN
ABOVE

OV
REF

PAN.

RAILING

DN

UP
FOYER

DINING
14 x 14
STEPPED CLG

ENTRY

B C

P

GARAGE
24 x 34(+)

PORCH

9–FT DOORS

FIRST FLOOR

60–2

SHWR

T

M/BATH
CATH CLG

WD
LDY

LINEN

B 2

BR 4
14–6 x 12

MBR
14 x 18–6

DN

FOYER
BELOW

HALL

T

BR 3
10 x 12(+)

RAILING
BALCONY

ROOF

BR 2
14 x 12

ROOF

ROOF

SECOND FLOOR

A Whisper of Victorian

Price Code: H

■ This plan features:

— Four bedrooms

— Two full and one half baths

■ A formal Living Room with wraparound windows and access to the cozy Den

■ An elegant Dining Room accented by a stepped ceiling

■ An efficient Kitchen equipped with a cooktop island/eating bar, a huge walk-in Pantry and a Dinette with a window seat and Deck access

■ A Family Room with a fireplace and a tray ceiling topping a circle-head window

■ A Master Suite with a decorative ceiling and a Bath with a raised Atrium tub, and two vanities

■ This home is designed with a basement foundation

FIRST FLOOR — 1,743 SQ. FT.
SECOND FLOOR — 1,455 SQ. FT.

TOTAL LIVING AREA:
3,198 SQ. FT.

European-Style Elegance

Price Code: H

■ This plan features:
— Four bedrooms
— Three full and two half baths

■ Grand two-story Foyer with graceful, landing staircase, opens to formal Living and Dining rooms

■ Central Great Room with a decorative ceiling, inviting fireplace, wetbar and backyard views

■ Master Bedroom wing enhanced by a decorative ceiling, arched window, dual walk-in closets and vanities, and a skylit whirlpool tub

FIRST FLOOR — 1,981 SQ. FT.
SECOND FLOOR — 1,103 SQ. FT.
GARAGE — 544 SQ. FT.

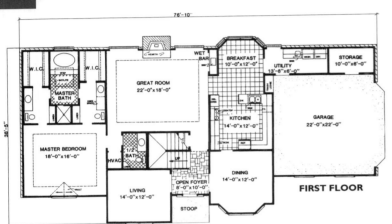

**TOTAL LIVING AREA:
3,084 SQ. FT.**

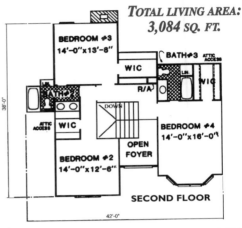

Lasting Elegance

Price Code: G

■ This plan features:
— Four bedrooms
— Three full and one half baths

■ Large Foyer leads directly into huge Den with hearth fireplace and built-ins

■ Both the Living and Dining Rooms have bays which add style and character

■ This home is designed with crawlspace and slab foundation options

FIRST FLOOR — 2,008 SQ. FT.
SECOND FLOOR — 943 SQ. FT.
GARAGE — 556 SQ. FT.

**TOTAL LIVING AREA:
2,951 SQ. FT.**

FIRST FLOOR

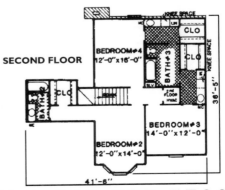

SECOND FLOOR

Traditional Brick with Detailing

Price Code: C

■ This plan features:
— Three bedrooms
— Two full baths

■ Covered Entry leading into the Foyer, the formal Dining Room and the Den

■ Expansive Den with a decorative ceiling over a hearth fireplace and sliding glass doors to the rear yard

■ Country Kitchen with a built-in Pantry, double ovens and a cooktop island easily serves the Breakfast Nook and Dining Room

■ Private Master Bedroom has a decorative ceiling and walk-in closet, connecting to a double vanity and a whirlpool tub

■ Two additional Bedrooms share a full Bath

■ This home is designed with slab and crawlspace foundation options

MAIN FLOOR — 1,869 SQ. FT.
GARAGE — 561 SQ. FT.

TOTAL LIVING AREA:
1,869 SQ. FT.

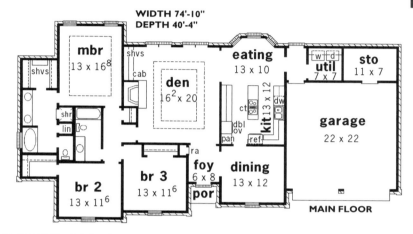

WIDTH 74'-10"
DEPTH 40'-4"

MAIN FLOOR

Country Cottage Charm

Price Code: I

■ This plan features:
— Four bedrooms
— Two full and one half baths

■ Vaulted Master Bedroom has a private skylight Bath and large walk-in closet with a built-in chest of drawers

■ Three more Bedrooms (one possibly a Study) have walk-in closets and share a full Bath

■ A Loft and Bonus Room above the Living Room

■ Family Room has built-in bookshelves and a fireplace, while overlooking the covered Veranda in the backyard

■ The huge three-car Garage has a separate Shop Area

■ This home is designed with crawlspace and slab foundation options

FIRST FLOOR — 2,787 SQ. FT.
SECOND FLOOR — 636 SQ. FT.
GARAGE — 832 SQ. FT.

TOTAL LIVING AREA:
3,423 SQ. FT.

WIDTH 101'-0"
DEPTH 58'-8"

SECOND FLOOR

FIRST FLOOR

PLAN NO. 92582

Plenty of Attention to Detail

Price Code: I

- This plan features:
— Four bedrooms
— Three full and one half baths
- The exterior of the home gives a hint of the attention to detail that is also found inside
- The Dining Room has three windows with segmented keystone arches above them
- The long Kitchen is a chef's delight, including a center island
- The centrally located Den has a fireplace with built-in cabinets and shelves to either side
- The Master Bedroom is located in its own wing and has a huge walk-in closet
- The Garage has two storage areas
- This home is designed with slab and crawlspace foundation options

FIRST FLOOR — 2,545 SQ. FT.
SECOND FLOOR — 711 SQ. FT.
GARAGE — 484 SQ. FT.

TOTAL LIVING AREA:
3,256 SQ. FT.

WIDTH 59'-10"
DEPTH 72'-10"

FIRST FLOOR

SECOND FLOOR

PLAN NO. 99454

Captivating Colonial

Price Code: F

- This plan features:
— Four bedrooms
— Two full and one half baths
- Decorative windows and brick detailing accent the exterior
- Dining Room is highlighted by decorative ceiling, French doors, and hutch space
- The Family Room has a fireplace and a bow window
- The Breakfast Nook and Kitchen are perfectly set up for meals on the run
- Upstairs find the Master Bedroom and Bath fully complemented
- Three more Bedrooms and a Bath complete the second floor plan
- This home is designed with basement and slab foundation options
- Alternate foundation options available at an additional charge. Please call 1-800-235-5700 for more information

FIRST FLOOR — 1,362 SQ. FT.
SECOND FLOOR — 1,223 SQ. FT.
GARAGE — 734 SQ. FT.

TOTAL LIVING AREA:
2,585 SQ. FT.

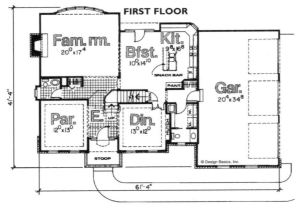

FIRST FLOOR

SECOND FLOOR

© Design Basics, Inc.

To order your Blueprints, call 1-800-235-5700

Luxury Personified

Price Code: F

PLAN NO. 92623

■ This plan features:
— Four bedrooms
— Two full and one half baths
■ A tray ceiling in the formal Living Room and Dining Room with corner columns pulling these two rooms into a large and charming area for entertaining
■ An island Kitchen which includes a corner sink with windows to flood the counter with natural light
■ A sunken Family Room with a cozy fireplace
■ A luxurious Master Bedroom with double walk-in closets, tray ceiling and private Master Bath
■ Three additional Bedrooms that share a skylit full Bath with Laundry chute located close by
■ A balcony overlooking the Foyer with a plant shelf and arched window
■ This home is designed with a basement foundation

FIRST FLOOR — 1,365 SQ. FT.
SECOND FLOOR — 1,288 SQ. FT.

TOTAL LIVING AREA:
2,653 SQ. FT.

WIDTH 61'-0"
DEPTH 37'-6"

FIRST FLOOR

SECOND FLOOR

Mind Your Manor

Price Code: I

PLAN NO. 98514

■ This plan features:
— Five bedrooms
— Two full, one three-quarter, and one half baths
■ The front Covered Porch leads into the Entry/Gallery which features a grand spiral staircase
■ In the front of the house find the formal Living Room and Dining Room, each with two palladian windows
■ The Study has built-in bookcases centered around a window
■ The large Family Room has a fireplace and a built-in stereo cabinet
■ The bayed Breakfast Nook has a door leading to the backyard Covered Patio
■ The first-floor Master Suite has two walk-in closets with a built-in chest of drawers, and a Bath with a cathedral ceiling
■ This home is designed with crawlspace and slab foundation options

FIRST FLOOR — 2,208 SQ. FT.
SECOND FLOOR — 1,173 SQ. FT.
BONUS ROOM — 224 SQ. FT.
GARAGE — 520 SQ. FT.

TOTAL LIVING AREA:
3,381 SQ. FT.

FIRST FLOOR

SECOND FLOOR

WIDTH 72'-0"
DEPTH 63'-10"

Turn of the Century Charm

Price Code: I

- This plan features:
  — Four bedrooms
  — Three full and two half baths
- Old fashioned turn of the century exterior
- Gourmet Kitchen is open to the Sunroom and the Breakfast Nook
- Large Family Room features a cozy fireplace
- Master Suite has a luxurious Bath and large Sitting Area
- Three additional Bedrooms on the second floor share two full Baths
- This home is designed with a basement foundation

FIRST FLOOR — 2,470 SQ. FT.
SECOND FLOOR — 1,000 SQ. FT.
BASEMENT — 2,470 SQ. FT.

TOTAL LIVING AREA:
3,470 SQ. FT.

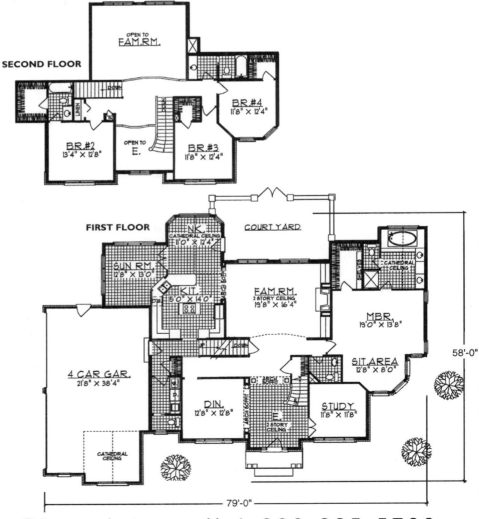

Outstanding Appeal

Price Code: K

- This plan features:
— Five bedrooms
— Four full and one half baths
- The Formal Dining and Living Rooms are located off the two-story Foyer
- A Butler's Pantry located between the Kitchen and formal Dining Room for convenience
- An island Kitchen with a walk-in Pantry and a peninsula counter/serving bar
- The Breakfast Room with access to the backyard through a French door
- The second floor Master Suite is topped by a tray ceiling in the Bedroom and by a vaulted ceiling above the Sitting Room and Bath
- Three additional Bedrooms with private access to full Baths and closet space
- This home is designed with basement and crawlspace foundation options

FIRST FLOOR — 2,002 SQ. FT.
SECOND FLOOR — 1,947 SQ. FT.
BASEMENT — 2,002 SQ. FT.
GARAGE — 737 SQ. FT.

TOTAL LIVING AREA:
3,949 SQ. FT.

FIRST FLOOR

SECOND FLOOR

Country Brick

Price Code: E

- This plan features:
— Three bedrooms
— Two full and one half baths
- Friendly front Porch leads into a gracious open Foyer and Great Room beyond
- Secluded Library offers a quiet space with built-in shelves
- Expansive Great Room is enhanced by focal point fireplace and topped by sloped ceiling
- Country-size Kitchen with island snack bar, bright Breakfast Area, Pantry, and nearby Laundry/Garage access
- Private Master Bedroom offers a deluxe Bath and spacious walk-in closet
- Two additional bedrooms with walk-in closets and window seats share a double-vanity Bath
- This home is designed with a basement foundation

FIRST FLOOR — 1,710 SQ. FT.
SECOND FLOOR — 733 SQ. FT.
BASEMENT — 1,697 SQ. FT.
BONUS ROOM — 181 SQ. FT.
GARAGE — 499 SQ. FT.

TOTAL LIVING AREA:
2,443 SQ. FT.

WIDTH 78'-4"
DEPTH 47'-8"

FIRST FLOOR

SECOND FLOOR

Modern Luxury

Price Code: F

- This plan features:

— Four bedrooms

— Three full and one half baths

- A feeling of spaciousness is created by the two-story Foyer and volume ceilings

- Arched openings and decorative windows enhance the Dining and Living Rooms

- The efficient Kitchen has a work island, a Pantry and a Breakfast Area open to the Family Room

- The plush Master Suite features a tray ceiling and an alcove of windows

- This home is designed with basement and crawlspace foundation options

FIRST FLOOR — 1,883 SQ. FT.
SECOND FLOOR — 803 SQ. FT.
BASEMENT — 1,883 SQ. FT.
GARAGE — 495 SQ. FT.

TOTAL LIVING AREA:
2,686 SQ. FT.

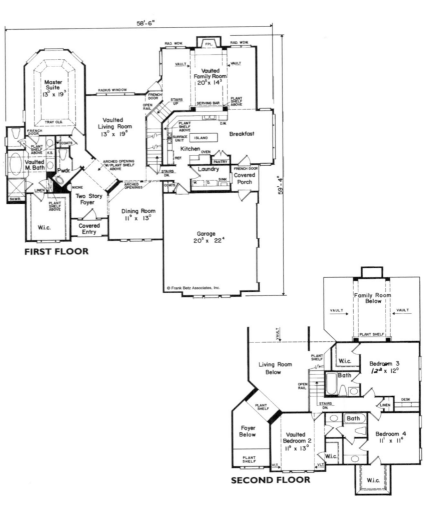

To order your Blueprints, call 1-800-235-5700

FIRST FLOOR

OPEN TO
FAMILY RM.

BEDROOM #2
13'-0" x 11'-0"

BEDROOM #4
13'-0" x 13'-0"

OPEN TO
FOYER

BEDROOM #3
17'-0" x 11'-0"

Contemporary Plan with an Old-Fashioned Look

Price Code: I

■ This plan features:

— Four bedrooms

— Three full and one half baths

■ Gracious Entry with arched window, sidelights and two-story Foyer

■ Formal Dining Room and quiet Study have decorative windows

■ Convenient Kitchen with cooktop island, opens to Eating Area

■ This home is designed with a basement foundation

■ This plan cannot be built within a 25 mile radius of Cedar Rapids, IA.

FIRST FLOOR — 2,385 SQ. FT.
SECOND FLOOR — 1,012 SQ. FT.
GARAGE — 846 SQ. FT.
BASEMENT — 2,385 SQ. FT.

TOTAL LIVING AREA:
3,397 SQ. FT.

WIDTH 79'-0"
DEPTH 55'-0"

EATING AREA
11'-0" x 8'-0"

SUNROOM
17'-0" x 13'-0"

KITCHEN
13'-0" x 14'-0"

FAMILY ROOM
20'-0" x 15'-0"

MASTER BEDROOM
15'-0" x 14'-0"

4 CAR GARAGE
21'-0" x 38'-0"

DINING ROOM
13'-0" x 13'-0"

SITTING AREA
10'-0" x 8'-0"

STUDY
17'-0" x 11'-0"

FOYER

SECOND FLOOR

Photography supplied by Studer Residential Designs, Inc.

Arched Windows

Price Code: L

■ This plan features:
— Three bedrooms
— Two full, one three-quarter, and one half baths
■ The Foyer and Gallery accent the stairs that lead to the lower floor
■ The impressive Master Bedroom has a walk-in closet, Dressing Area, and Bath with a dual vanity
■ Two Bedrooms on the lower floor share a full Bath
■ Accented by columns, the Dining Room and Great Room are perfect for formal occasions
■ An Exercise Room, Billiard Room, Media Room, and a full Bath complete the living space on the lower floor
■ This home is designed with a basement foundation

MAIN FLOOR — 2,582 SQ. FT.
LOWER FLOOR — 1,746 SQ. FT.
BASEMENT — 871 SQ. FT.

TOTAL LIVING AREA:
4,328 SQ. FT.

MAIN FLOOR

Deck

Kitchen 15'1" x 18'7"
Breakfast 13'8" x 13'8"
Great Room 15'6" x 21'5'
Master Bedroom 14'4" x 19'1"
walk in closet
Laun.
Hall
Bath
Gallery
Dressing
Three-car Garage 22'2" x 29'8"
Dining Room 16'2" x 14'2"
Foyer
Library 11'8" x 12'7"
Porch

LOWER FLOOR

Patio
Media Room 17'10" x 21'6"
Bedroom 14'1" x 12'9"
Bath
Basement
Bedroom 10'9" x 14'10"
Bath
Exercise Room 10'11" x 10'10"
Billiard Room 15'8" x 16'8"
Basement

Brick and Stone in Perfect Harmony

Price Code: F

■ This plan features:
— Four bedrooms
— Two full and one half baths
■ A sheltered front Entry has sidelight windows beside and a transom window above the door
■ Inside the Foyer there is a sloped ceiling and an open rail staircase
■ Columns delineate the sunken Great Room and the Dining Room
■ The Master Bedroom on the first floor has a bay window and a tray ceiling
■ This home is designed with a basement foundation

FIRST FLOOR — 1,767 SQ. FT.
SECOND FLOOR — 873 SQ. FT.
BASEMENT — 1,749 SQ. FT.
GARAGE — 440 SQ. FT.

TOTAL LIVING AREA:
2,640 SQ. FT.

FIRST FLOOR

Breakfast 12'4" x 9'5"
Dining Room 11'10" x 15'11"
Kitchen
Family Center 13'5" x 12'3"
Laun.
walk in closet
Hall
Bath
Sunken Great Room 15'1" x 19'6" high ceiling
Foyer
Bath
Master Bedroom 15'6" x 14'8"
Two-car Garage 20' x 22'
66'4"

SECOND FLOOR

Bedroom 11'1" x 13'6"
Bath
Bedroom 11'0" x 14'2"
Balcony
Bedroom 13'10" x 11'0"
55'

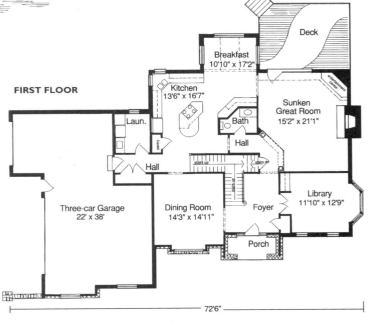

FIRST FLOOR

Deck

Breakfast
10'10" x 17'2"

Kitchen
13'6" x 16'7"

Laun.

Bath

Sunken
Great Room
15'2" x 21'1"

Hall

Hall

stairs up

stairs dn

Three-car Garage
22' x 38'

Dining Room
14'3" x 14'11"

Foyer

Library
11'10" x 12'9"

Porch

55'8"

72'6"

SECOND FLOOR

Bath

Bedroom
12'4" x 13'3"

walk-in closet

Bath

Dressing

Bedroom
12'1" x 12'7"

Balcony

walk-in closet

Bedroom
14'3" x 16'5"

Foyer
Below

Master Bedroom
14'2" x 17'6"

walk-in closet

Bath

stairs dn

The Ultimate in Style

Price Code: I

■ This plan features:

— Four bedrooms

— Three full and one half baths

■ A variety of exterior materials combine with a well-planned interior for impeccable style

■ The open Kitchen has ample counter space and features a center island

■ Upstairs find the Master Bedroom, which has a walk-in closet and a sumptuous Bath

■ Three additional Bedrooms all have access to Baths

■ This home is designed with a basement foundation

FIRST FLOOR — 1,678 SQ. FT.
SECOND FLOOR — 1,766 SQ. FT.
BASEMENT — 1,639 SQ. FT.
GARAGE — 761 SQ. FT.

TOTAL LIVING AREA:
3,444 SQ. FT.

Covered Front Porch

Price Code: F

■ This plan features:

— Four bedrooms

— Two full and one half baths

■ A covered front Porch coupled with the field-stone and brick exterior provides a warm and welcoming effect

■ A Butler's Pantry is located between the Kitchen and Dining Room for ease in serving

■ A tray ceiling tops the formal Dining Area, adding style and charm

■ The oversized Kitchen offers an abundance of storage and work space

■ This home is designed with a basement foundation

FIRST FLOOR — 1,573 SQ. FT.
SECOND FLOOR — 1,152 SQ. FT.
BASEMENT — 1,534 SQ. FT.
GARAGE — 680 SQ. FT.

TOTAL LIVING AREA:
2,725 SQ. FT.

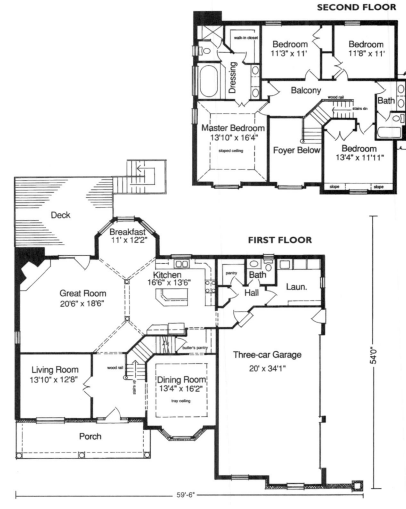

SECOND FLOOR

walk-in closet

Bedroom 11'3" x 11'

Bedroom 11'8" x 11'

Dressing

Balcony

wood rail   stairs dn

Bath

Master Bedroom 13'10" x 16'4"

sloped ceiling

Foyer Below

Bedroom 13'4" x 11'11"

slope   slope

FIRST FLOOR

Deck

Breakfast 11' x 12'2"

Kitchen 16'6" x 13'6"

pantry   Bath

Hall   Laun.

Great Room 20'6" x 18'6"

butler's pantry

Living Room 13'10" x 12'8"

wood rail   up dn

Dining Room 13'4" x 16'2"

tray ceiling

Three-car Garage 20' x 34'1"

54'0"

Porch

59'-6"

To order your Blueprints, call 1-800-235-5700

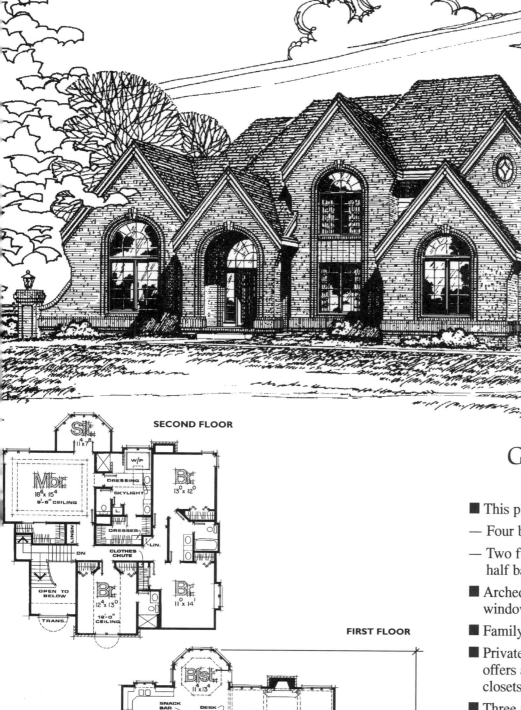

Sit.
11⁴ x 7⁸

W/P

Mbr.
18⁶ x 15⁴
9'-6" CEILING

DRESSING

SKYLIGHT

Br.
13⁰ x 12⁰

DN

DRESSER

LIN.

LINEN

CLOTHES CHUTE

OPEN TO BELOW

Br.
12⁴ x 13⁰

Br.
11 x 14

12'-0" CEILING

TRANS.

FIRST FLOOR

Bfst.
11 x 13⁴

SNACK BAR

DESK

Kit.
22⁰ x 15⁰

Fam. rm.
21⁸ x 15⁰

WET BAR

SALAD SINK

TRANS.

11'-0" CEILING

Din.
12 x 13⁶

UP

DN

LAUNDRY

Gar.
22⁴ x 31⁴

ARCHED CEILING

Liv. rm.
15⁴ x 12¹⁰

UP

Libr.
13⁰ x 11⁷

BOOKS

COVERED STOOP

© Design Basics, Inc.

55'-4"

62'-0"

Glorious Gables

Price Code: I

■ This plan features:

— Four bedrooms

— Two full, one three-quarter and one half baths

■ Arched ceiling topping decorative windows

■ Family Room with hearth fireplace

■ Private Master Bedroom Suite offers a Sitting Area, two walk-in closets, and luxurious Bath

■ Three additional Bedrooms with ample closets and private access to a full Bath

■ This home is designed with a basement foundation

■ Alternate foundation options available at an additional charge. Please call 1-800-235-5700 for more information.

FIRST FLOOR — 1,709 SQ. FT.
SECOND FLOOR — 1,597 SQ. FT.
GARAGE — 721 SQ. FT.
BASEMENT — 1,709 SQ. FT.

TOTAL LIVING AREA:
3,306 SQ. FT.

To order your Blueprints, call 1-800-235-5700

129

Georgian Style

Price Code: L

■ This plan features:

— Four bedrooms

— Three full and two half baths

■ Covered Porch and open Foyer with magnificent staircase welcome you home

■ Living Room with a fireplace flows into the Dining Room

■ Butler's Pantry connects the Dining Room to the Breakfast and Kitchen Areas

■ Sunken Hearth Room has a cozy fireplace and access the rear Deck

■ Master Suite encompasses much of the second floor and contains many luxuries

■ This home is designed with a basement foundation

FIRST FLOOR — 2,094 SQ. FT.
SECOND FLOOR — 2,169 SQ. FT.
BASEMENT — 2,049 SQ. FT.

TOTAL LIVING AREA:
4,263 SQ. FT.

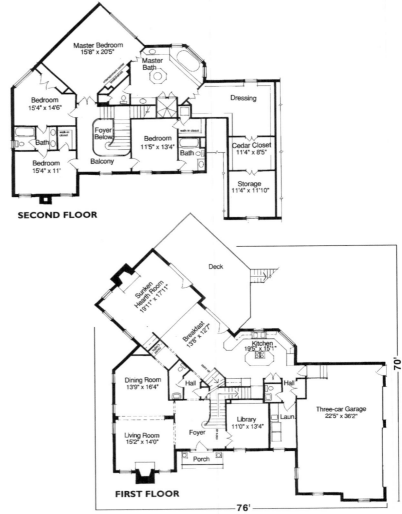

130

Stucco Accents

Price Code: H

- This plan features:
- — Four bedrooms
- — Two full, one three-quarter and one half baths
- Stucco accents and graceful window treatments enhance the front of this home
- Double doors open to the private Den, which features brilliant bayed windows
- French doors open to a large Screened Veranda ideal for outdoor entertaining
- The open Living Room and handsome curved staircase add drama to the Entry Area
- The gourmet Kitchen, Dinette Bay and Family Room flow together for easy living
- The elegant Master Bedroom has a 10-foot vaulted ceiling
- Two walk-in closets, his and her vanities and a whirlpool tub highlight the Master Bath
- Three additional Bedrooms have private access to full Baths
- This home is designed with a basement foundation
- Alternate foundation options available at an additional charge. Please call 1-800-235-5700 for more information.

FIRST FLOOR — 1,631 SQ. FT.
SECOND FLOOR — 1,426 SQ. FT.
BASEMENT — 1,631 SQ. FT.
GARAGE — 681 SQ. FT.

TOTAL LIVING AREA: 3,057 SQ. FT.

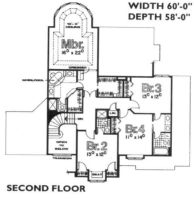

WIDTH 60'-0"
DEPTH 58'-0"

SECOND FLOOR

FIRST FLOOR

Exceptional Family Living

Price Code: L

- This plan features:
- — Four bedrooms
- — Three full and one half baths
- Decorative dormers, a bay window and an eyebrow arched window provide for a pleasing country farmhouse facade
- The cozy Study has its own fireplace and a bay window
- The large formal Living Room has a fireplace and built-in bookcases
- The huge Kitchen is open to the Breakfast Bay and the Family Room
- The Master Suite includes a large Bath with a unique closet
- Three more Bedrooms located at the other end of the home each have private access to a full Bath
- This home is designed with a slab foundation

MAIN FLOOR — 4,082 SQ. FT.
GARAGE — 720 SQ. FT.

TOTAL LIVING AREA: 4,082 SQ. FT.

MAIN FLOOR

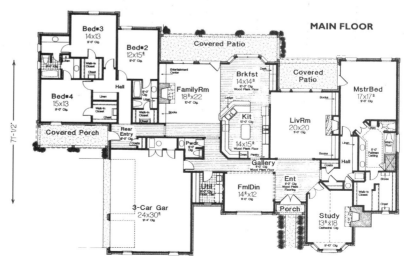

Southern Mansion

Price Code: I

- ■ This plan features:
- — Four bedrooms
- — Three full and one half baths
- ■ Covered Porches, intricate detailing and illuminating transom windows enhance this home
- ■ The prominent Entry opens to the formal Dining and Living Rooms
- ■ French doors open to the Master Suite, which includes his and her walk-in closets, a large Dressing Area, two vanities, and an oval whirlpool bath
- ■ This home is designed with a basement foundation
- ■ Alternate foundation options available at an additional charge. Please call 1-800-235-5700 for more information.

FIRST FLOOR — 1,598 SQ. FT.
SECOND FLOOR — 1,675 SQ. FT.

TOTAL LIVING AREA:
3,273 SQ. FT.

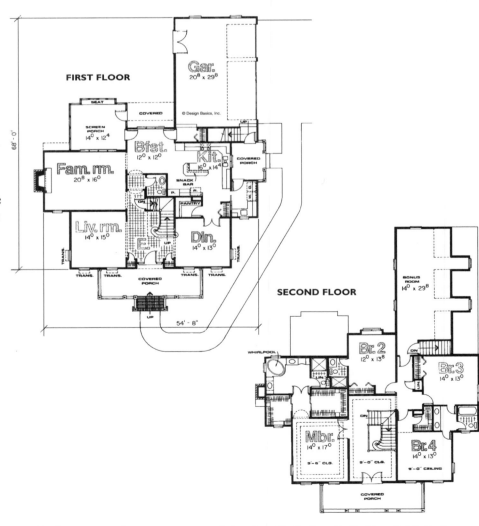

132

An Estate of Epic Proportion

Price Code: K

- This plan features
- — Four bedrooms
- — Three full and one half baths
- The front door opens into a grand Entry with a 20-foot ceiling and a curved staircase
- Flanking the Entry on the right is the Living Room with a cathedral ceiling and fireplace, and on the left is the bayed formal Dining Room
- Walk down the Gallery to the Study with a full wall built-in bookcase
- The enormous Master Bedroom has a walk-in closet, sumptuous Bath and a bayed Sitting Area
- The Family Room has a wetbar, a fireplace and a door leading outside to the covered Veranda
- This home is designed with basement and slab foundation options

FIRST FLOOR — 2,751 SQ. FT.
SECOND FLOOR — 1,185 SQ. FT.
BONUS — 343 SQ. FT.
GARAGE — 790 SQ. FT.

TOTAL LIVING AREA: 3,936 SQ. FT.

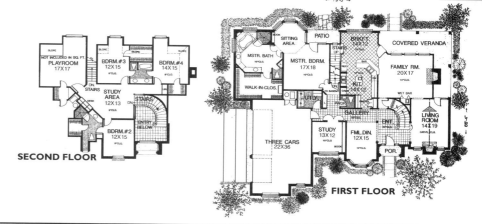

SECOND FLOOR

FIRST FLOOR

A Home for Today's Lifestyle

Price Code: G

- This plan features:
- — Four bedrooms
- — Three full baths
- Family living area comprised of a Family Room, Breakfast Area, and island Kitchen
- Formal Dining Room with easy access from the Kitchen
- Pampering Master Suite with private Master Bath and an abundance of storage space
- Three additional full Baths with ample closet space
- Screened Porch and Covered Patio extending living space outdoors
- This home is designed with a slab foundation

MAIN FLOOR — 2,782 SQ. FT.
GARAGE — 685 SQ. FT.

TOTAL LIVING AREA: 2,787 SQ. FT.

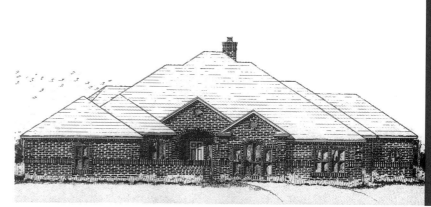

WIDTH 78'-0"
DEPTH 78'-6"

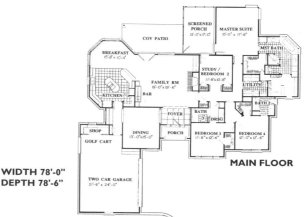

MAIN FLOOR

Photography supplied by Larry E. Belk

Towering Windows
Enhance Elegance

Price Code: G

■ This plan features:

— Four bedrooms

— Three full baths

■ Designed for a corner or pie-shaped lot

■ Spectacular split-staircase highlights Foyer

■ Expansive Great Room with hearth fireplace opens to formal Dining Room and Patio

■ Quiet Study easily another Bedroom or Home Office

■ Secluded Master Bedroom suite offers private Porch, two walk-in closets and vanities, and a corner whirlpool tub

■ This home is designed with basement, slab, and crawlspace foundation options

FIRST FLOOR — 1,966 SQ. FT.
SECOND FLOOR — 872 SQ. FT.
GARAGE — 569 SQ. FT.

TOTAL LIVING AREA:
2,838 SQ. FT.

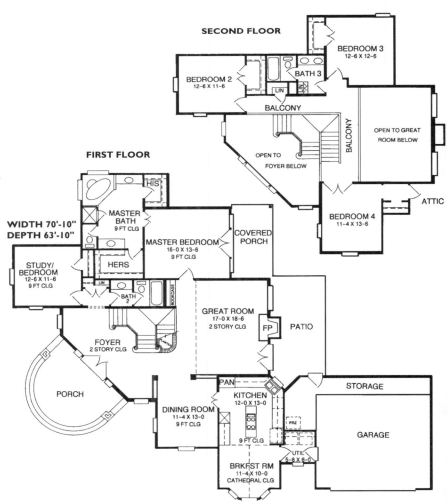

134

To order your Blueprints, call 1-800-235-5700

WIDTH 64'-4"
DEPTH 53'-4"

MASTER BDRM.
LIVING RM.
DINING RM.
FAMILY ROOM
MASTER BATH
BREAKFAST
HALL
KITCHEN
CLO.
ENTRY
PDR.
UTIL.
PORCH
GARAGE

FIRST FLOOR

OPEN TO LIVING ROOM BELOW
STUDIO/ BEDROOM 5
OPEN TO FAMILY ROOM BELOW
CLO.
OPEN TO FOYER BELOW
LOFT
BEDROOM 4
DOWN
BATH 2
HALL
BEDROOM 3
BEDROOM 2
CLO. CLO.

SECOND FLOOR

Two-Story Entry Adds Grace

Price Code: H

■ This plan features:

— Five bedrooms

— Two full and one half baths

■ A stucco design is accented by an arched two-story Entry

■ The Kitchen, Breakfast Room and Family Room are adjacent and open to one another

■ An island cooktop and double sinks, along with an abundance of storage space, make the Kitchen even more convenient

■ The Master Bath has an angled whirlpool tub, separate shower and his-and-her vanities

■ This home is designed with crawlspace and slab foundation options

FIRST FLOOR — 1,974 SQ. FT.
SECOND FLOOR — 1,060 SQ. FT.
GARAGE — 531 SQ. FT.

TOTAL LIVING AREA:
3,034 SQ. FT.

Opulent Luxury

Price Code: K

■ This plan features:

— Four bedrooms

— Two full and one three-quarter and one half baths

■ Columns frame elegant two-story Entry with a graceful banister staircase

■ A stone hearth fireplace and built-in bookshelves enhance the Living Room

■ Comfortable Family Room with a huge fireplace, cathedral ceiling and access to covered Veranda

■ Lavish Master Bedroom with a Sitting Area, private Patio and a huge Bath with two walk-in closets and a whirlpool tub

■ This home is designed with basement and slab foundation options

FIRST FLOOR — 2,804 SQ. FT.
SECOND FLOOR — 979 SQ. FT.
BASEMENT — 2,804 SQ. FT.
GARAGE — 802 SQ. FT.

TOTAL LIVING AREA:
3,783 SQ. FT.

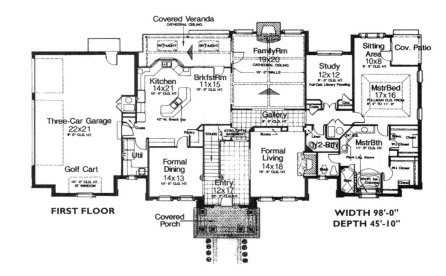

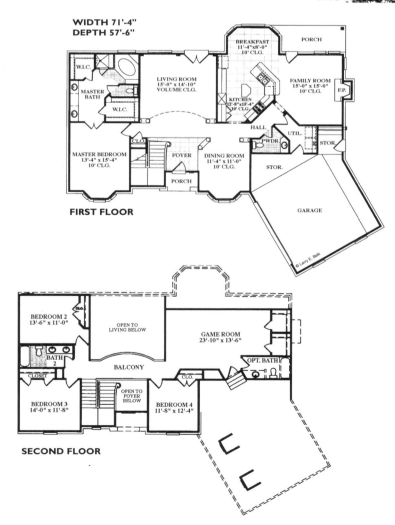

WIDTH 71'-4"
DEPTH 57'-6"

FIRST FLOOR

W.I.C.

MASTER BATH

W.I.C.

MASTER BEDROOM
13'-4" x 15'-4"
10' CLG.

CLO.

FOYER

PORCH

LIVING ROOM
15'-0" x 14'-10"
VOLUME CLG.

KITCHEN
12'-8" x 15'-4"
10' CLG.

DINING ROOM
11'-4" x 11'-0"
10' CLG.

BREAKFAST
11'-4" x 8'-0"
10' CLG.

PORCH

FAMILY ROOM
15'-0" x 15'-0"
10' CLG.

F.P.

HALL

PWDR.

UTIL.

STOR.

STOR.

GARAGE

© Larry E. Belk

SECOND FLOOR

BEDROOM 2
13'-6" x 11'-0"

BATH 2

CLOSET

BEDROOM 3
14'-0" x 11'-8"

OPEN TO LIVING BELOW

BALCONY

OPEN TO FOYER BELOW

GAME ROOM
23'-10" x 13'-6"

OPT. BATH

CLO.

BEDROOM 4
11'-8" x 12'-4"

Traditional Elegance

Price Code: G

■ This plan features:

— Four bedrooms

— Two full and one half baths

■ A tiled Foyer that opens to a two-story Living Room

■ A formal Dining Room that includes one of the lovely bay windows

■ An island Kitchen, with a peninsula counter and eating bar, connecting with a Breakfast Room that flows easily into the Family Room

■ A spacious Family Room that includes a focal point fireplace

■ A Master Suite with an intimate Sitting Area and a Master Bath

■ This home is designed with crawlspace and slab foundation options

FIRST FLOOR — 1,832 SQ. FT.
SECOND FLOOR — 1,163 SQ. FT.
GARAGE — 591 SQ. FT.

TOTAL LIVING AREA:
2,995 SQ. FT.

To order your Blueprints, call 1-800-235-5700

A Commanding Presence

Price Code: I

■ This plan features:

— Four bedrooms

— Three full and one half bath

■ An arresting double arch gives this European style home a commanding presence

■ Two-story Foyer opens the view directly through the Living Room to the rear grounds

■ Kitchen/Breakfast Area and Family Room are conveniently grouped for informal entertaining

■ This home is designed with basement, slab, and crawlspace foundation options

MAIN FLOOR — 2,469 SQ. FT.
SECOND FLOOR — 1,025 SQ. FT.
BONUS ROOM — 320 SQ. FT.
GARAGE — 795 SQ. FT.

TOTAL LIVING AREA:
3,494 SQ. FT.

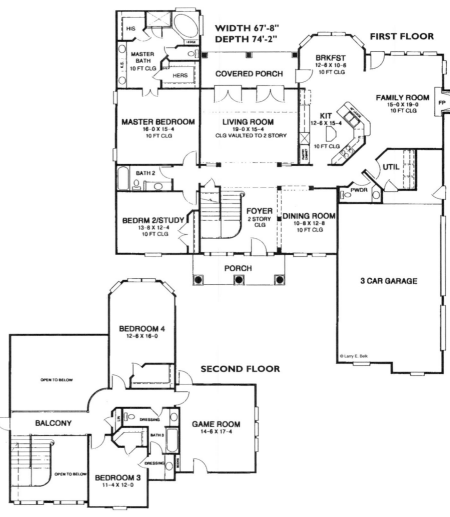

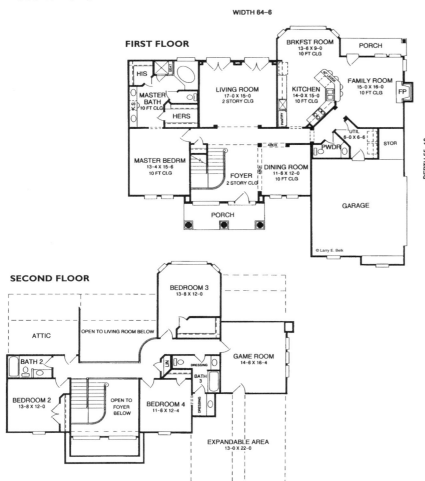

FIRST FLOOR

WIDTH 64–6

BRKFST ROOM
13-6 X 9-0
10 FT CLG

PORCH

HIS

MASTER
BATH
10 FT CLG

LIVING ROOM
17-0 X 15-0
2 STORY CLG

KITCHEN
14-0 X 15-0
10 FT CLG

FAMILY ROOM
15-0 X 16-0
10 FT CLG

FP

HERS

PANTRY

UTIL
6-0 X 6-6

STOR

MASTER BEDRM
13-4 X 15-6
10 FT CLG

FOYER
2 STORY CLG

DINING ROOM
11-6 X 12-0
10 FT CLG

PWDR

DEPTH 55–10

PORCH

GARAGE

© Larry E. Belk

SECOND FLOOR

BEDROOM 3
13-8 X 12-0

ATTIC

OPEN TO LIVING ROOM BELOW

BATH 2

GAME ROOM
14-6 X 16-4

DRESSING

BEDROOM 2
13-8 X 12-0

OPEN TO
FOYER
BELOW

BATH 3

BEDROOM 4
11-6 X 12-4

DRESSING

EXPANDABLE AREA
13-0 X 22-0

A European Influence
Price Code: H

■ This plan features:

— Four bedrooms

— Three full and one half baths

■ European styling is prevalent in the exterior of this design

■ The grand Entry Porch gives way to the equally impressive two-story Foyer

■ The Dining Room is separated from the Foyer by columns

■ The Living Room has a set of French doors to the rear yard and a two-story ceiling

■ An oversized Garage with storage space completes this plan

■ This home is designed with basement, slab, and crawlspace foundation options

FIRST FLOOR — 1,919 SQ. FT.
SECOND FLOOR — 1,190 SQ. FT.
BONUS SPACE — 286 SQ. FT.
GARAGE — 561 SQ. FT.

TOTAL LIVING AREA:
3,109 SQ. FT.

Designed for Entertaining

Price Code: J

- This plan features:
  — Three bedrooms
  — Three full and one half baths

- Large open floor plan with an array of amenities

- Grand Room and Dining Area separated by three-sided fireplace

- Secluded Master Suite enhanced by a private Spa Deck

- This home is designed with pier and post foundation options

- Alternate foundation options available at an additional charge. Please call 1-800-235-5700 for more information.

MAIN FLOOR — 2,066 SQ. FT.
UPPER FLOOR — 809 SQ. FT.
BONUS — 1,260 SQ. FT.
GARAGE — 798 SQ. FT.

TOTAL LIVING AREA:
2,875 SQ. FT.

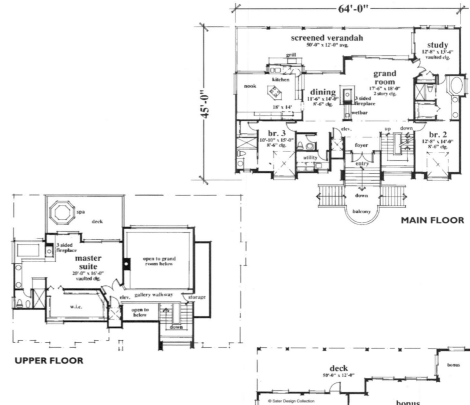

MAIN FLOOR

UPPER FLOOR

LOWER FLOOR

To order your Blueprints, call 1-800-235-5700

Just Past the Garden Gate

Price Code: G

- This plan features:
— Four bedrooms
— Two full and one half baths
- The quaint exterior is reminiscent of a European cottage
- From the covered front Porch step through double doors into the Foyer with a 10-foot ceiling
- There is an arched entry from the Foyer into the Dining Room
- The Family Room and Breakfast Room are warmed by a fireplace and share a sloped ceiling
- The Living Room has French doors that open to the rear Porch
- All the Bedrooms, including the Master Suite, are located in one wing
- The Kitchen is located in the rear of the home and conveniently accesses the Garage
- This home is designed with basement, slab, and crawlspace foundation options

MAIN FLOOR — 2,757 SQ. FT.
GARAGE — 484 SQ. FT.

TOTAL LIVING AREA:
2,757 SQ. FT.

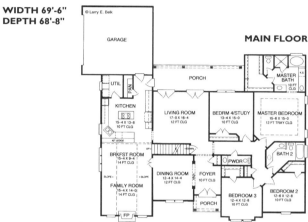

WIDTH 69'-6"
DEPTH 68'-8"
© Larry E. Belk

MAIN FLOOR

Classic Styling

Price Code: E

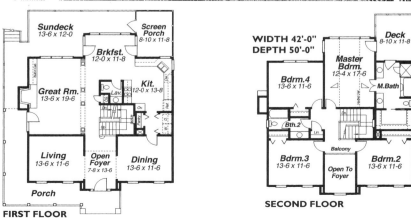

- This plan features:
— Four bedrooms
— Two full and one half baths
- A wraparound Porch adds a cozy touch to this classic style
- The two-story Foyer is open to the formal Dining and Living Rooms
- The large Great Room is accentuated by columns and a fireplace
- A sunny Breakfast Area provides direct access to the Sun Deck, Screen Porch and the Kitchen
- A convenient Kitchen is situated between the formal Dining Room and informal Breakfast Area
- A private Deck highlights the Master Suite, which includes a luxurious Bath and a walk-in closet
- Three additional Bedrooms share a full Bath
- This home is designed with a basement foundation

FIRST FLOOR — 1,250 SQ. FT.
SECOND FLOOR — 1,166 SQ. FT.
BASEMENT — 448 SQ. FT.
GARAGE — 706 SQ. FT.

TOTAL LIVING AREA:
2,464 SQ. FT.

WIDTH 42'-0"
DEPTH 50'-0"

FIRST FLOOR

SECOND FLOOR

Luxurious Masterpiece
Price Code: K

- This plan features:
  - Four bedrooms
  - Three full and one half baths
- An elegant and distinguished exterior
- An expansive formal Living Room with a 14-foot ceiling and a raised hearth fireplace
- Informal Family Room offers another fireplace, wetbar, cathedral ceiling and access to the covered Patio
- A hub Kitchen with a cooktop island, peninsula counter/snack bar, and a bright Breakfast Area
- French doors lead into a quiet Study offering many uses
- Private Master Bedroom enhanced by a pullman ceiling, lavish his and her Baths, and a garden window tub
- Three additional Bedrooms with walk-in closets and private access to full Baths
- This home is designed with basement and slab foundation options

MAIN FLOOR — 3,818 SQ. FT.
GARAGE — 816 SQ. FT.

TOTAL LIVING AREA:
3,818 SQ. FT.

WIDTH 107'-4"
DEPTH 68'-7"

107' - 4"

68' - 7"

X

Her Bath

His Bath

MstrBed
15x17
11' Pullman Clg

LivRm
23x17
14' Clg

Covered Patio

Wet Bar

FamilyRm
16x21
Cathedral Clg

Brkfst
11x14

Bed#3
13x14

Bed#4
13x12

Util

Kit
14x16

Gallery

Bed#2
13x14

Study
14x13
14' Clg

Ent
14' Clg

FmlDin
14x14
12' Clg

3-Car Gar
24x34

Covered Porch

MAIN FLOOR

Traditional French Touches
Price Code: J

- This plan features:
  - Four bedrooms
  - Three full and one half baths
- Traditional French touches adorn this Country classic
- Interior details include a tiled Entry with columns and an arched soffit
- The Den and the Dining Room both have decorative ceiling treatments
- The Great Room has a fireplace with built-in cabinets beside it
- The Kitchen has a walk-in Pantry and a cooktop island
- The Master Bedroom is located on the first floor for privacy
- This home is designed with a basement foundation

FIRST FLOOR — 2,575 SQ. FT.
SECOND FLOOR — 1,075 SQ. FT.
BASEMENT — 2,575 SQ. FT.

TOTAL LIVING AREA:
3,650 SQ. FT.

Photography supplied by Ahmann Designs, Inc.

WIDTH 85'-0"
DEPTH 53'-4"

4 CAR GAR.
23'6" X 39'6"

KIT.
10'6" X 16'6"

NK.
11' X 14'4"

GRT. RM.
16'9" X 23'

CATHEDRAL CEILING

M.B.R.
STEP CEILING
18'9" X 19'3"

WALK IN PANTRY

DIN.
STEP CEILING
15' X 15'

DEN
TRAY CEILING
14' X 16'8"

BUILT IN CAB.

FIRST FLOOR

OPEN TO
GRT. RM.

BR. 2
12'8" X 17'0"

BR. 3
12'8" X 16'6"

BR. 4
14'0" X 13'8"

STUDY AREA
10' X 10'

PLANT LEDGE

OPEN TO E.

SECOND FLOOR

English Tudor Styling

Price Code: G

- This plan features:
  — Four bedrooms
  — Three full and one half baths
- This Tudor-styled gem has a unique mix of exterior materials
- Inside the Entry either turn left to the Living Room or right into the Dining Room
- At the end of the Gallery is the Master Bedroom, which has dual walk-in closets
- The Family Room has a sloped ceiling and a rear wall fireplace
- The Kitchen has a center island and opens to the Breakfast Area
- A skylight brightens the staircase to the second floor
- Upstairs find three large Bedrooms and two full Baths
- Also upstairs is the future bonus room, located over the Garage
- This home is designed with basement, slab, and crawlspace foundation options

FIRST FLOOR — 2,082 SQ. FT.
SECOND FLOOR — 904 SQ. FT.
BONUS ROOM — 408 SQ. FT.
GARAGE — 605 SQ. FT.

TOTAL LIVING AREA:
2,986 SQ. FT.

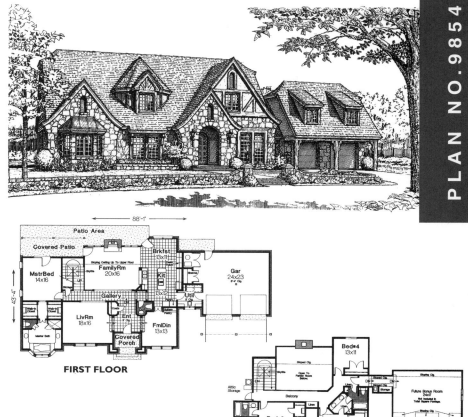

FIRST FLOOR

SECOND FLOOR

Kitchen on Lanai

Price Code: G

- This plan features:
  — Three bedrooms
  — Two full, two three-quarter, and two half baths
- Columns in the grand Foyer direct guests into the Living and Dining Rooms
- The Master Suite arrangement allows access to the closets and luxury Bath without passing through the Bedroom
- This home is designed with a slab foundation
- Alternate foundation options available at an additional charge. Please call 1-800-235-5700 for more information.

MAIN FLOOR — 3,896 SQ. FT.
BONUS ROOM — 356 SQ. FT.
GARAGE — 846 SQ. FT.

TOTAL LIVING AREA:
3,896 SQ. FT.

WIDTH 90'-0"
DEPTH 128'-8"

BASEMENT STAIRS OPTION

MAIN FLOOR

Poetic Symmetry

Price Code: G

- This plan features:
- — Three bedrooms
- — Three full and one half baths
- The open Living and Dining Areas are defined by French doors with windows above
- The Master Suite is located on the main floor for maximum in privacy
- Also upstairs is a Gallery Loft and a Computer Loft, which overlook the Grand Room
- The lower floor features a two-car Garage and plenty of storage space
- This home is designed with pier and post foundation options
- Alternate foundation options available at an additional charge. Please call 1-800-235-5700 for more information.

MAIN FLOOR — 1,642 SQ. FT.
UPPER FLOOR — 1,165 SQ. FT.
LOWER FLOOR — 150 SQ. FT.

TOTAL LIVING AREA: 2,957 SQ. FT.

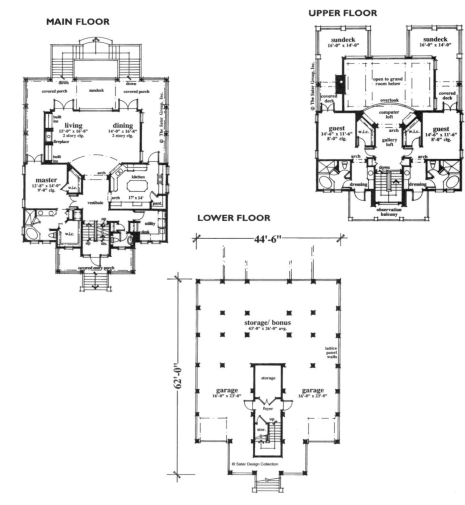

MAIN FLOOR

UPPER FLOOR

LOWER FLOOR

144

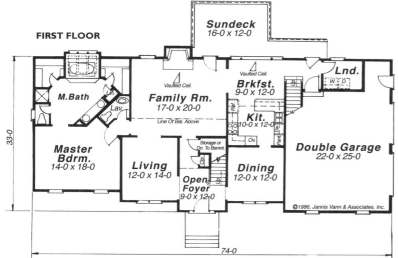

FIRST FLOOR

Sundeck
16-0 x 12-0

Vaulted Ceil.

Vaulted Ceil.

Brkfst.
9-0 x 12-0

Lnd.
W. D.

M.Bath

Lav.

Family Rm.
17-0 x 20-0

Kit.
10-0 x 12-0

Line Of Bal. Above

Double Garage
22-0 x 25-0

33-0

Master
Bdrm.
14-0 x 18-0

Living
12-0 x 14-0

Storage or
Dn. To Bsmnt.

Dining
12-0 x 12-0

Open
Foyer
9-0 x 12-0

©1986, Jannis Vann & Associates, Inc.

74-0

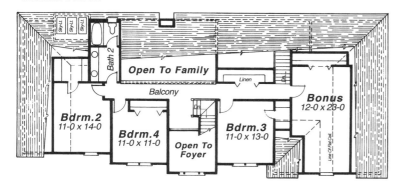

SECOND FLOOR

Bath 2

Open To Family

Linen

Balcony

Bonus
12-0 x 28-0

Bdrm.2
11-0 x 14-0

Bdrm.4
11-0 x 11-0

Open To
Foyer

Bdrm.3
11-0 x 13-0

Line Of Flat Ceil.

Master Suite on the First Floor

Price Code: F

■ This plan features:

— Four bedrooms

— Two full and one half baths

■ The first floor Master Bedroom is a private retreat

■ This home has formal Living and Dining Rooms located in the front of the home

■ The large Family Room has a rear wall fireplace and access to the Sun Deck

■ Convenient appliance placement highlights the Kitchen

■ This home is designed with basement, slab, and crawlspace foundation options

FIRST FLOOR — 1,719 SQ. FT.
SECOND FLOOR — 917 SQ. FT.
BONUS — 294 SQ. FT.
BASEMENT — 1,719 SQ. FT.
GARAGE — 614 SQ. FT.

TOTAL LIVING AREA:
2,636 SQ. FT.

Luxurious Bedrooms Abound

Price Code: I

■ This plan features:

— Five bedrooms

— Three full and one half baths

■ The formal Living Room and Dining Room have special window treatments

■ The Family Room has a focal point fireplace and access to the rear Sun Deck

■ The Kitchen, Family Room, and Breakfast Nook are all open to each other

■ The Master Suite has a decorative ceiling, a fireplace enjoyed also from the Sitting Area, a private Bath and a Screen Porch

■ This home is designed with a basement foundation

FIRST FLOOR — 1,491 SQ. FT.
SECOND FLOOR — 1,811 SQ. FT.
BASEMENT — 1,164 SQ. FT.
GARAGE — 564 SQ. FT.

TOTAL LIVING AREA:
3,302 SQ. FT.

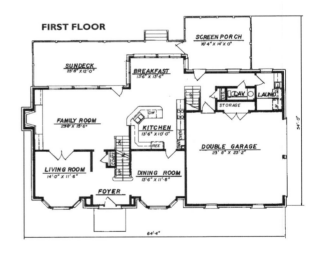

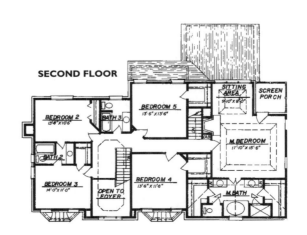

146

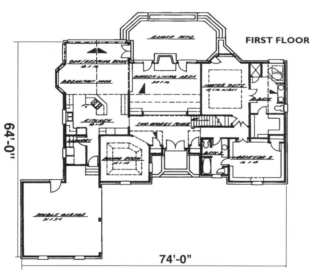

FIRST FLOOR

64'-0"

74'-0"

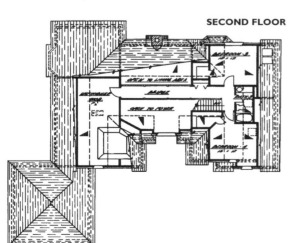

SECOND FLOOR

Exquisite Home
Price Code: G

- This plan features:
  - Four bedrooms
  - Three full baths
- A two-story Foyer greets you as you enter this home
- The elegant formal Dining Room has a decorative ceiling
- The Kitchen features a cooktop island
- The dramatic sunken Living Room has a rear wall fireplace
- The Master Suite features a private Bath and a walk-in closet
- This home is designed with basement and crawlspace foundation options

FIRST FLOOR — 2,177 SQ. FT.
SECOND FLOOR — 661 SQ. FT.
BONUS — 312 SQ. FT.
BASEMENT — 2,149 SQ. FT.
GARAGE — 534 SQ. FT.

TOTAL LIVING AREA:
2,838 SQ. FT.

Quoins and Keystones Accent Stucco

Price Code: K

■ This plan features:

— Three bedrooms

— Two full and four half baths

■ Impressive entrance with two-story window Foyer, curved staircase and Balcony

■ Spacious Living Room with a vaulted ceiling above a wall of windows, Sun Deck access and an inviting fireplace

■ Ideal Kitchen with extended cooktop serving counter, octagonal glass Breakfast Area, Keeping Room with a cozy fireplace, and nearby Laundry and Garage Entry

■ This home is designed with a basement foundation

FIRST FLOOR — 2,656 SQ. FT.
SECOND FLOOR — 1,184 SQ. FT.
GARAGE — 528 SQ. FT.

TOTAL LIVING AREA:
3,840 SQ. FT.

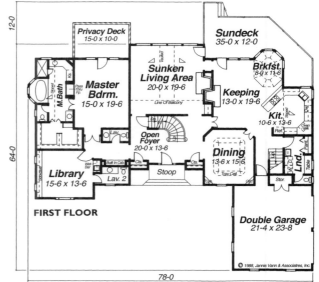

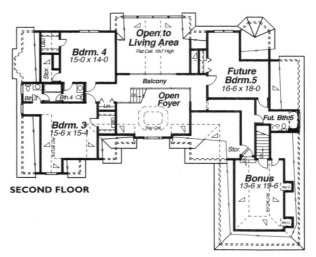

148

To order your Blueprints, call 1-800-235-5700

Family Room with a Fireplace

Price Code: E

■ This plan features:

— Four bedrooms

— Two full and one half baths

■ An island Kitchen with a built-in Pantry, double sink and convenient Dinette Area

■ A cozy fireplace enhancing the Family Room

■ A formal Living Room and Dining Room

■ A luxurious Master Suite with an ultra Bath and walk-in closet

■ This home is designed with a basement foundation

FIRST FLOOR — 1,228 SQ. FT.
SECOND FLOOR — 1,191 SQ. FT.
BASEMENT — 1,228 SQ. FT.
GARAGE — 528 SQ. FT.

TOTAL LIVING AREA:
2,419 SQ. FT.

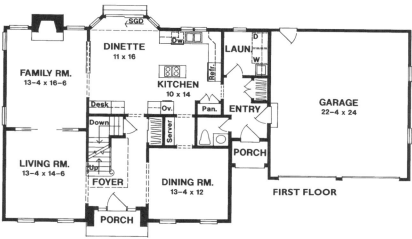

FIRST FLOOR

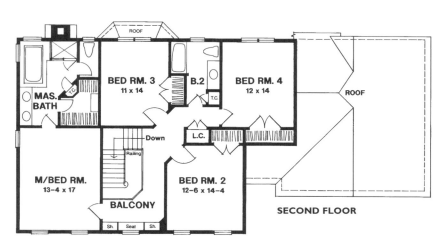

SECOND FLOOR

A Tasteful Elegance

Price Code: I

- This plan features:
- — Four bedrooms
- — Two full and one half baths

- A Foyer with a vaulted ceiling, giving a great first impression

- A large Family Room with a beamed ceiling, bay window and a cozy fireplace

- A tray ceiling as the crowning touch to the formal Living Room, which also has a terrific fireplace

- A Master Bedroom with a stepped ceiling, double vanity private Bath and a huge walk-in closet

- This home is designed with a basement foundation

FIRST FLOOR — 1,947 SQ. FT.
SECOND FLOOR — 1,390 SQ. FT.
BASEMENT — 1,947 SQ. FT.
GARAGE — 680 SQ. FT.

TOTAL LIVING AREA:
3,337 SQ. FT.

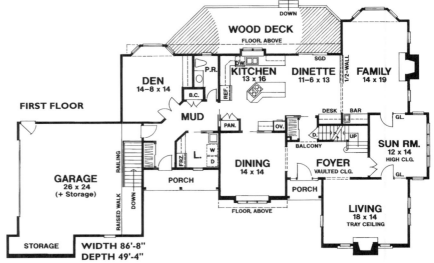

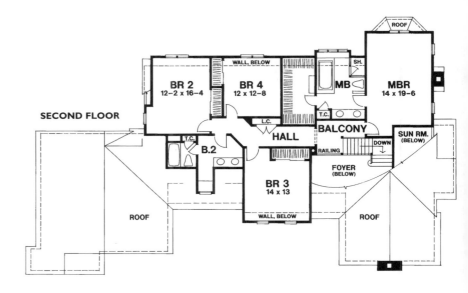

Unique V-Shaped Home

Price Code: I

■ This plan features:
— Two bedrooms
— Three full baths
■ Bookshelves, interspersed with windows, line the long hallway that provides access to the owner's wing
■ Skylights brighten the already sunny Eating Nook in the huge Country Kitchen
■ A walk-in Pantry, range-top work island, built-in barbecue, and a sink add to the amenities of the Kitchen
■ A wide window bay and an entire wall of windows along its length illuminate the Living Room
■ Master Suite with adjacent Sitting Area plus a luxurious private Bath
■ A Guest Suite with a full Bath
■ This home is designed with a crawlspace foundation

MAIN FLOOR — 3,417 SQ. FT.
GARAGE — 795 SQ. FT.

TOTAL LIVING AREA:
3,417 SQ. FT.

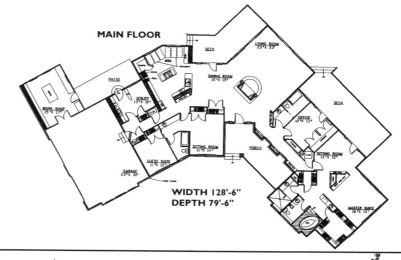

MAIN FLOOR

WIDTH 128'-6"
DEPTH 79'-6"

Great Room with Vaulted Ceiling

Price Code: F

■ This plan features:
— Four Bedrooms
— Three full and two half baths
■ Cozy covered Porch leading into an impressive two-story Foyer
■ Formal Dining Room accented by a bay window
■ A gas fireplace in the Great Room
■ Kitchen and Dinette topped by a vaulted ceiling, with only a peninsula counter between them
■ Island Kitchen has an abundance of work and storage space
■ First floor Master Bedroom affording privacy and luxury
■ This home is designed with a basement foundation

FIRST FLOOR — 1,845 SQ. FT.
SECOND FLOOR — 876 SQ. FT.
BASEMENT — 1,832 SQ. FT.

TOTAL LIVING AREA:
2,721 SQ. FT.

WIDTH 75'-6"
DEPTH 45'-4"

FIRST FLOOR

SECOND FLOOR

A Grand Presence

Price Code: J

- This plan features:
- — Four bedrooms
- — Two full and one half baths
- A gourmet Kitchen with a cooktop island, built-in Pantry and planning Desk
- Pocket doors that separate the formal Dining Room from the informal Dinette Area
- An expansive Family Room with a fireplace and a built-in entertainment center
- A luxuriant Master Bath that highlights the Master Bedroom
- This home is designed with a basement foundation

First floor — 2,093 sq. ft.
Second floor — 1,527 sq. ft.
Basement — 2,093 sq. ft.
Garage — 816 sq. ft.

Total living area: *3,620 sq. ft.*

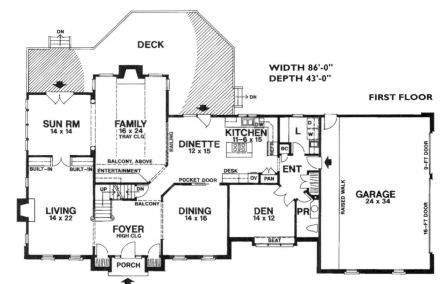

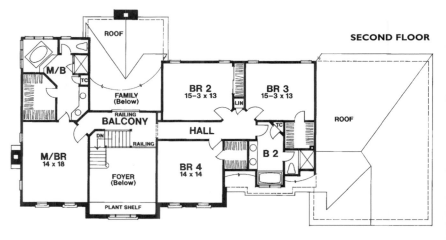

WIDTH 82'-0"
DEPTH 48'-8"

SUN RM
15 x 12
CATHEDRAL CLG

SGD

FLOOR ABOVE

DINETTE
12–4 x 10

FAMILY
21 x 15

DN   DESK

DW

KITCHEN
15–8 x 13

L   D
W

REF

ENTRY

BC

GARAGE
24 x 34

9-FT DOORS

OPEN
ABOVE

PAN.

PARLOR
14 x 16

UP

FOYER

OV

DINING
14 x 15
STEPPED CLG

P

PORCH

FIRST FLOOR

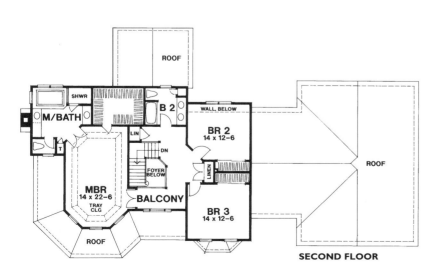

ROOF

SHWR

B 2

WALL BELOW

M/BATH

LIN

BR 2
14 x 12–6

T

ROOF

FOYER
BELOW

DN

LINEN

MBR
14 x 22–6
TRAY
CLG

BALCONY

BR 3
14 x 12–6

ROOF

SECOND FLOOR

That Old-Fashion Feeling

Price Code: F

- ■ This plan features:
- — Three bedrooms
- — Two full and one half baths

■ An inviting front Porch wrapping around the unique octagonal Parlor and Master Bedroom above

■ A large island Kitchen with a double sink, built-in Pantry and a peninsula counter/eating bar leading through a large Entry to both the Garage and Laundry Room

■ An elegant Master Bedroom with a tray ceiling, a room-sized walk-in closet and a plush Bath, featuring a raised, corner window tub and two vanities

■ This home is designed with a basement foundation

FIRST FLOOR — 1,484 SQ. FT.
SECOND FLOOR — 1,223 SQ. FT.

TOTAL LIVING AREA:
2,707 SQ. FT.

Luxury Living

Price Code: H

■ This plan features:

— Four bedrooms

— Two full and one three-quarter baths

■ A Living Room with a vaulted ceiling and elegant fireplace

■ A formal Dining Room, featuring a built-in buffet that adjoins the Living Room

■ An island cook top in the well-appointed Kitchen with a walk-in Pantry and an open layout to the Family Room

■ A vaulted ceiling in the Family Room with a cozy corner fireplace

■ A huge walk-in closet, built-in entertainment center and a full Bath with every amenity in the Master Suite

■ This home is designed with basement, slab, and crawlspace foundation options

FIRST FLOOR — 2,125 SQ. FT.
SECOND FLOOR — 1,095 SQ. FT.

TOTAL LIVING AREA:

3,220 SQ. FT.

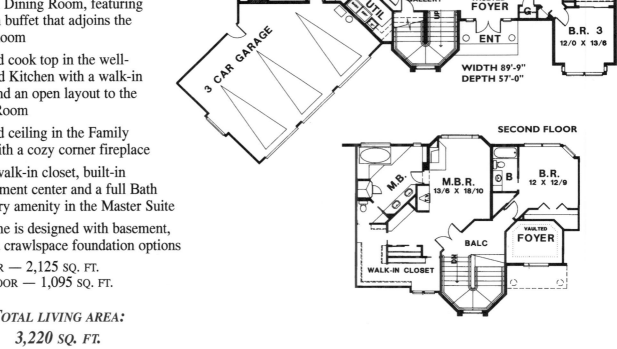

Bath

walk-in closet

Bedroom
14' x 11'4"

Master Bedroom
13'8" x 16'

Hall

wood rail
stairs dn

linen

Bath

Foyer
Below

Bedroom
12' x 13'

Sitting Area
13'8" x 7'3"

SECOND FLOOR

Breakfast
11' x 12'4"

Great Room
20'6" x 18'2"

Kitchen
17'5" x 13'6"

Laun.

computer center

Hall

stairs dn
butler's pantry

wood rail

Foyer

Dining Room
12' x 15'4"

Two-car Garage
20' x 35'4"

Library
13'7" x 12'9"

Porch

53'4"

FIRST FLOOR

57'7"

Countrified Luxury

Price Code: G

■ This plan features:

— Three bedrooms

— Two full and one half baths

■ A Library is located off of the Foyer

■ The Dining Room is distinguished by decorative ceiling treatment

■ The Great Room and the Kitchen converge at the wetbar

■ The dreamy L-shaped Kitchen incorporates a center island into its design

■ The upstairs Master Bedroom has a Sitting Area

■ An oversized two-car Garage has space for storage or a workshop

■ This home is designed with a basement foundation

FIRST FLOOR — 1,625 SQ. FT.
SECOND FLOOR — 1,188 SQ. FT.
BASEMENT — 1,625 SQ. FT.
GARAGE — 592 SQ. FT.

TOTAL LIVING AREA:
2,813 SQ. FT.

Stately Columns and Keystones

Price Code: H

- This plan features:
- — Four bedrooms
- — Three full and one half baths

- Gracious two-story Foyer opens to vaulted Living Room and arched Dining Room

- Expansive, two-story Grand Room with impressive fireplace between outdoor views

- Spacious and efficient Kitchen with a work island, Breakfast Area with backyard access and nearby Laundry/Garage Entry

- Private Master Bedroom offers a decorative ceiling, two walk-in closets and a garden window tub

- This home is designed with basement and slab foundation options

First floor — 2,115 sq. ft.
Second floor — 914 sq. ft.
Garage — 448 sq. ft.

Total living area:
3,029 sq. ft.

156

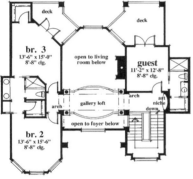

SECOND FLOOR

deck

br. 3
13'-6" x 15'-0"
8'-8" clg.

open to living
room below

guest
11'-2" x 12'-8"
8'-8" clg.

deck

gallery loft

arch

art
niche
down

arch

open to foyer below

br. 2
13'-6" x 15'-6"
8'-8" clg.

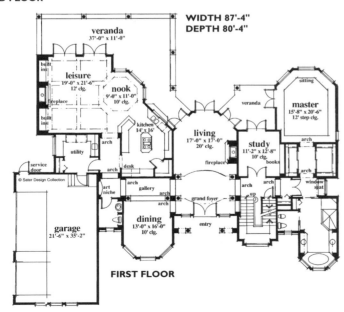

FIRST FLOOR

WIDTH 87'-4"
DEPTH 80'-4"

veranda
37'-0" x 11'-0"

built
ins

leisure
19'-0" x 21'-6"
12' clg.

fireplace

built
ins

nook
9'-0" x 11'-0"
10' clg.

kitchen
14' x 16'

desk

utility

service
door

art
niche

gallery

arch

arch

arch

arch

© Sater Design Collection

garage
21'-6" x 35'-2"

dining
13'-0" x 16'-0"
10' clg.

entry

grand foyer

up

living
17'-0" x 17'-0"
20' clg.

fireplace

study
11'-2" x 12'-8"
10' clg.

books

sitting

veranda

master
15'-8" x 20'-6"
12' step clg.

arch

arch

arch

window
seat

Spectacular Stucco and Stone

Price Code: L

■ This plan features:

— Four bedrooms

— One full, two three-quarter and one half baths

■ Open Living Room with fireplace and multiple doors to rear grounds

■ Formal Dining Room has a conveniently located bay window

■ Master wing offers a step ceiling, two walk-in closets and a lavish Bath

■ This home is designed with basement, slab and combo basement/slab foundation options

■ Alternate foundation options available at an additional charge. Please call 1-800-235-5700 for more information.

FIRST FLOOR — 3,027 SQ. FT.
SECOND FLOOR — 1,079 SQ. FT.
BASEMENT — 3,027 SQ. FT.
GARAGE — 802 SQ. FT.

TOTAL LIVING AREA:
4,106 SQ. FT.

PLAN NO. 94622

Multiple Porches Provide Added Interest

Price Code: H

■ This plan features:
— Four bedrooms
— Three full and one half baths
■ Two-story central Foyer flanked by Living and Dining Rooms
■ Spacious Great Room with large fireplace between french doors to Porch and Deck
■ Country-size Kitchen with cooktop work island, walk-in Pantry and Breakfast Area with Porch access
■ Pampering Master Bedroom offers a decorative ceiling, Sitting Area, Porch and Deck access, a huge walk-in closet and lavish Bath
■ Three second floor Bedrooms, all with walk-in closets, have private access to full Baths
■ This home is designed with slab and pier/post foundation options

First Floor — 2,033 sq. ft.
Second Floor — 1,116 sq. ft.

Total Living Area:
3,149 sq. ft.

WIDTH 66'-0"
DEPTH 56'-0"

SECOND FLOOR

FIRST FLOOR

PLAN NO. 93604

With Attension to Detail

Price Code: H

■ This plan features:
— Four bedrooms
— Three full and one half bath
■ A two story Foyer
■ A formal Living Room and Dining Room perfect for entertaining
■ A two story Grand Room with a focal point fireplace that can be seen from the Foyer
■ A gourmet Kitchen with a work island, walk-in Pantry, built-in planning desk, double sink and ample cabinet and counter space
■ A first floor Master Suite with a decorative ceiling and a luxurious Master Bath
■ Three upstairs Bedrooms with direct access to full Bath
■ This home is designed with basement and slab foundation options
■ This plan is not to be built within a 50 mile radius of Atlanta, GA.

First Floor — 2,115 sq. ft.
Second Floor — 914 sq. ft.
Basement — 2,115 sq. ft.
Garage — 448 sq. ft.

Total Living Area:
3,029 sq. ft.

WIDTH 60'-0"
DEPTH 52'-0"

FIRST FLOOR

SECOND FLOOR

Dramatic Design

Price Code: F

■ This plan features:
— Four bedrooms
— Two full and one half baths

■ Dramatic two-story Foyer flows into the formal Dining Area, which is defined by a cluster of columns

■ Great Room shares a two-way fireplace with the Morning Room that opens onto the a Deck

■ The Kitchen features a built-in Pantry, island and a planning desk

■ The Master Bedroom has a private double vanity Bath and a walk-in closet

■ Three upstairs Bedrooms contain abundant closet space and share an oversized Bath

■ This home is designed with a crawlspace foundation

FIRST FLOOR — 1,910 SQ. FT.
SECOND FLOOR — 697 SQ. FT.

TOTAL LIVING AREA:
2,607 SQ. FT.

PLAN NO. 93709

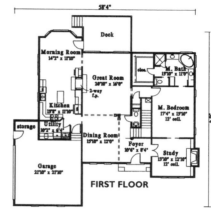

FIRST FLOOR

SECOND FLOOR

Expansive Family Living Area

Price Code: E

■ This plan features:
— Four bedrooms
— Two full and one half baths

■ A vaulted ceiling tops the Foyer, achieving a feeling of volume

■ The Living Room showcases a tray ceiling and is enhanced by a boxed bay window

■ The Dining Room adjoins the Living Room, having direct access to the Kitchen

■ The Kitchen features a cooktop island and flows into the Dinette

■ The Family Room includes a fireplace framed by windows and adjoins the Dinette

■ Double doors add privacy to the Den

■ A tray ceiling tops the Master Bedroom which also includes a walk-in closet and a full Bath

■ The secondary Bedrooms are in close proximity to a full Bath

■ This home is designed with a basement foundation

FIRST FLOOR — 1,378 SQ. FT.
SECOND FLOOR — 1,084 SQ. FT.
BASEMENT — 1,378 SQ. FT.
GARAGE — 448 SQ. FT.

TOTAL LIVING AREA:
2,462 SQ. FT.

PLAN NO. 93340

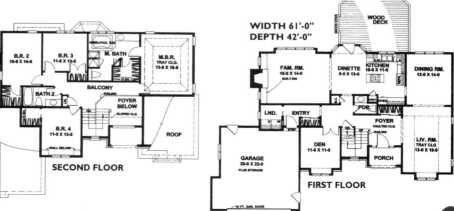

WIDTH 61'-0"
DEPTH 42'-0"

SECOND FLOOR

FIRST FLOOR

Grand Design

Price Code: L

- This plan features:

— Four bedrooms

— Two full, one three-quarter, and one half baths

- Triple arches at Entry lead into Grand Foyer and Gallery with arched entries to all areas

- Triple French doors catch the breeze and access rear grounds in Living and Leisure Rooms

- Spacious Kitchen with large walk-in Pantry, cooktop/work island, angled serving counter/snack bar, glass Nook, and easy access to Utility Room and Garage

- This home is designed with a slab foundation

- Alternate foundation options available at an additional charge. Please call 1-800-235-5700 for more information.

FIRST FLOOR — 3,546 SQ. FT.
SECOND FLOOR — 1,213 SQ. FT.
GARAGE — 822 SQ. FT.

TOTAL LIVING AREA:
4,759 SQ. FT.

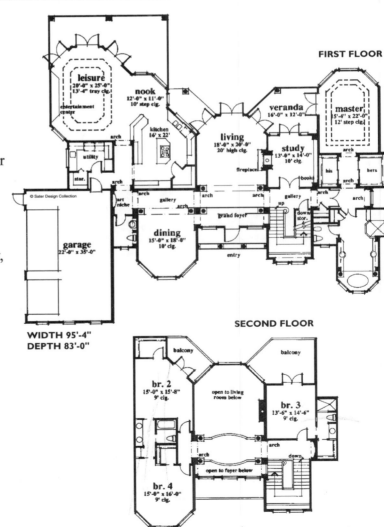

160

Impressive Elevation

Price Code: H

■ This plan features:
— Three bedrooms
— Two full and one three-quarter baths
■ Glass arch entrance into Foyer and Grand Room accented by fireplace between built-ins and multiple French doors leading to Veranda
■ Decorative windows highlight Study and formal Dining Room
■ Spacious Kitchen with walk-in Pantry and peninsula serving counter easily serves Nook, Veranda and Dining Room
■ Luxurious Master Suite with step ceiling, Sitting Area, his and her closets and pampering Bath
■ Two additional Bedrooms, one with a private Deck, have bay windows and walk-in closets
■ This home is designed with basement and slab foundation options
■ Alternate foundation options available at an additional charge. Please call 1-800-235-5700 for more information

FIRST FLOOR — 2,181 SQ. FT.
SECOND FLOOR — 710 SQ. FT.
GARAGE —658 SQ. FT.

TOTAL LIVING AREA: 2,891 SQ. FT.

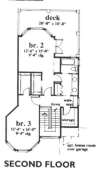

WIDTH 66'-4"
DEPTH 79'-0"

FIRST FLOOR

SECOND FLOOR

Spectacular Curving Stairway

Price Code: H

■ This plan features:
— Four bedrooms
— Two full and one three-quarter and one half baths
■ Spacious formal Entry with arched transom, is enhanced by a curved staircase
■ Great Room is inviting with a cozy fireplace, a wetbar, and three arched windows
■ Open Kitchen, Breakfast, and Hearth Area combine efficiency and comfort for all
■ Master Bedroom offers a private back door, a double walk-in closet, and a whirlpool Bath
■ Generous closets and Baths enhance the three second floor Bedrooms
■ This home is designed with a basement foundation
■ Alternate foundation options available at an additional charge. Please call 1-800-235-5700 for more information

FIRST FLOOR — 2,252 SQ. FT.
SECOND FLOOR — 920 SQ. FT.
BASEMENT — 2,252 SQ. FT.
GARAGE — 646 SQ. FT.

TOTAL LIVING AREA: 3,172 SQ. FT.

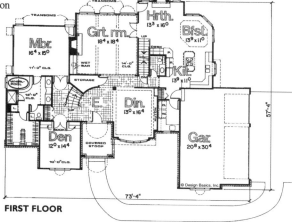

FIRST FLOOR

SECOND FLOOR

To order your Blueprints, call 1-800-235-5700

One Floor Convenience

Price Code: F

■ This plan features:

— Four bedrooms

— Three full baths

■ A Formal Entry/Gallery opens to a large Living Room with a hearth fireplace

■ The Efficient Kitchen, with angled counters and serving bar, easily serves the Breakfast Room, Patio, and formal Dining Room

■ The Master Bedroom is enhanced by a vaulted ceiling and pampering Bath with a large walk-in closet

■ This home is designed with a slab foundation

MAIN FLOOR — 2,675 SQ. FT.
GARAGE — 638 SQ. FT.

TOTAL LIVING AREA:
2,675 SQ. FT.

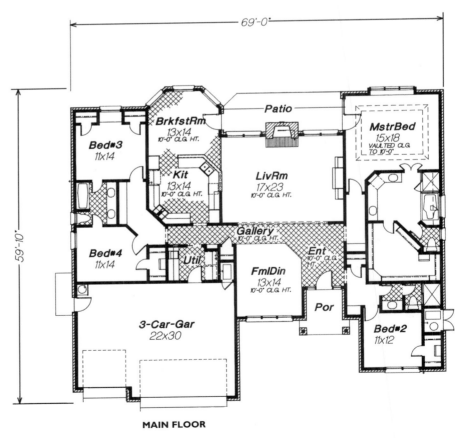

MAIN FLOOR

Soft Arches Accent Country Design

Price Code: F

- **This plan features:**
- — Four or five bedrooms
- — Two full and one half baths
- Entry Porch with double dormers and doors enhances Country charm
- Pillared arches frame Foyer, Dining Room, and Great Room
- Open Great Room with optional built-ins and sliding glass doors to Veranda
- Comfortable Master Suite with his and her closets and vanities and a garden tub
- This home is designed with basement and slab foundation options
- Alternate foundation options available at an additional charge. Please call 1-800-235-5700 for more information.

FIRST FLOOR — 1,676 SQ. FT.
SECOND FLOOR — 851 SQ. FT.
GARAGE — 304 SQ. FT.

TOTAL LIVING AREA:
2,527 SQ. FT.

FIRST FLOOR

55'-0"
50'-0"

study/br. 4
14'-0" x 11'-2"
9'-4" clg.

opt. desk closet

nook
10' x 12'

veranda
26'-0" x 10'-0"

master
13'-0" x 15'-6"
9'-4" clg.

optional built ins

great room
18'-0" x 13'-0" avg.
9'-4" clg.

kitchen
12' x 13'

his   hers

utility

arch   arch

arch   foyer

hers

garage
18'-0" x 21'-6"

dining
11'-4" x 11'-6"
9'-4" clg.

his

entry porch

© Sater Design Collection

SECOND FLOOR

balcony

br. 2
11'-10" x 11'-0"
8' clg.

br. 3
15'-0" x 10'-0"
8' clg

attic room

computer loft/
built ins

books

br. 1
11'-8" x 14'-4"
8' clg.

open to
foyer
below

wdw.
seat

Luxurious Elegance

Price Code: H

- ■ This plan features:
- — Four bedrooms
- — Two full and one three-quarter and one half baths
- ■ Double doors lead into Entry with an exquisite curved staircase
- ■ Formal Living Room features a marble hearth fireplace, triple window and built-in bookshelves
- ■ The Kitchen has a cooktop/work island and a Utility/Garage Entry
- ■ Expansive Great Room with entertainment center and fieldstone fireplace
- ■ Vaulted ceiling crowns Master Bedroom offering a plush Bath and two walk-in closets
- ■ This home is designed with basement and slab foundation options

FIRST FLOOR — 2,190 SQ. FT.
SECOND FLOOR — 920 SQ. FT.
GARAGE — 624 SQ. FT.

TOTAL LIVING AREA:

3,110 SQ. FT.

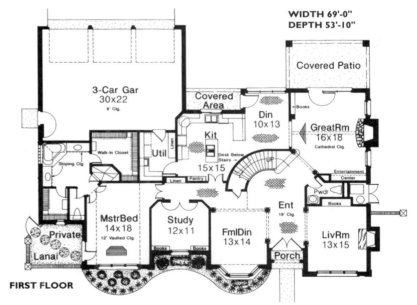

WIDTH 69'-0"
DEPTH 53'-10"

FIRST FLOOR

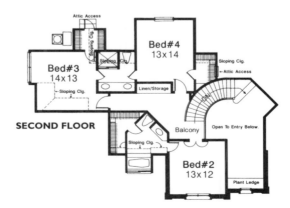

SECOND FLOOR

To order your Blueprints, call 1-800-235-5700

Traditional Elegance

Price Code: K

- This plan features:
- — Four bedrooms
- — Three full and one half baths
- A elegant entrance leading into a two-story Foyer with an impressive staircase highlighted by a curved window
- Floor to ceiling windows in both the formal Living and Dining Rooms
- A spacious Den with a hearth fireplace, built-in bookshelves, a wetbar and a wall of windows viewing the backyard
- A large, efficient Kitchen, equipped with lots of counter and storage space, a bright Breakfast Area, and access to the Dining Room, Utility Room, walk-in Pantry and Garage
- A grand Master Suite with decorative ceilings, a private Porch, an elaborate Bath and two walk-in closets
- Three additional Bedrooms on the second floor with walk-in closets, sharing adjoining full Baths and an ideal Children's Den
- This home is designed with slab and crawlspace foundation options

FIRST FLOOR — 2,553 SQ. FT.
SECOND FLOOR — 1,260 SQ. FT.
GARAGE — 714 SQ. FT.

TOTAL LIVING AREA: 3,813 SQ. FT.

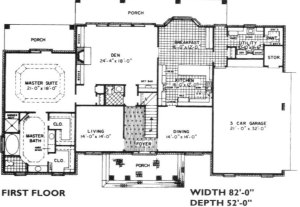

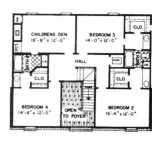

FIRST FLOOR

WIDTH 82'-0"
DEPTH 52'-0"

SECOND FLOOR

Elegant Stone Two-Story

Price Code: H

- This plan features:
- — Four bedrooms
- — Two full and one half baths
- The two-story Entry leads into the Great Room
- The Kitchen has a center island and is open to the large Nook
- The Master Bedroom has an access door to the rear Deck
- Upstairs are two Bedrooms serviced by a full Bath
- Also upstairs is a large Bonus Room for all the kids' toys
- A three-season Porch with a cathedral ceiling rounds out this plan
- This home is designed with a basement foundation

FIRST FLOOR — 2,039 SQ. FT.
SECOND FLOOR — 970 SQ. FT.

TOTAL LIVING AREA: 3,009 SQ. FT.

WIDTH 69'-8"
DEPTH 72'-0"

FIRST FLOOR

SECOND FLOOR

Stunning Home
Price Code: I

■ This plan features:
— Three bedrooms
— Three full and one half baths
■ Twin arched covered Entry leading through double doors into a grand Foyer
■ A side by side living and formal Dining Room
■ Arches and niche space highlighting the Gallery hallways
■ Nook with curved glass views the rear yard
■ Master Suite with bayed Sitting Room, French doors to the covered Lanai and a step ceiling
■ This home is designed with a slab foundation
■ Alternate foundation options available at an additional charge. Please call 1-800-235-5700 for more information.

MAIN FLOOR — 3,250 SQ. FT.

TOTAL LIVING AREA:
3,250 SQ. FT.

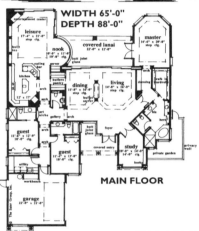

WIDTH 65'-0"
DEPTH 88'-0"

MAIN FLOOR

Family Room at the Heart of the Home
Price Code: F

■ This plan features:
— Four bedrooms
— Three full baths
■ The Living Room and Dining Room are to the right and left of the Foyer
■ The Dining Room with French doors opens to the Kitchen
■ An extended counter maximizes the work space in the Kitchen
■ The Breakfast Room includes access to the Utility Room and the secondary Bedroom wing
■ The Master Bedroom is equipped with a double vanity Bath, two walk-in closets and a linear closet
■ A cozy fireplace and a decorative ceiling highlight the Family Room
■ Secondary Bedrooms have easy access to two full Baths
■ This home is designed with slab and crawlspace foundation options

MAIN FLOOR — 2,558 SQ. FT.
GARAGE — 549 SQ. FT.

TOTAL LIVING AREA:
2,558 SQ. FT.

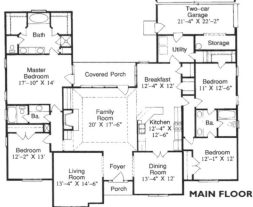

WIDTH 63'-6"
DEPTH 71'-6"

MAIN FLOOR

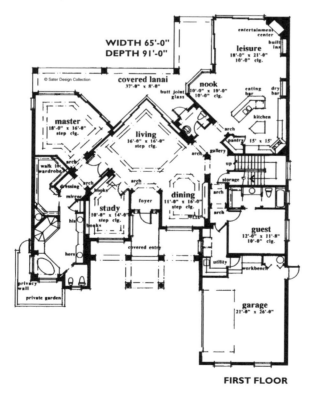

WIDTH 65'-0"
DEPTH 91'-0"

© Sater Design Collection

covered lanai
37'-0" x 8'-0"

butt joint glass

leisure
18'-0" x 21'-0"
10'-0" clg.

entertainment center

built ins

nook
10'-0" x 10'-0"
10'-0" clg.

eating bar

dry bar

kitchen

master
18'-0" x 16'-0"
step clg.

living
16'-0" x 16'-0"
step clg.

arch

pantry

15' x 15'

gallery

arch

up

arch

walk in wardrobe

dressing

mirror

arch

study
10'-0" x 14'-0"
step clg.

hooks

books

foyer

arch

arch

dining
11'-0" x 16'-0"
step clg.

storage

arch

arch

guest
12'-0" x 11'-8"

his

hers

covered entry

utility

workbench

privacy wall

private garden

garage
21'-0" x 26'-0"

FIRST FLOOR

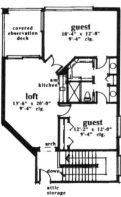

covered observation deck

guest
18'-4" x 12'-0"
9'-4" clg.

am kitchen

loft
13'-6" x 20'-0"
9'-4" clg.

guest
12'-2" x 12'-0"
9'-4" clg.

arch

down

attic storage

SECOND FLOOR

Grand Style
Price Code: K

■ This plan features:

— Four bedrooms

— Three full and one half baths

■ A raised covered Entry leads into the Foyer with the grand Living Room just beyond

■ The Living Room has corner glass doors out to the rear Lanai

■ The Dining Room features a step ceiling and a built-in server

■ The impeccable Master Suite has a private outdoor garden

■ This home is designed with a slab foundation

■ Alternate foundation options available at an additional charge. Please call 1-800-235-5700 for more information.

FIRST FLOOR — 3,010 SQ. FT.
SECOND FLOOR — 948 SQ. FT.
GARAGE — 604 SQ. FT.

TOTAL LIVING AREA:
3,958 SQ. FT.

High Pitched Roof Lines

Price Code: G

- This plan features:
  — Three bedrooms
  — Three full baths

- The facade is clean and elegant with a mix of brick and stucco and high pitched roof lines

- The Living Room opens to a covered Lanai facing the rear yard through pocketing sliding glass doors

- The Master Suite has a tray ceiling and glass doors to the rear Lanai

- This home is designed with a slab foundation

- Alternate foundation options available at an additional charge. Please call 1-800-235-5700 for more information.

MAIN FLOOR — 2,802 SQ. FT.
GARAGE — 619 SQ. FT.
PORCH — 266 SQ. FT.

TOTAL LIVING AREA:
2,802 SQ. FT.

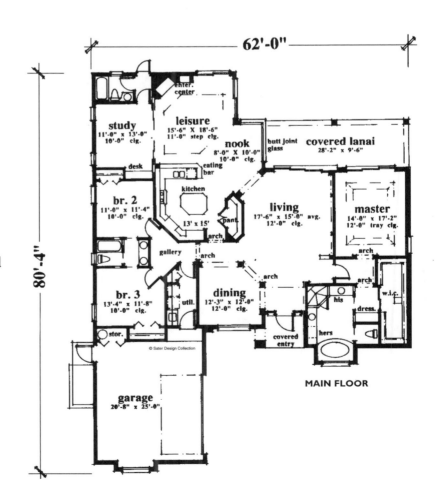

62'-0"

80'-4"

study
11'-0" x 13'-0"
10'-0" clg.

leisure
15'-6" X 18'-6"
11'-0" step clg.

enter. center

nook
8'-0" X 10'-0"
10'-0" clg.

butt joint glass

covered lanai
28'-2" x 9'-6"

desk

eating bar

kitchen

br. 2
11'-0" x 11'-4"
10'-0" clg.

13' x 15'

living
17'-6" x 15'-0" avg.
12'-0" clg.

master
14'-0" x 17'-2"
12'-0" tray clg.

pant.

gallery

arch

arch

arch

arch

arch

arch

br. 3
13'-4" x 11'-8"
10'-0" clg.

util.

dining
12'-3" x 12'-0"
12'-0" clg.

his

dress.

w.i.c.

stor.

© Sater Design Collection

covered entry

hers

MAIN FLOOR

garage
20'-8" x 25'-0"

Unique Traditional

Price Code: H

- This plan features:
  - Three bedrooms
  - Two full and one three-quarter and one half baths
- A raised Entry with a double gable roof line, detailed columns and a brick and stucco mixture exterior
- Slump arched top windows at the Entry and Study give a custom look divided light design
- Raised Entry is surrounded glass and open to the home's Foyer
- Formal Living and Dining Room are side by side and view the rear yard through three pairs of French doors
- Two Guest Suites sharing a full Bath are separated from the owner's wing
- The Master Suite has glass doors to the Lanai and a tray ceiling
- Master Bath highlighted by a Dressing Area mirror, walk-in wardrobe, his and her vanities with a make-up space, a walk-in shower and a garden tub
- This home is designed with a slab foundation
- Alternate foundation options available at an additional charge. Please call 1-800-235-5700 for more information.

MAIN FLOOR — 2,850 SQ. FT.

GARAGE — 588 SQ. FT.

TOTAL LIVING AREA:
2,850 SQ. FT.

WIDTH 63'-4"
DEPTH 86'-0"

MAIN FLOOR

Superb Southern Styling

Price Code: G

- This plan features:
  - Five bedrooms
  - Three full baths
- Terrific front Porch and dormers create a homey Southern-style entrance
- A corner fireplace enhances the Family Room
- A cooktop island and a peninsula counter add to the efficiency of the Kitchen
- Convenient peninsula counter separates the Kitchen from the Breakfast Room
- Lavish Master Suite includes a whirlpool tub and a walk-in closet
- Secondary Bedrooms sit in close proximity to a full Bath
- This home is designed with a crawlspace foundation

FIRST FLOOR — 2,135 SQ. FT.

SECOND FLOOR — 763 SQ. FT.

BONUS — 538 SQ. FT.

GARAGE — 436 SQ. FT.

TOTAL LIVING AREA:
2,898 SQ. FT.

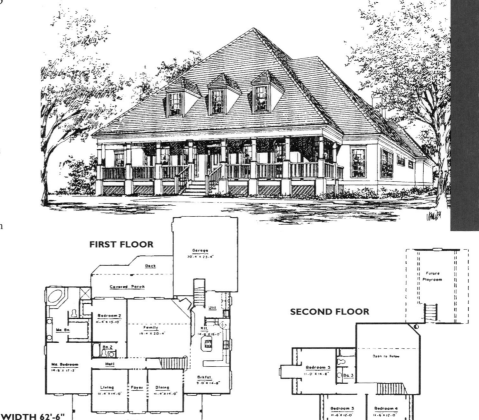

FIRST FLOOR

SECOND FLOOR

WIDTH 62'-6"
DEPTH 70'-0"

Luxurious Features

Price Code: I

■ This plan features:

— Four bedrooms

— Two full and one half baths

■ An open staircase leading to the Bedrooms and dividing the space between the vaulted Living and Dining Rooms

■ A wide family area including the Kitchen, Dinette and Family Room

■ A Master Bedroom with a vaulted ceiling, spacious closets and access to a Jacuzzi

■ This home is designed with a basement foundation

FIRST FLOOR — 1,786 SQ. FT.
SECOND FLOOR — 1,490 SQ. FT.
BASEMENT — 1,773 SQ. FT.
GARAGE — 579 SQ. FT.

TOTAL LIVING AREA:
3,276 SQ. FT.

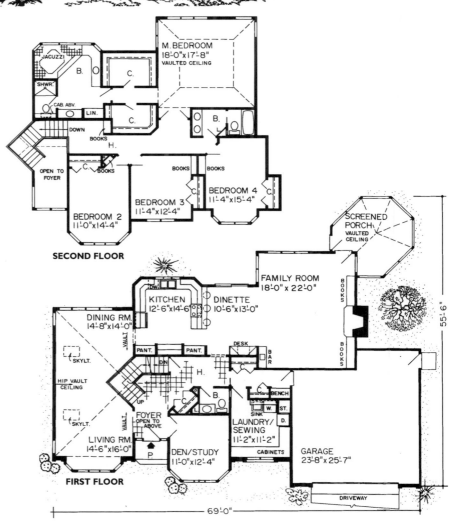

Brick and Stucco

Price Code: J

■ This plan features:
— Four bedrooms
— Two full, two three-quarter and one half baths
■ The brick, stucco wing walls and dual chimneys add elegant eye appeal to this home
■ A large front Courtyard adds intrigue to the front
■ The spider-beamed Den with French doors includes arched transom windows
■ The formal Dining Room opens to a dramatic high ceiling in the Entry
■ The Great Room features a fireplace, wall with entertainment center, bookcases, and wetbar
■ Informal areas include the Gazebo-shaped Breakfast Area, Kitchen with wrapping counters, large island/snack bar, walk-in Pantry, and private stairs accessing the second floor
■ The exquisite first-floor Master Bedroom includes a Sitting Room with a built-in bookcase and a fireplace
■ This home is designed with a basement foundation
■ Alternate foundation options available at an additional charge. Please call 1-800-235-5700 for more information.

FIRST FLOOR — 2,603 sq. ft.
SECOND FLOOR — 1,020 sq. ft.
BASEMENT — 2,603 sq. ft.
GARAGE — 801 sq. ft.

TOTAL LIVING AREA: 3,623 SQ. FT.

WIDTH 76'-8"
DEPTH 68'-0"

FIRST FLOOR

SECOND FLOOR

Wonderful Presence

Price Code: H

■ This plan features:
— Three bedrooms
— Four full baths
■ Double front doors welcome you into this spacious home
■ The Dining Room has a bay of windows at its front and also sports a step ceiling
■ Across the Foyer is the Study with a barrel vaulted ceiling and an immense front window
■ The Great Room is truly that with its fireplace, entertainment center and high ceiling
■ The Master Suite comprises the width of one side of the home
■ There are two separate covered Lanais in the rear
■ Upstairs find two Bedrooms and an optional Bonus Room
■ This home is designed with a slab foundation
■ Alternate foundation options available at an additional charge. Please call 1-800-235-5700 for more information

FIRST FLOOR — 2,341 sq. ft.
SECOND FLOOR — 797 sq. ft.
GARAGE — 635 sq. ft.

TOTAL LIVING AREA: 3,138 SQ. FT.

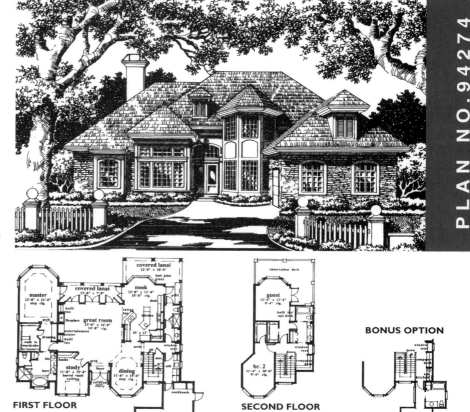

FIRST FLOOR

SECOND FLOOR

BONUS OPTION

WIDTH 65'-0"
DEPTH 79'-0"

Grand Country Porch

Price Code: F

■ This plan features:

— Four bedrooms

— Three full baths

■ Large front Porch provides shade and Southern hospitality

■ Spacious Living Room with access to Covered Porch and Patio and a cozy fireplace between built-in shelves

■ Country Kitchen with a cooktop island, bright Breakfast bay, Utility Room, Garage Entry, and adjoining Dining Room

■ Corner Master Bedroom with a walk-in closet and private Bath

■ This home is designed with crawlspace and slab foundation options

FIRST FLOOR — 1,916 SQ. FT.
SECOND FLOOR — 749 SQ. FT.
GARAGE — 479 SQ. FT.

TOTAL LIVING AREA:
2,665 SQ. FT.

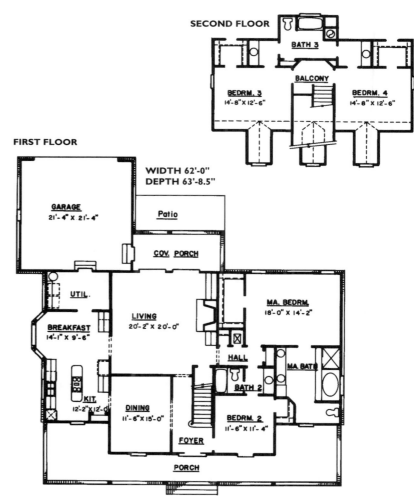

SECOND FLOOR

BATH 3

BEDRM. 3
14'-8" X 12'-6"

BALCONY

BEDRM. 4
14'-8" X 12'-6"

FIRST FLOOR

GARAGE
21'-4" X 21'-4"

Patio

COV. PORCH

WIDTH 62'-0"
DEPTH 63'-8.5"

UTIL.

BREAKFAST
14'-1" X 9'-6"

LIVING
20'-2" X 20'-0"

MA. BEDRM.
18'-0" X 14'-2"

HALL

MA. BATH

KIT.
12'-2" X 12'-0"

DINING
11'-6" X 15'-0"

BATH 2

BEDRM. 2
11'-6" X 11'-4"

FOYER

PORCH

172

Striking Brick Detailing and Arched Transoms

Price Code: H

■ This plan features:
— Four bedrooms
— Three full and one half baths

■ The formal Living Room has oak flooring and a 12-foot-high ceiling

■ There is a decorative ceiling and hutch space in the formal Dining Room

■ The gourmet Kitchen includes a central island, a roomy Pantry, and a lazy susan

■ The comfortable Family Room is enhanced by a brick fireplace

■ The Master Suite contains a vaulted ceiling and a built-in Kitchenette

■ This home is designed with a basement foundation

■ Alternate foundation options available at an additional charge. Please call 1-800-235-5700 for more information.

MAIN FLOOR — 1,561 SQ. FT.
SECOND FLOOR — 1,458 SQ. FT.
BONUS ROOM — 160 SQ. FT.
BASEMENT — 1,561 SQ. FT.
GARAGE — 748 SQ. FT.

TOTAL LIVING AREA:
3,019 SQ. FT.

WIDTH 65'-4"
DEPTH 50'-0"

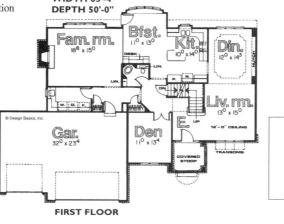

FIRST FLOOR

SECOND FLOOR

Lap of Luxury

Price Code: E

■ This plan features:
— Four bedrooms
— Three full and one half baths

■ Entertain in grand style in the formal Living Room, the Dining Room, or under the covered Patio in the backyard

■ A Family Room crowned in a cathedral ceiling enhanced by a center fireplace, and built-in bookshelves

■ An efficient Kitchen is highlighted by a wall oven, plentiful counter space and a Pantry

■ A Master Bedroom with a Sitting Area, huge walk in closet and private Bath, has access to a covered Lanai

■ A secondary Bedroom wing contains three additional Bedrooms with ample closet space and two full Baths

■ This home is designed with slab and crawlspace foundation options

MAIN FLOOR — 2,445 SQ. FT.
GARAGE — 630 SQ. FT.

TOTAL LIVING AREA:
2,445 SQ. FT.

WIDTH 65'-0"
DEPTH 68'-8"

MAIN FLOOR

Low-Maintence Brick

Price Code: J

- This plan features:
- — Three bedrooms
- — Two full and one half baths

- Three fireplaces keep things cozy: a vent-free fireplace in the Living Room, a hearth fireplace in the Family Room, and a see-through fireplace in the Master Suite

- A wide family area including the Kitchen, Breakfast Area, and Family Room

- This home is designed with basement and crawlspace foundation options

FIRST FLOOR — 1,711 SQ. FT.
SECOND FLOOR — 1,880 SQ. FT.
BASEMENT — 1,705 SQ. FT.
GARAGE — 441 SQ. FT.

TOTAL LIVING AREA:
3,591 SQ. FT.

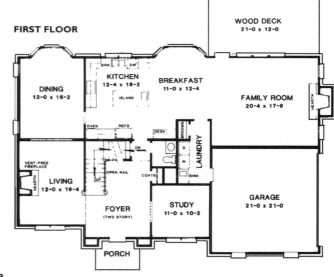

FIRST FLOOR

WOOD DECK
21-0 x 12-0

DINING
12-0 x 16-2

KITCHEN
12-4 x 16-2

BREAKFAST
11-0 x 12-4

FAMILY ROOM
20-4 x 17-8

ISLAND

OVEN   REFG   DESK   BROOMS

VENT-FREE
FIREPLACE

LIVING
12-0 x 16-4

LAUNDRY

COATS   SINK

STUDY
11-0 x 10-2

GARAGE
21-0 x 21-0

FOYER
(TWO STORY)

OPEN RAIL

PORCH

SECOND FLOOR

WIDTH 58'-4"
DEPTH 39'-10"

WALK-IN
CLOSET

BEDROOM
14-0 x 12-4

WALK-IN
CLOSET

HERS

SPA
TUB

HIS

VAULT

BATH

VAULT

MASTER
BATH

SHOWER

CLOSET

OPEN RAIL

BALCONY

SHELVES

BEDROOM
12-2 x 13-10

OPEN RAIL

FOYER
(BELOW)

SEE-THRU
FIREPLACE

SITTING
11-0 x 11-0

TRAY CEILING

MASTER
BEDROOM
20-4 x 20-4

PLANT SHELF

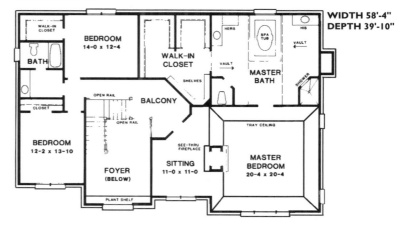

Columns Separate Interior Spaces

Price Code: L

- This plan features:
  — Four bedrooms
  — Three full and one half baths
- Stucco, stone, and varied windows add character to this home
- The Foyer is separated from the Dining Room and Great Room by columns
- The Great Room has a two-story ceiling and a fireplace with built-ins surrounding it
- Located in a quiet spot, the Study is a fine retreat
- The U-shaped Kitchen has a center island
- The bay shaped Breakfast Area is perfect for casual meals
- The warm Keeping Room has a vaulted ceiling
- The Master Bedroom on the first floor features a quiet Sitting Area
- This home is designed with a basement foundation

FIRST FLOOR — 3,687 SQ. FT.
SECOND FLOOR — 1,299 SQ. FT.
BONUS ROOM — 233 SQ. FT.
BASEMENT — 3,036 SQ. FT.
GARAGE — 683 SQ. FT.

TOTAL LIVING AREA:
4,986 SQ. FT.

Delightful Detailing

Price Code: F

- This plan features:
  — Three bedrooms
  — Two full and one half baths
- The vaulted ceiling extends from the Foyer into the Living Room
- The Dining Room is delineated by columns with a plant shelf above
- Family Room has a vaulted ceiling and a wall of radius windows
- The Kitchen is equipped with an island serving bar, a desk, a wall oven, a Pantry, and a Breakfast Bay
- The Master Suite is highlighted by a Sitting Room, a walk-in closet and a Bath with a vaulted ceiling
- Two additional large Bedrooms share a full Bath in the Hall
- There is an optional Bonus Room located over the Garage
- This home is designed with basement and crawlspace foundation options

MAIN FLOOR — 2,622 SQ. FT.
BONUS ROOM — 478 SQ. FT.
BASEMENT — 2,622 SQ. FT.
GARAGE — 506 SQ. FT.

TOTAL LIVING AREA:
2,622 SQ. FT.

Grandeur Personified

Price Code: I

■ This plan features:

— Four bedrooms

— Two full, one three-quarter, and one half bath

■ A Master Bedroom with a decorative ceiling and a luxurious Bath

■ French doors and an arched window accenting the Den

■ A Dining Room with a built-in hutch and an adjacent Butler's Pantry

■ A Great Room with an 11-foot ceiling, bowed transom windows, and a fireplace

■ This home is designed with a basement foundation

■ Alternate foundation options available at an additional charge. Please call 1-800-235-5700 for more information

FIRST FLOOR — 2,375 SQ. FT.
SECOND FLOOR — 1,073 SQ. FT.
GARAGE — 672 SQ. FT.

TOTAL LIVING AREA:
3,448 SQ. FT.

FIRST FLOOR

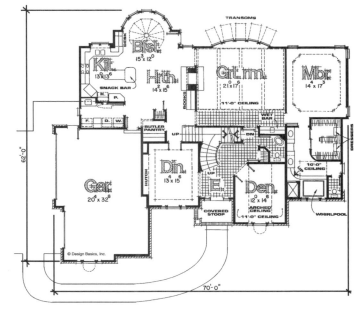

SECOND FLOOR

176

FIRST FLOOR

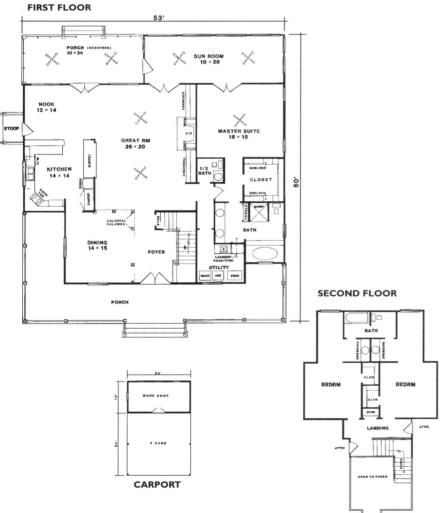

53'

PORCH (SCREENED)
10 × 24

SUN ROOM
10 × 28

NOOK
12 × 14

STOOP

MASTER SUITE
18 × 15

CREDENZA

GREAT RM
26 × 20

F/P

KITCHEN
14 × 14

BUFFET

OVEN

CREDENZA

1/2 BATH

CLOSET

SHELVES

SHELVES

PANTRY

COOK

COLONIAL COLUMNS

STOR

BATH

60'

DINING
14 × 15

FOYER

LAUNDRY PASS-THRU

UTILITY

WASH DRY FRZR

PORCH

SECOND FLOOR

BATH

24'

WORK SHOP

DRESSING DRESSING

CLOS

BEDRM

BEDRM

2 CARS

CLOS

STOR

LANDING

ATTIC

ATTIC

CARPORT

DOWN

OPEN TO FOYER

Friendly Front Porch

Price Code: H

- This plan features:
- — Three bedrooms
- — Two full and one half baths

- Wraparound front Porch and double French doors are an inviting sight

- Central Foyer with a lovely landing staircase opens to the Dining and Great Rooms

- The fireplace is framed by a built-in credenza in the Great Room

- Kitchen boasts a buffet, Pantry and a peninsula counter/snack bar

- Master Bedroom offers direct access to the Sunroom, a walk-in closet and a luxurious Bath

- This home is designed with crawlspace and slab foundation options

FIRST FLOOR — 2,361 SQ. FT.
SECOND FLOOR — 650 SQ. FT.
DETACHED CARPORT — 864 SQ. FT.

TOTAL LIVING AREA:
3,011 SQ. FT.

With A European Influence

Price Code: F

- This plan features:
- — Four bedrooms
- — Two full and one half baths
- The old world Country French influence in this home is evident
- The Foyer opens to the well-proportioned Dining Room
- Double French doors with transoms lead off the Living Room to the rear Porch
- The spacious Kitchen is adjacent to the Breakfast and Family Room
- A vaulted ceiling tops the Breakfast Room and the Family Room
- The Master Bedroom features a tray ceiling and a luxurious Master Bath
- This home is designed with basement, slab, and crawlspace foundation options

MAIN FLOOR — 2,745 SQ. FT.
GARAGE — 525 SQ. FT.

TOTAL LIVING AREA:
2,745 SQ. FT.

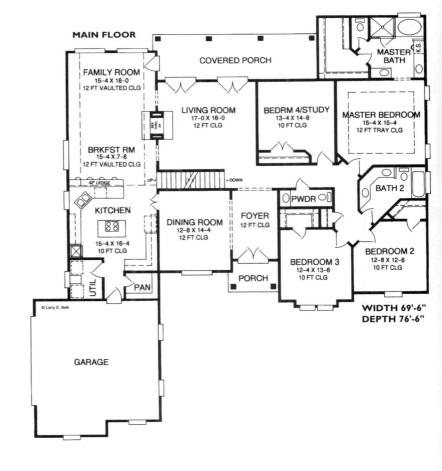

To order your Blueprints, call 1-800-235-5700

WIDTH 70'-10"
DEPTH 67'-4"

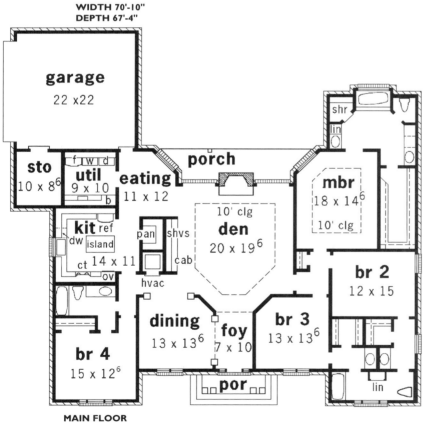

garage
22 x22

sto
10 x 8⁶

util
9 x 10

eating
11 x 12

porch

shr

lin

mbr
18 x 14⁶

10' clg

kit
ref
dw
island
ct 14 x 11
ov

10' clg
den
20 x 19⁶

pan

shvs

cab

hvac

br 2
12 x 15

br 4
15 x 12⁶

dining
13 x 13⁶

foy
7 x 10

br 3
13 x 13⁶

lin

por

MAIN FLOOR

Lavish Accommodations

Price Code: F

■ This plan features:

— Four bedrooms

— Three full baths

■ A central Den with a large fireplace, built-in shelves and cabinets and a decorative ceiling

■ A well planned island Kitchen that includes a walk-in Pantry

■ An informal Breakfast Room that is directly accessible from either the Kitchen or the Den

■ A Master Bedroom enhanced by a decorative ceiling and a walk-in closet as well as a luxurious Master Bath

■ This home is designed with crawlspace and slab foundation options

MAIN FLOOR — 2,733 SQ. FT.
GARAGE AND STORAGE — 569 SQ. FT.

TOTAL LIVING AREA:
2,733 SQ. FT.

Two-Story Family Room

Price Code: F

■ This plan features:

— Four bedrooms

— Two full and one half baths

■ A wraparound covered Porch is the highlight of the exterior elevation

■ The Family Room has a fireplace and a French door to the Porch

■ The Kitchen features a convenient serving bar for quick meals and snacks

■ The second floor Master Suite has a tray ceiling and an optional plan for a Sitting Area

■ This home is designed with a basement foundation

FIRST FLOOR — 1,351 SQ. FT.
SECOND FLOOR — 1,257 SQ. FT.
BONUS ROOM — 115 SQ. FT.
GARAGE — 511 SQ. FT.
BASEMENT — 1,351 SQ. FT.

TOTAL LIVING AREA: 2,608 SQ. FT.

FIRST FLOOR

WIDTH 60'-0"
DEPTH 46'-4"

FPL.

OPEN RAIL · FRENCH DOOR · PANTRY

Breakfast

Two Story Family Room
14² x 19³

Covered Porch

FRENCH DOOR

FRENCH DOORS

Living Room
13³ x 12⁵

STAIRS DN.

STAIRS UP

STAIRS UP

Kitchen

SERVING BAR

D.W. · RANGE

REF.

BUTLER'S PANTRY

BROOM · COATS

Laundry
W. · D.

Pwdr.

Storage

Garage

Two Story Foyer

Dining Room
12³ x 14⁵

Covered Porch

© Frank Betz Associates, Inc.

SECOND FLOOR

Bedroom 4
12⁰ x 13¹

Family Room Below

PLANT SHELF ABOVE · SHWR.

LINEN

Vaulted M. Bath

W.i.c. · K.S.

PLANT SHELF ABOVE

OPEN RAIL

STAIRS DN.

OPEN RAIL

Bath

LIN.

Bedroom 2
13³ x 12⁵

OVERLOOK

Foyer Below

Master Suite
17⁹ x 13¹⁰

TRAY CLG.

ARCHED OPENING

Bedroom 3
12³ x 11⁰

W.i.c.

Opt. Sitting Room

180

To order your Blueprints, call 1-800-235-5700

FIRST FLOOR

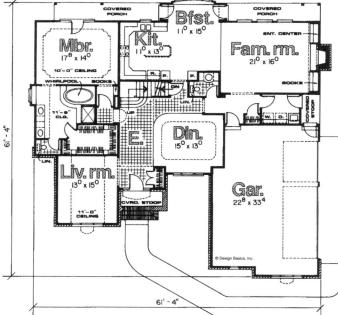

Mbr.
17⁸ x 14⁰
10'-0" CEILING

Bfst.
11⁰ x 15⁰

Kit.
11⁰ x 13⁰

Fam. rm.
21⁰ x 16⁰

WHIRLPOOL   BOOKS

Liv. rm.
13⁰ x 15⁰

11'-0" CEILING

Din.
15⁰ x 13⁰

Gar.
22⁸ x 33⁴

COVERED PORCH

COVERED PORCH

ENT. CENTER

BOOKS

61'-4"

61'-4"

© Design Basics, Inc.

SECOND FLOOR

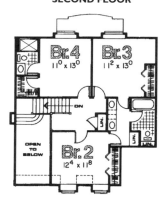

Br. 4
11⁰ x 13⁰

Br. 3
11² x 13⁰

OPEN TO BELOW

Br. 2
12⁴ x 11⁸

Spaciousness is Dominating Feature

Price Code: G

■ This plan features:

— Four bedrooms

— Two full, one three-quarter and one half baths

■ Pair of narrow dormers, double gables and extensive detailing highlight the exterior

■ An island counter and two Pantries add to Kitchen's efficiency

■ Rear covered Porches can be accessed from the Breakfast Area, the Family Room or Master Suite

■ This home is designed with a basement foundation

■ Alternate foundation options available at an additional charge. Please call 1-800-235-5700 for more information

FIRST FLOOR — 2,098 SQ. FT.
SECOND FLOOR — 790 SQ. FT.
GARAGE — 739 SQ. FT.

TOTAL LIVING AREA:
2,888 SQ. FT.

Manor Styled

Price Code: G

- This plan features:
— Four bedrooms
— Two full and one half baths
- Shutters and round pilasters perfectly contrast the all-brick facade
- The two-story Living Room and stairhall share a see-through fireplace
- An angled Kitchen is positioned to serve the Breakfast Room
- Angled lines in the Master Suite help direct a view to the backyard
- This home is designed with a slab foundation
- Alternate foundation options available at an additional charge. Please call 1-800-235-5700 for more information.

FIRST FLOOR — 2,069 SQ. FT.
SECOND FLOOR — 897 SQ. FT.
GARAGE — 688 SQ. FT.

TOTAL LIVING AREA:
2,966 SQ. FT.

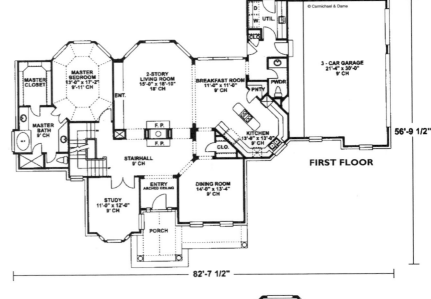

60'-0"

Deck

Breakfast
13'-8" X 11'-5"

Laun.

Hearth Room
16'-0" X 18'-2"

Garage
21'-10" X 31'-10"

Kitchen
13'-8" X 15'-10"

Hall | Bath

Dining Room
12'-6" X 15'-4"

45'-6"

Living Room
14'-0" X 15'-0"

Library
12'-0" X 12'-0"

Foyer

Porch

FIRST FLOOR

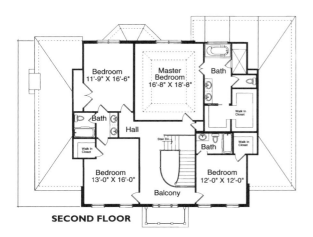

Bedroom
11'-9" X 16'-6"

Master
Bedroom
16'-8" X 18'-8"

Bath

Bath

Walk In
Closet

Hall

Walk In
Closet

Bath

Walk In
Closet

Bedroom
13'-0" X 16'-0"

Bedroom
12'-0" X 12'-0"

Balcony

SECOND FLOOR

The Perfect Balance

Price Code: I

- This plan features:
  — Four bedrooms
  — Three full and one half baths

- The Entry leads into a graceful curved staircase

- Pocket doors introduce you to the spacious Hearth Room

- An island with seating defines the functional Kitchen, which serves the Breakfast Area and the Dining Room

- A Library located for privacy completes the first floor

- The spacious Master Bedroom has a tray ceiling and access to a walk-in closet

- This home is designed with a basement foundation

FIRST FLOOR — 1,670 SQ. FT.
SECOND FLOOR — 1,641 SQ. FT.
BASEMENT — 1,670 SQ. FT.
GARAGE — 750 SQ. FT.

TOTAL LIVING AREA:
3,311 SQ. FT.

To order your Blueprints, call 1-800-235-5700

183

Luxurious Yet Cozy

Price Code: I

■ This plan features:

— Four bedrooms

— Three full and one half baths

■ Covered Porch leads into two-story Foyer and Living Room

■ Decorative columns define Dining Room and Great Room

■ Open and convenient Kitchen with a work island

■ Corner Master Suite includes a cozy fireplace

■ Three second floor Bedrooms with ample closet space

■ This home is designed with basement, slab and crawlspace foundation options

FIRST FLOOR — 2,467 SQ. FT.
SECOND FLOOR — 928 SQ. FT.
BONUS — 296 SQ. FT.
BASEMENT — 2,467 SQ. FT.
GARAGE — 566 SQ. FT.

TOTAL LIVING AREA:
3,395 SQ. FT.

SECOND FLOOR

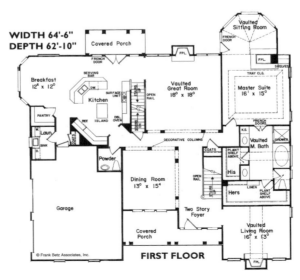

FIRST FLOOR

WIDTH 64'-6"
DEPTH 62'-10"

To order your Blueprints, call 1-800-235-5700

Music Room and Library

Price Code: L

- This plan features:
  - Four bedrooms
  - Four full and one half baths
- Large rear windows bring in light and a panoramic view
- Architectural details add impact to the exterior
- The spacious Kitchen offers workspace for more than one cook
- This home is designed with a basement foundation

MAIN FLOOR — 2,782 SQ. FT.
UPPER FLOOR — 1,027 SQ. FT.
LOWER FLOOR — 1,316 SQ. FT.
GARAGE — 607 SQ. FT.

TOTAL LIVING AREA:
5,125 SQ. FT.

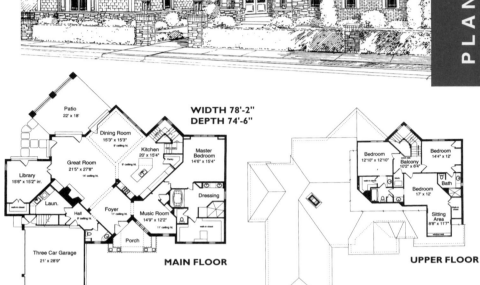

WIDTH 78'-2"
DEPTH 74'-6"

LOWER FLOOR

MAIN FLOOR

UPPER FLOOR

Windows Distinguish Design

Price Code: J

- This plan features:
  - Five bedrooms
  - Four full and one half baths
- Light shines into the Dining and Living Room through their respective elegant windows
- A Hall through the Butler's Pantry leads the way into the Breakfast Nook
- The two-story Family Room has a fireplace with built-in bookcases on either side
- The upstairs Master Suite has a Sitting Room and a French door that leads into the Master Bath
- There are three additional Bedrooms upstairs
- This home is designed with basement and crawlspace foundation options

FIRST FLOOR — 1,786 SQ. FT.
SECOND FLOOR — 1,739 SQ. FT.
BASEMENT — 1,786 SQ. FT.
GARAGE — 704 SQ. FT.

TOTAL LIVING AREA:
3,525 SQ. FT.

FIRST FLOOR

SECOND FLOOR

WIDTH 59'-0"
DEPTH 53'-0"

© Frank Betz Associates, Inc.

Luxurious Living

Price Code: I

- This plan features:
- — Four bedrooms
- — Two full and one three-quarter baths
- Decorative windows enhance front Entry of elegant home
- Formal Living Room accented by fireplace
- Breakfast Bar, work island, and an abundance of storage and counter space featured in Kitchen
- Spacious Master Bedroom with access to covered Patio
- This home is designed with a slab foundation

MAIN FLOOR — 3,254 SQ. FT.
GARAGE — 588 SQ. FT.

TOTAL LIVING AREA:
3,254 SQ. FT.

MAIN FLOOR

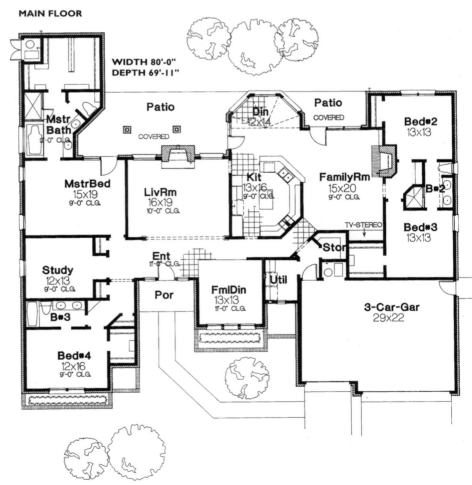

WIDTH 80'-0"
DEPTH 69'-11"

Patio
COVERED

Din
12x14

Patio
COVERED

Bed#2
13x13

Mstr Bath
2'-0" CLG.

MstrBed
15x19
9'-0" CLG.

LivRm
16x19
10'-0" CLG.

Kit
13x16
9'-0" CLG.

FamilyRm
15x20
9'-0" CLG.

B#2

Bed#3
13x13

TV-STEREO

Stor

Study
12x13
9'-0" CLG.

Ent
11'-0" CLG.

Util

B#3

Por

FmlDin
13x13
11'-0" CLG.

3-Car-Gar
29x22

Bed#4
12x16
9'-0" CLG.

Golf Cart Storage

Price Code: J

- This plan features:
  — Four bedrooms
  — Three full, one three-quarter, and one half baths
- The Master Bedroom and Library share a two-sided fireplace
- A walk-in bar located off the gallery hall is convenient when entertaining
- This home is designed with basement, slab, and crawlspace foundation options

FIRST FLOOR — 2,658 SQ. FT.
SECOND FLOOR — 1,012 SQ. FT.
GARAGE — 640 SQ. FT.

TOTAL LIVING AREA:
3,670 SQ. FT.

WIDTH 80'-0"
DEPTH 67'-4"

FIRST FLOOR

SECOND FLOOR

Brick Magnificence

Price Code: G

- This plan features:
  — Four bedrooms
  — Three full baths
- Large windows and attractive brick detailing using segmented arches give fantastic curb appeal
- Convenient Ranch layout allows for step-saving one floor ease
- A fireplace in the Living Room adds a warm ambience
- The Family Room sports a second fireplace and built-in shelving
- Two additional Bedrooms include private access to a full double vanity Bath
- This home is designed with a slab foundation

MAIN FLOOR — 2,858 SQ. FT.
GARAGE — 768 SQ. FT.

TOTAL LIVING AREA:
2,858 SQ. FT.

WIDTH 89'-7"
DEPTH 68'-4"

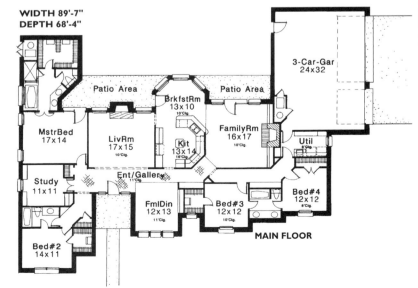

MAIN FLOOR

To order your Blueprints, call 1-800-235-5700

European Style

Price Code: F

- This plan features:
— Four bedrooms
— Three full and one half baths
- Central Foyer between spacious Living and Dining Rooms with arched windows
- Hub Kitchen with extended counter and nearby Utility/Garage Entry, easily serves Breakfast Area and Dining Room
- Spacious Den with a hearth fireplace between built-ins and sliding glass doors to Porch
- Master Bedroom wing with decorative ceiling, plush Bath with two walk-in closets
- This home is designed with crawlspace and slab foundation options

MAIN FLOOR — 2,727 SQ. FT.
GARAGE — 569 SQ. FT.

TOTAL LIVING AREA:
2,727 SQ. FT.

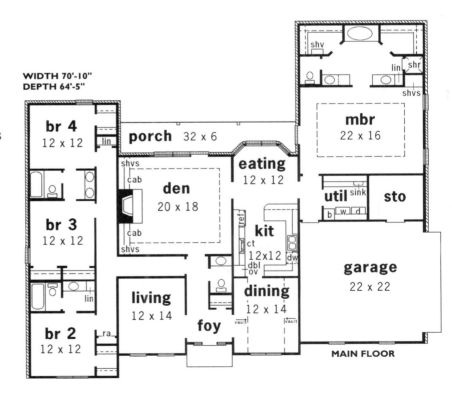

WIDTH 70'-10"
DEPTH 64'-5"

br 4
12 x 12

porch 32 x 6

mbr
22 x 16

den
20 x 18

eating
12 x 12

util   sto

br 3
12 x 12

kit
12x12

garage
22 x 22

living
12 x 14

dining
12 x 14

foy

br 2
12 x 12

MAIN FLOOR

WIDTH 76'-10.5"
DEPTH 77'-7"

FIRST FLOOR

SECOND FLOOR

Central Gallery Links Main Floor Rooms

Price Code: L

■ This plan features:

— Four bedrooms

— Two full, two three-quarter, and one half baths

■ Every Bedroom adjoins a private Bath and a walk-in closet

■ The Family Room features a pass-through ledge from the Kitchen

■ This home is designed with a slab foundation

FIRST FLOOR — 2,856 SQ. FT.
SECOND FLOOR — 1,148 SQ. FT.
BONUS ROOM — 561 SQ. FT.
GARAGE — 650 SQ. FT.

TOTAL LIVING AREA:
4,004 SQ. FT.

Luxurious Details
Price Code: L

- This plan features:
  — Four bedrooms
  — Four full and two half baths
- Elegant columns and French doors grace the entrances into the formal rooms that open from the Entry
- Family atmosphere is defined by the gourmet Kitchen with open views to the Family Room and circular Breakfast Area
- The Master Bathroom is a stunning oasis with private Exercise Area and huge walk-in closet
- This home is designed with a slab foundation

MAIN FLOOR — 4,615 SQ. FT.
GARAGE — 748 SQ. FT.

TOTAL LIVING AREA:
4,615 SQ. FT.

WIDTH 113'-4"
DEPTH 69'-4"

MAIN FLOOR

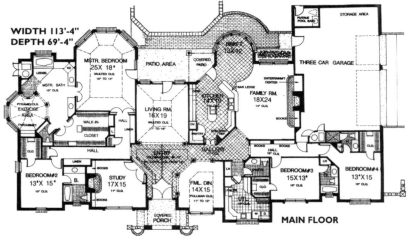

Executive Features
Price Code: H

- This plan features:
  — Four bedrooms
  — Three full and one half baths
- High volume ceilings
- An extended staircase highlighting the Foyer as columns define the Dining Room and the Grand Room
- A massive glass exterior rear wall and high ceiling in the Master Bedroom
- His and her walk-in closets and a lavish five-piece Bath highlight the Master Bedroom
- The island Kitchen, Keeping Room, and Breakfast Room creating an open living space
- Fireplaces accenting both the Keeping Room and the two-story Grand Room
- Three additional Bedrooms with private Bathroom access and ample closet space
- This home is designed with basement and crawlspace foundation options

FIRST FLOOR — 2,035 SQ. FT.
SECOND FLOOR — 1,028 SQ. FT.
BASEMENT — 2,035 SQ. FT.
GARAGE — 530 SQ. FT.

TOTAL LIVING AREA:
3,063 SQ. FT.

WIDTH 56'-0"
DEPTH 62'-6"

FIRST FLOOR

SECOND FLOOR

To order your Blueprints, call 1-800-235-5700

FIRST FLOOR

WIDTH 60'-6"
DEPTH 53'-4"

SECOND FLOOR

Angled Master Suite Walls

Price Code: F

■ This plan features:

— Four bedrooms

— Two full and one half baths

■ The Breakfast Area features built-ins on two walls and a vaulted ceiling

■ Bedroom 3 has space for a Sitting Area

■ This home is designed with a basement foundation

FIRST FLOOR — 1,803 SQ. FT.
SECOND FLOOR — 748 SQ. FT.
BASEMENT — 1,803 SQ. FT.

TOTAL LIVING AREA:
2,551 SQ. FT.

Exquisite Detail

Price Code: I

■ This plan features:

— Four bedrooms

— Three full and one half baths

■ Formal Living Room with access to covered Porch and an arched opening to Family Room

■ Spacious and efficient Kitchen with Pantry, cooktop/serving bar, two-story Breakfast Area and a Butler's Pantry

■ Expansive Master Bedroom offers a tray ceiling, a cozy Sitting Room, a luxurious Bath and a huge walk-in closet

■ This home is designed with basement and crawlspace foundation options

FIRST FLOOR — 1,418 SQ. FT.
SECOND FLOOR — 1,844 SQ. FT.
BASEMENT — 1,418 SQ. FT.
GARAGE — 820 SQ. FT.

TOTAL LIVING AREA:
3,262 SQ. FT.

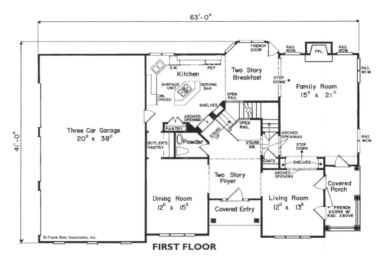

FIRST FLOOR

SECOND FLOOR

WIDTH 61'-6"
DEPTH 64'-0"

FIRST FLOOR

KEEPING ROOM 12'4" X 13'8"

BREAKFAST 11'0" X 10'6"

M. BATH

HIS   HERS

LIVING ROOM 15'0" X 21'6"

PANT.

KITCHEN 16'6" X 11'0"

M. BEDROOM 18'4" X 15'0"

BALCONY ABOVE

OPEN RAIL

REF

LAUNDRY

W   D

REF   P. RM.

COATS

ARCH

STUDY 15'4" X 13'2"

FOYER 8'0" X 13'0"

DINING ROOM 13'8" X 15'0"

3 CAR GARAGE 21'4" X 29'4"

Sun–Drenched Spaces

Price Code: H

■ This plan features:

— Four bedrooms

— Three full and one half baths

■ The Study, which has a fireplace and sloped ceiling, is secluded behind double doors

■ Windows line the rear of the home

■ A morning bar sits beside the Master Suite

■ This home is designed with a basement foundation

FIRST FLOOR — 2,253 SQ. FT.
SECOND FLOOR — 890 SQ. FT.
BASEMENT — 2,253 SQ. FT.
GARAGE — 630 SQ. FT.

TOTAL LIVING AREA:
3,143 SQ. FT.

OPEN TO LIVING ROOM BELOW

BATH

BEDROOM #4 17'8" X 14'0"

CLO.

ATTIC

OPEN TO FOYER BELOW

BEDROOM #2 13'8" X 14'10"

CLO.   CLO.

BEDROOM #3 12'0" X 13'4"

BATH

SECOND FLOOR

It's All in the Details

Price Code: G

- This plan features:
- — Five bedrooms
- — Four full baths
- The exterior is appointed with keystones, arches and shutters
- The Living Room and Dining Room meet through an arched opening
- The Kitchen, Breakfast and Family Room are open to each other
- The Master Suite has a tray ceiling in the Bedroom and a vaulted ceiling in the Master Bath
- This home is designed with basement and crawlspace foundation options

FIRST FLOOR — 1,447 SQ. FT.
SECOND FLOOR — 1,325 SQ. FT.
BONUS ROOM — 301 SQ. FT.
BASEMENT — 1,447 SQ. FT.
GARAGE — 393 SQ. FT.

TOTAL LIVING AREA:
2,772 SQ. FT.

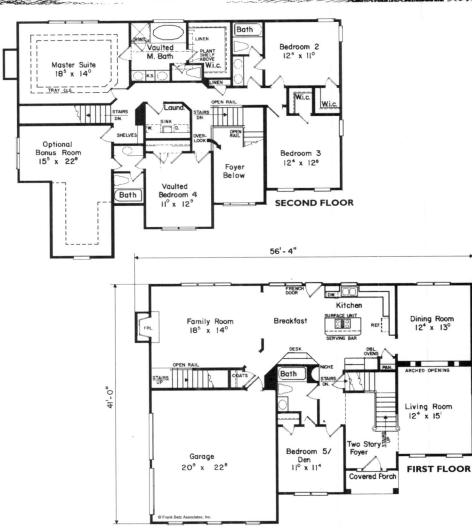

Turret Study Creates Impact

Price Code: I

PLAN NO. 94220

■ This plan features:
— Three bedrooms
— Two full and one three-quarter and one half baths
■ Entry doors opening into the formal Living Room focusing to the Lanai through sliding glass doors and a mitered glass corner
■ Double sided fireplace in the Living Room shared by the Master Suite
■ Wetbar easily serves the Living Room, Dining Room and Lanai
■ Island Kitchen easily serves all informal family areas
■ Octagonal Nook with windows spanning to all views
■ Leisure Room with fireplace and built-ins along the back wall
■ Spacious Master Suite including a fireplace, morning Kitchen bar, and Lanai access
■ This home is designed with a slab foundation
■ Alternate foundation options available at an additional charge. Please call 1-800-235-5700 for more information.

MAIN FLOOR — 3,477 SQ. FT.
GARAGE — 771 SQ. FT.

TOTAL LIVING AREA:
3,477 SQ. FT.

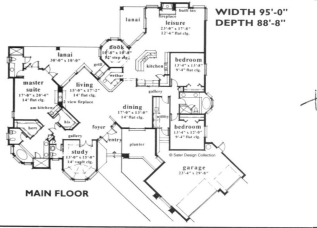

WIDTH 95'-0"
DEPTH 88'-8"

MAIN FLOOR

Living Large

Price Code: I

PLAN NO. 98228

■ This plan features:
— Four bedrooms
— Three full and one half baths
■ Box bay windows in the Dining Room and the Parlor add character to this home
■ Inside the two-story Foyer find a grand staircase and columns to separate the space
■ The Family Room shares a see-through fireplace with the Parlor
■ The Kitchen is open to the interesting Breakfast Room
■ The Master Bedroom has a Sitting Area with a fireplace, as well as a sumptuous Bath
■ Three large additional Bedrooms all have walk in closets
■ A three-car Garage completes this home plan
■ This home is designed with basement and slab foundation options

FIRST FLOOR — 1,597 SQ. FT.
SECOND FLOOR — 1,859 SQ. FT.
GARAGE — 694 SQ. FT.
BASEMENT — 1,597 SQ. FT.

TOTAL LIVING AREA:
3,456 SQ. FT.

WIDTH 62'-0"
DEPTH 46'-0"

FIRST FLOOR

SECOND FLOOR

Curb Appeal

Price Code: F

- ■ This plan features:
- — Four bedrooms
- — Three full baths
- ■ A private Master Bedroom with a raised ceiling and attached Bath with a Spa tub
- ■ A wing of three Bedrooms that share two full Baths on the right side of the home
- ■ An efficient Kitchen is straddled by an Eating Nook and a Dining Room
- ■ A cozy Den with a raised ceiling and a fireplace is the focal point of the home
- ■ A two-car Garage with a Storage Area
- ■ This home is designed with crawlspace and slab foundation options

MAIN FLOOR — 2,735 SQ. FT.
GARAGE — 561 SQ. FT.

TOTAL LIVING AREA:
2,735 SQ. FT.

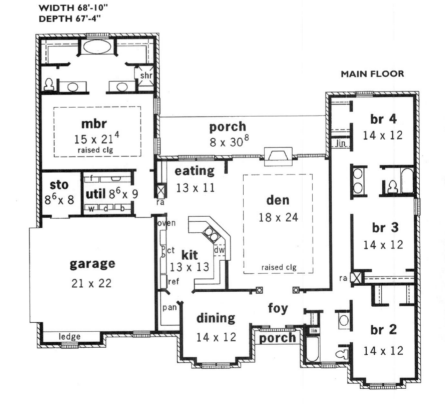

WIDTH 68'-10"
DEPTH 67'-4"

MAIN FLOOR

mbr 15 x 21⁴ raised clg	porch 8 x 30⁸
sto 8⁶ x 8	util 8⁶ x 9	eating 13 x 11
garage 21 x 22	kit 13 x 13	den 18 x 24 raised clg
	dining 14 x 12	foy

br 4 14 x 12
br 3 14 x 12
br 2 14 x 12

FIRST FLOOR

61'-3"

49'-0"

Bedroom 5/ Study 13² x 12⁰

Bath

Breakfast

FRENCH DOOR

W.i.c.

SERVING BAR

DW

Kitchen

Two Story Family Room 20³ x 16⁰

FPL

REF.

SURFACE UNIT

PANTRY

DBL OVENS

DECORATIVE COLUMNS

ARCHED OPENING

COATS

Pwdr.

BUTLER'S PANTRY

STAIRS DN.

OPEN RAIL

OPEN RAIL

STAIRS

ARCHED OPENING

Living Room 12⁰ x 13⁰

Three Car Garage 21⁶ x 33²

Dining Room 13⁶ x 16⁹

Two Story Foyer

Covered Porch

© Frank Betz Associates, Inc.

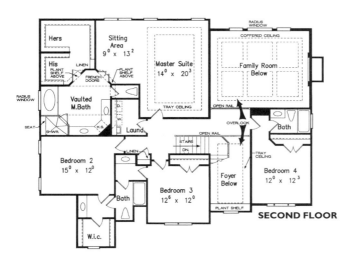

SECOND FLOOR

Hers

Sitting Area 9⁰ x 13²

RADIUS WINDOW

COFFERED CEILING

His

LINEN

Master Suite 14⁰ x 20³

Family Room Below

PLANT SHELF ABOVE

FRENCH DOORS

PLANT SHELF ABOVE

RADIUS WINDOW

Vaulted M.Bath

D. W.

OPEN RAIL

SEAT

SHWR.

K.S.

Laund.

TRAY CEILING

OVERLOOK

Bath

LINEN

OPEN RAIL

Bedroom 2 15⁰ x 12⁰

LINEN

STAIRS DN.

TRAY CEILING

Bedroom 4 12⁰ x 13³

Bath

Bedroom 3 12⁶ x 12⁰

Foyer Below

PLANT SHELF

W.i.c.

Home Sweet Home

Price Code: I

■ This plan features:

— Five bedrooms

— Four full and one half baths

■ An arched opening leads into the Living Room from the two-story Foyer

■ The Dining Room has a bay window that overlooks the front yard

■ The Breakfast Nook has a French door to the rear yard

■ The second floor Master Suite has many special features

■ This home is designed with basement and crawlspace foundation options

FIRST FLOOR — 1,615 SQ. FT.
SECOND FLOOR — 1,763 SQ. FT.
BASEMENT — 1,615 SQ. FT.
GARAGE — 747 SQ. FT.

TOTAL LIVING AREA:
3,378 SQ. FT.

Bricks and Arches
Detail this Ranch

Price Code: F

■ This plan features:

— Two bedrooms

— Two full and one half baths

■ A Master Bedroom with a vaulted ceiling luxurious Bath is complimented by a skylit walk-in closet

■ Columns and arched windows define the elegant Dining Room

■ A Great Room shares a see-through fireplace with the Hearth Room, which also has a built-in entertainment center

■ This home is designed with a basement foundation

■ Alternate foundation options available at an additional charge. Please call 1-800-235-5700 for more information.

MAIN FLOOR — 2,512 SQ. FT.
GARAGE — 783 SQ. FT.

TOTAL LIVING AREA:
2,512 SQ. FT.

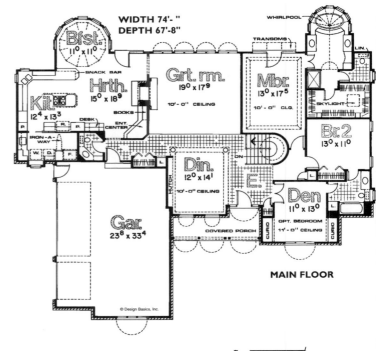

WIDTH 74'- "
DEPTH 67'-8"

MAIN FLOOR

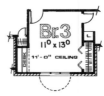

BEDROOM OPTION

Elegant Presense

Price Code: G

■ This plan features:
— Four Bedrooms
— Two full, one three-quarter, and one half baths

■ An elegant Entry and an abundance of windows create a larger than life feeling

■ There is a double-door entrance into the grand Foyer, and an attached double-door Entry gives access to the Library

■ The Living Room is to the left of the Foyer and steps up into the Dining Room

■ A vaulted ceiling crowns the Family Room and the Breakfast Room

■ The Master Bedroom is topped by a vaulted ceiling and includes a his and her Bath

■ Three additional Bedrooms enjoy ample closet space and easy access to a full Bath

■ This home is designed with basement and slab foundation options

FIRST FLOOR — 1,396 SQ. FT.
SECOND FLOOR — 1,584 SQ. FT.
BASEMENT — 1,396 SQ. FT.

TOTAL LIVING AREA:
2,980 SQ. FT.

WIDTH 48'-0"
DEPTH 52'-0"

FIRST FLOOR

SECOND FLOOR

Glorious Arches

Price Code: G

■ This plan features:
— Four bedrooms
— Three full and one half baths

■ Glorious arched openings distinguish the Family Room

■ From the two-story Foyer, you may enter either the Living Room or the Dining Room

■ A three-car Garage completes this home design

■ This home is designed with basement and crawlspace foundation options

FIRST FLOOR — 1,347 SQ. FT.
SECOND FLOOR — 1,493 SQ. FT.
BONUS ROOM — 243 SQ. FT.
BASEMENT — 1,347 SQ. FT.
GARAGE — 778 SQ. FT.

TOTAL LIVING AREA:
2,840 SQ. FT.

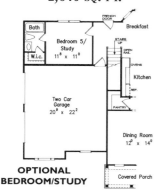

OPTIONAL BEDROOM/STUDY

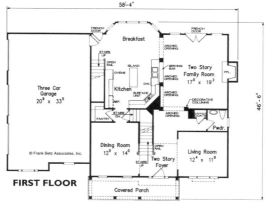

FIRST FLOOR

SECOND FLOOR

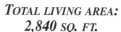

To order your Blueprints, call 1-800-235-5700

199

Distinctive Brick with Room to Expand

Price Code: F

■ This plan features:

— Four bedrooms

— Two full and one half baths

■ Arched entrance with decorative glass leads into two-story Foyer

■ Formal Dining Room with tray ceiling above decorative window

■ Kitchen with island cooktop and built-in desk and Pantry

■ The Master Bedroom, topped with a tray ceiling, has a French door to the Patio and a lavish Bath

■ This home is designed with basement, slab and crawlspace foundation options

FIRST FLOOR — 2,577 SQ. FT.
BONUS ROOM — 619 SQ. FT.
BASEMENT — 2,561 SQ. FT.
BRIDGE — 68 SQ. FT.
GARAGE — 560 SQ. FT.

TOTAL LIVING AREA:
2,645 SQ. FT.

FIRST FLOOR

Sundeck
17-0 x 16-0

Master Bdrm.
15-6 x 17-6

Tray Ceil.

M. Bath

Family Rm.
22-4 x 13-6

Cathedral Ceil.

Living
13-6 x 15-6

Two Story Ceil. Line

Bath 2

Bdrm.2
11-6 x 13-4

Brkfst.
13-4 x 9-6

Lav.

Line Of Bridge

Kit.
13-4 x 12-0

Ref.

Dining
13-8 x 13-6

Tray Ceil.

Line Of Bridge

Open Foyer
12-0 x 9-4

Bdrm.4
13-6 x 11-2

Bdrm.3
11-6 x 11-6

Stoop

Double Garage
21-4 x 23-8

WIDTH 74'-0"
DEPTH 70'-0"

© 1988, Jannis Vann & Associates, Inc.

SECOND FLOOR

Open To Living

Fut. Bth.

Sky Lt.

Storage
15-8 x 11-8

Bridge

Future Bdrm.
18-4 x 16-8

Sky Lt.

Open Foyer

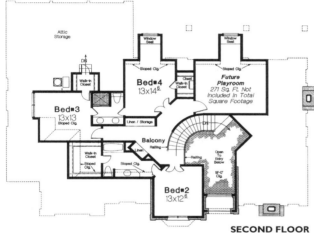

SECOND FLOOR

← 73'-0" →

56'-6 1/2"

FIRST FLOOR

Country Estate Home
Price Code: I

■ This plan features:
— Four bedrooms
— Three full and one half baths

■ Impressive two-story Entry with a lovely curved staircase

■ Formal Living and Dining Rooms have columns and decorative windows

■ Wood plank flooring, a large fireplace and Veranda access accent Great Room

■ Hub Kitchen with brick pavers, extended serving counter, bright Breakfast Area, and nearby Utility/Garage Entry

■ Private Master Bedroom offers a Private Lanai and plush Dressing Area

■ Future Playroom offers many options

■ This home is designed with a slab foundation

FIRST FLOOR — 2,441 SQ. FT.
SECOND FLOOR — 1,039 SQ. FT.
BONUS — 271 SQ. FT.
GARAGE — 660 SQ. FT.

TOTAL LIVING AREA:
3,480 SQ. FT.

Timeless Beauty

Price Code: G

■ This plan features:

— Four bedrooms

— Two full, two three-quarter and one half baths

■ Two-story Entry accesses formal Dining and Living Room

■ Spacious Great Room with cathedral ceiling and fireplace

■ Ideal Kitchen with Pantry

■ Master Bedroom wing offers a decorative ceiling, and luxurious Dressing/Bath Area

■ This home is designed with a basement foundation

■ Alternate foundation options available at an additional charge. Please call 1-800-235-5700 for more information.

FIRST FLOOR — 2,063 SQ. FT.
SECOND FLOOR — 894 SQ. FT.
GARAGE — 666 SQ. FT.
BASEMENT — 2,063 SQ. FT.

TOTAL LIVING AREA:
2,957 SQ. FT.

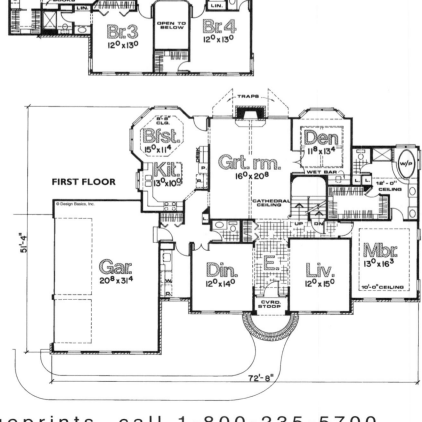

Elegant Row House

Price Code: F

- This plan features:
- — Three bedrooms
- — Two full and one half baths
- Arched columns define the formal and casual spaces
- Wraparound Porches on two levels provide views to the living areas
- Four sets of French doors let the outside into the Great Room
- The Master Suite features a private Bath designed for two people
- Generous bonus space awaits your ideas for completion
- The Guest Bedroom leads to a Gallery hallway with Deck access
- This home is designed with slab and pier/post foundation options
- Alternate foundation options available at an additional charge. Please call 1-800-235-5700 for more information.

MAIN FLOOR — 1,305 SQ. FT.
UPPER FLOOR — 1,215 SQ. FT.
LOWER FLOOR — 935 SQ. FT.
GARAGE — 480 SQ. FT.

TOTAL LIVING AREA:
2,520 SQ. FT.

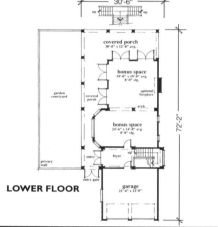

LOWER FLOOR

MAIN FLOOR

UPPER FLOOR

Sensational Entry

Price Code: L

- This plan features:
- — Four bedrooms
- — Three full and one half baths
- Grand columns frame two-story Portico leading into a gracious Foyer with a curved staircase
- Two-story Living Room accented by columns, a massive fireplace and French doors to the rear yard
- Vaulted Family Room highlighted by outdoor views and a cozy fireplace, opens to Kitchen/Breakfast Area
- Ideal Kitchen with a cooktop island/serving bar, walk-in Pantry, Breakfast Area, and nearby Laundry and Garage Entry
- Secluded Master Suite offers a vaulted Sitting Area with radius windows and decorative columns, two walk-in closets, and a lavish Bath
- Three second floor Bedrooms with walk-in closets and private access to full Baths
- This home is designed with basement and crawlspace foundation options

FIRST FLOOR — 2,764 SQ. FT.
SECOND FLOOR — 1,598 SQ. FT.
GARAGE — 743 SQ. FT.

TOTAL LIVING AREA:
4,362 SQ. FT.

FIRST FLOOR

SECOND FLOOR

Lavish Appointments

Price Code: L

- This plan features:
- — Four bedrooms
- — Four full and one half baths
- Glassed two-story Entry
- The staircase to the second floor accents the marble Entry hall
- A sloped ceiling and a fireplace enhance the Living Room
- The Dining Room has a rear wall of windows
- The Kitchen has a center island with a cooktop
- The Study has a fireplace
- This home is designed with a slab foundation

FIRST FLOOR — 3,145 SQ. FT.
SECOND FLOOR — 1,181 SQ. FT.
GARAGE — 792 SQ. FT.

TOTAL LIVING AREA:
4,326 SQ. FT.

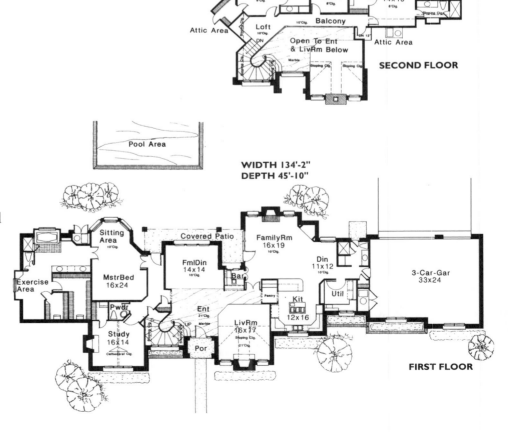

FIRST FLOOR

SECOND FLOOR

Traditional Home

Price Code: G

- This plan features:
- — Four bedrooms
- — Two full, one three-quarter and one half baths
- Dining Room has a built-in hutch and a bay window
- Cozy Den and Great Room have high ceilings and transom windows
- The warm Gathering Room features a fireplace and a cathedral ceiling
- This home is designed with a basement foundation
- Alternate foundation options available at an additional charge. Please call 1-800-235-5700 for more information.

FIRST FLOOR — 2,158 SQ. FT.
SECOND FLOOR — 821 SQ. FT.
BASEMENT — 2,158 SQ. FT.
GARAGE — 692 SQ. FT.

TOTAL LIVING AREA:
2,979 SQ. FT.

Stately Exterior with an Open Interior

Price Code: F

- This plan features:
- — Four bedrooms
- — Two full and one half baths

- Central Family Room with an inviting fireplace and a cathedral ceiling extending into Kitchen

- Spacious Kitchen offers a work island/snack bar, built-in Pantry, glass Breakfast Area and nearby Porch, Utilities and Garage Entry

- This home is designed with basement and slab foundation options

- Alternate foundation options available at an additional charge. Please call 1-800-235-5700 for more information.

FIRST FLOOR — 1,906 SQ. FT.
SECOND FLOOR — 749 SQ. FT.
BASEMENT — 1,906 SQ. FT.
GARAGE — 682 SQ. FT.

TOTAL LIVING AREA:
2,655 SQ. FT.

SECOND FLOOR

FIRST FLOOR

© Carmichael & Dame

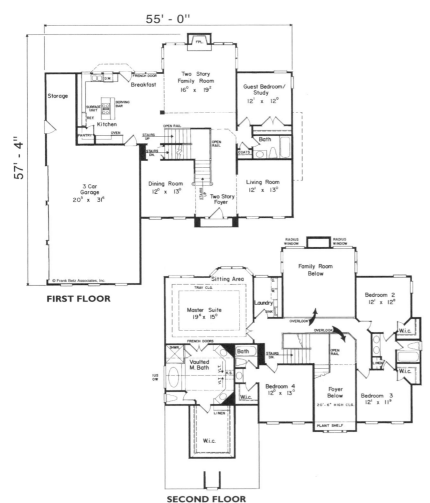

55' - 0"

Storage

Breakfast

D.W.

FRENCH DOOR

Two Story
Family Room
16⁰ x 19²

Guest Bedroom/
Study
12' x 12⁰

SERVING
BAR

SURFACE
UNIT

Kitchen

REF.

PANTRY

OVEN

OPEN RAIL

STAIRS
UP

STAIRS
DN.

OPEN
RAIL

Bath

COATS

57' - 4"

3 Car
Garage
20⁵ x 31⁶

Dining Room
12⁰ x 13⁰

STAIRS

Two Story
Foyer

Living Room
12' x 13⁰

FPL

© Frank Betz Associates, Inc.

FIRST FLOOR

RADIUS
WINDOW

RADIUS
WINDOW

Family Room
Below

Sitting Area

TRAY CLG.

Laundry

D.

SINK

Bedroom 2
12' x 12⁶

Master Suite
19⁶ x 15⁰

OVERLOOK

W.i.c.

FRENCH DOORS

OVERLOOK

SHWR.

Vaulted
M. Bath

Bath

STAIRS
DN.

OPEN
RAIL

LINEN

W.i.c.

IUS
OW

W.i.c.

Bedroom 4
12⁰ x 13⁰

Foyer
Below
20'-6" HIGH CLG.

Bedroom 3
12' x 11⁵

LINEN

W.i.c.

PLANT SHELF

SECOND FLOOR

Regal Residence

Price Code: H

■ This plan features:

— Five bedrooms

— Four full baths

■ Keystone arched windows accent entrance into two-story Foyer between formal Living and Dining Rooms

■ Spacious two-story Family Room enhanced by a fireplace and lots of windows

■ First floor Guest Room/Study with roomy closet and adjoining full Bath

■ Luxurious Master Suite offers a tray ceiling, Sitting Area, a huge walk-in closet and a vaulted Bath with a radius window

■ This home is designed with basement and crawlspace foundation options

FIRST FLOOR — 1,488 SQ. FT.
SECOND FLOOR — 1,551 SQ. FT.
GARAGE — 667 SQ. FT.

TOTAL LIVING AREA:
3,039 SQ. FT.

Luxurious Residence

Price Code: L

■ This plan features:

— Three bedrooms

— Three full and one half baths

■ Vaulted ceilings in the formal Living and Dining Areas

■ Kitchen with cooking island opens to the round Nook and the Leisure Room

■ Spacious Master wing includes a Study, Exercise Room, captivating Bath and pampering Suite

■ This home is designed with a slab foundation

■ Alternate foundation options available at an additional charge. Please call 1-800-235-5700 for more information.

MAIN FLOOR — 4,565 SQ. FT.
GARAGE — 757 SQ. FT.

TOTAL LIVING AREA:
4,565 SQ. FT.

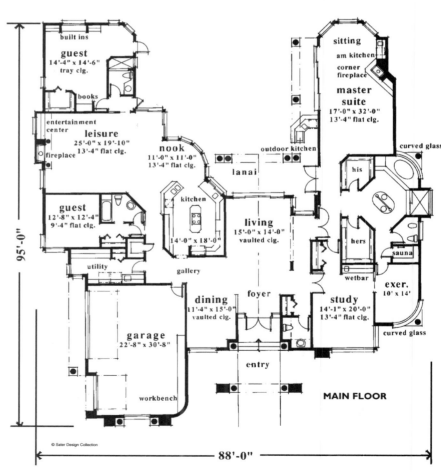

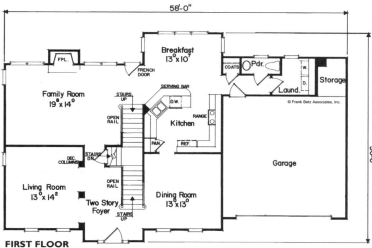

FIRST FLOOR

58'-0"

36'-6"

FPL.

Breakfast
13⁰x10⁷

FRENCH
DOOR

COATS

Pdr.

W.
D.
Laund.

Storage

Family Room
19⁰x14⁰

STAIRS
UP

SERVING BAR

D.W.

Kitchen

RANGE

© Frank Betz Associates, Inc.

OPEN
RAIL

STAIRS
DN.

PAN.

REF.

Garage

DEC.
COLUMNS

Living Room
13⁰x14²

OPEN
RAIL

Two Story
Foyer

Dining Room
13⁰x13⁰

STAIRS
UP

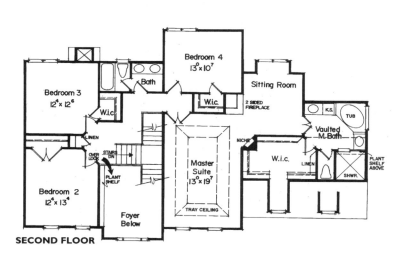

SECOND FLOOR

Bedroom 3
12⁴x12⁶

Bath

Bedroom 4
13⁰x10⁷

W.ic.

Sitting Room

2 SIDED
FIREPLACE

K.S.

TUB

Vaulted
M. Bath

W.ic.

LINEN

OVER
LOOK

STAIRS
DN.

PLANT
SHELF

NICHE

W.ic.

LINEN

PLANT
SHELF
ABOVE

Bedroom 2
12⁴x13⁴

Master
Suite
13⁰x19⁷

W.ic.

SHWR.

Foyer
Below

TRAY CEILING

Contemporary Plan with Old-World Charm

Price Code: F

■ This plan features:

— Four bedrooms

— Two full and one half baths

■ The elegant Dining Room has direct access to the Kitchen

■ The Family Room, enhanced by a fireplace, has direct access to the second floor

■ The Master Suite is enhanced by a two-sided fireplace, a Sitting Room, and a luxurious private Bath crowned by a vaulted ceiling

■ This home is designed with basement and crawlspace foundation options

FIRST FLOOR — 1,252 SQ. FT.
SECOND FLOOR — 1,348 SQ. FT.
BASEMENT — 1,252 SQ. FT.
GARAGE — 483 SQ. FT.

TOTAL LIVING AREA:
2,600 SQ. FT.

PLAN NO. 97633

Three Car Garage

Price Code: I

- ■ This plan features:
- — Five bedrooms
- — Four full and one half baths
- ■ The Living and Dining Rooms are located off the Foyer
- ■ Columns separate the Family Room from the Kitchen
- ■ A Study/Bedroom is tucked away on the first floor
- ■ The Laundry Room is located upstairs
- ■ The Master Suite is warmed by a fireplace in its Sitting Area
- ■ This home is designed with basement and crawlspace foundation options

FIRST FLOOR — 1,577 SQ. FT.
SECOND FLOOR — 1,689 SQ. FT.
BASEMENT — 1,577 SQ. FT.
GARAGE — 694 SQ. FT.

TOTAL LIVING AREA:
3,266 SQ. FT.

WIDTH 59'-4"
DEPTH 49'-0"

FIRST FLOOR

SECOND FLOOR

PLAN NO. 98439

Impressive Entrance

Price Code: L

- ■ This plan features:
- — Five bedrooms
- — Four full and one half baths
- ■ An impressive two-story Foyer leads through the arched openings that frame the formal Living Room and Dining Room
- ■ An island Kitchen offers an abundance of counter and work space as well as a Pantry and serving bar
- ■ The Breakfast Room opens to the Kitchen and has a French door to the rear yard
- ■ An arched opening leads into the two-story Family Room
- ■ A fireplace and built-in shelving highlight the Family Room
- ■ A Home Office or secondary Bedroom has a double-door entrance for privacy and a full Bath
- ■ The Master Suite has a Sitting Room, lavish Bath, and a huge his and her walk-in closets
- ■ This home is designed with basement and crawlspace foundation options

FIRST FLOOR — 2,058 SQ. FT.
SECOND FLOOR — 2,067 SQ. FT.
BASEMENT — 2,058 SQ. FT.
GARAGE — 819 SQ. FT.

TOTAL LIVING AREA:
4,125 SQ. FT.

FIRST FLOOR

WIDTH 62'-6"
DEPTH 59'-6"

SECOND FLOOR

To order your Blueprints, call 1-800-235-5700

SECOND FLOOR

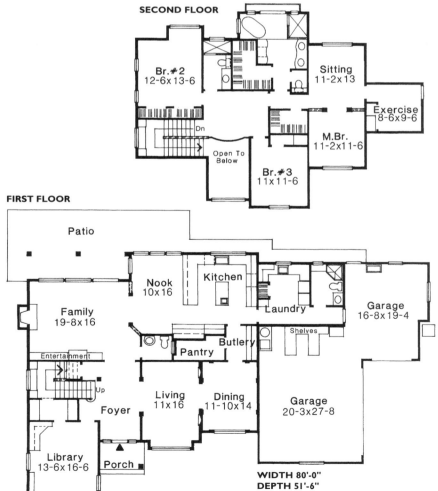

Br.#2
12-6x13-6

Sitting
11-2x13

Exercise
8-6x9-6

M.Br.
11-2x11-6

Open To
Below

Dn

Br.#3
11x11-6

FIRST FLOOR

Patio

Nook
10x16

Kitchen

Laundry

Garage
16-8x19-4

Family
19-8x16

Shelves

Entertainment

Butlery

Pantry

Up

Living
11x16

Dining
11-10x14

Garage
20-3x27-8

Foyer

Library
13-6x16-6

Porch

WIDTH 80'-0"
DEPTH 51'-6"

Rooms for Everything

Price Code: I

■ This plan features:

— Three bedrooms

— Two full and one half baths

■ English Country charm shines through in subtle curves and sharp angles

■ A Library, Exercise Room and Sitting Room offer something for everyone

■ Counter space, center island, Pantry, Butlery and separate Nook make an impressive Kitchen

■ Spanning the entire back of the house, the Patio creates a comfortable outdoorsy getaway

■ This home is designed with a crawlspace foundation

FIRST FLOOR — 2,057 SQ. FT.
SECOND FLOOR — 1,323 SQ. FT.
GARAGE — 886 SQ. FT.

TOTAL LIVING AREA:
3,380 SQ. FT.

Splendid Appointments

Price Code: H

■ This plan features:

— Three bedrooms

— Three full and one half baths

■ The two-story Foyer is highlighted by a staircase with an open rail

■ The formal Dining Room opens onto a terrace for expanded dining options

■ A luxurious Bath covered in a vaulted ceiling pampers the Master Suite

■ A two-story Family Room is accented by arched openings from the Dining Room and Foyer

■ This home is designed with basement and crawlspace foundation

FIRST FLOOR — 2,429 SQ. FT.
SECOND FLOOR — 654 SQ. FT.
BONUS ROOM — 420 SQ. FT.
BASEMENT — 2,429 SQ. FT.
GARAGE — 641 SQ. FT.

TOTAL LIVING AREA:
3,083 SQ. FT.

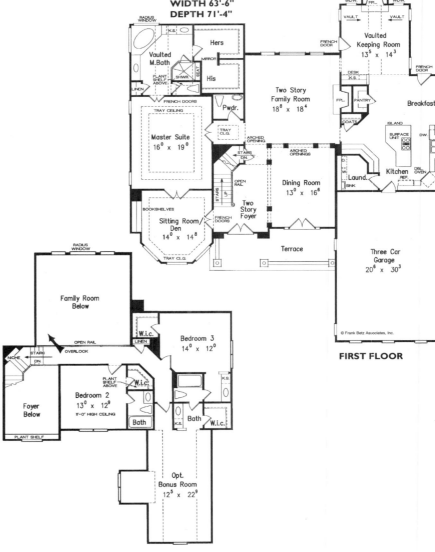

WIDTH 63'-6"
DEPTH 71'-4"

FIRST FLOOR

SECOND FLOOR

212

Living Room with Bay

Price Code: H

- This plan features:
— Four bedrooms
— Three full and one half baths
- Arches and columns distinguish the Entries into the Dining Room
- A French door provides elegant passage to the outdoors from the Family Room
- This home is designed with basement and crawlspace foundation options

FIRST FLOOR — 2,294 SQ. FT.
SECOND FLOOR — 869 SQ. FT.
BONUS ROOM — 309 SQ. FT.
GARAGE — 495 SQ. FT.

TOTAL LIVING AREA:
3,163 SQ. FT.

WIDTH 63'-6"
DEPTH 63'-0"

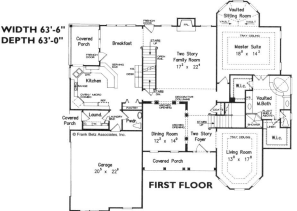

FIRST FLOOR

SECOND FLOOR

Essence of Style and Grace

Price Code: G

- This plan features:
— Four bedrooms
— Three full and one half baths
- French doors introduce the Study, and columns define the Gallery and formal areas
- The expansive Family Room, with an inviting fireplace and a cathedral ceiling, opens to the Kitchen
- The Kitchen features a cooktop island, Butler's Pantry, Breakfast Area, and Patio access
- The first floor Master Bedroom offers a private Patio, a vaulted ceiling, twin vanities and a walk-in closet
- This home is designed with basement and slab foundation options

FIRST FLOOR — 2,036 SQ. FT.
SECOND FLOOR — 866 SQ. FT.
GARAGE — 720 SQ. FT.

TOTAL LIVING AREA:
2,902 SQ. FT.

FIRST FLOOR

SECOND FLOOR

To order your Blueprints, call 1-800-235-5700

...auty

Price Code: F

- This plan featu...
- — Four bedroom...
- — Three full and ...e half baths
- The Living R... and the ...ng Room are each distinguished ...y ... impre...ve front window
- A Kitchen wi... ...opens into the Breakfast Nook which h...s ...ing ...s to the backyard Patio
- The enormous Family Room with a fireplace will be the central location of family activities
- A first floor Master Bedroom is removed from high traffic areas, and is complimented by a spacious Bath and walk-in closet
- Connected by the upstairs hallway are three Bedrooms and two full Baths
- This home is designed with slab and crawlspace foundation options

FIRST FLOOR — 1,842 SQ. FT.
SECOND FLOOR — 843 SQ. FT.

TOTAL LIVING AREA:
2,685 SQ. FT.

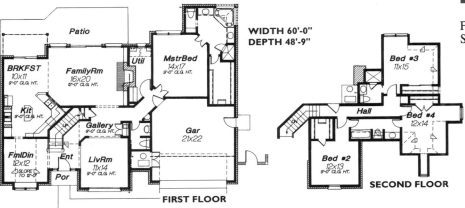

WIDTH 60'-0"
DEPTH 48'-9"

FIRST FLOOR

SECOND FLOOR

A Custom Look

Price Code: H

- This plan features:
- — Three bedrooms
- — Three full and one half baths
- Wonderfully balanced exterior highlighted by triple arched glass in Entry Porch, leading into the Gallery Foyer
- Triple arches leading into Formal Living and Dining Room, Veranda and beyond
- Kitchen, Nook, and Leisure Room easily flow together
- Owners' wing has a Master Suite with glass alcove to rear yard, a lavish Bath and a Study offering many uses
- Two additional Bedrooms with corner windows and oversized closets access a full Bath
- This home is designed with a slab foundation
- Alternate foundation options available at an additional charge. Please call 1-800-235-5700 for more information.

MAIN FLOOR — 2,978 SQ. FT
GARAGE — 702 SQ. FT.

TOTAL LIVING AREA:
2,978 SQ. FT.

MAIN FLOOR

WIDTH 84'-0"
DEPTH 90'-0"

To order your Blueprints, call 1-800-235-5700

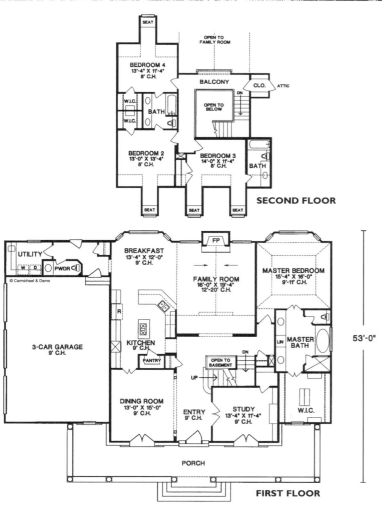

SECOND FLOOR

SEAT

OPEN TO FAMILY ROOM

BEDROOM 4
13'-4" X 11'-4"
8' C.H.

BALCONY

CLO. ATTIC

W.I.C.

BATH

W.I.C.

OPEN TO BELOW

DN

BEDROOM 2
13'-0" X 13'-4"
8' C.H.

BEDROOM 3
14'-0" X 11'-4"
8' C.H.

BATH

SEAT   SEAT   SEAT

UTILITY

W D

PWDR

© Carmichael & Dame

3-CAR GARAGE
9' C.H.

KITCHEN
9' C.H.

PANTRY

BREAKFAST
13'-4" X 12'-0"
9' C.H.

FP

FAMILY ROOM
16'-0" X 19'-4"
12'-20' C.H.

MASTER BEDROOM
15'-4" X 16'-0"
9'-11" C.H.

MASTER BATH

LIN

R

OPEN TO BASEMENT

DN

UP

W.I.C.

DINING ROOM
13'-0" X 15'-0"
9' C.H.

ENTRY
9' C.H.

STUDY
13'-4" X 11'-4"
9' C.H.

53'-0"

PORCH

FIRST FLOOR

67'-8"

Dormers and Porch Create Country Atmosphere

Price Code: H

- This plan features:
- — Four bedrooms
- — Three full and one half baths

- French doors lead from both the Dining Room and the Study onto the front Porch

- This home is designed with a basement and slab foundation options

- Alternate foundation options available at an additional charge. Please call 1-800-235-5700 for more information.

FIRST FLOOR — 2,116 SQ. FT.
SECOND FLOOR — 956 SQ. FT.
BASEMENT — 2,116 SQ. FT.
GARAGE — 675 SQ. FT.

TOTAL LIVING AREA:
3,072 SQ. FT.

Executive Estate

Price Code: J

■ This plan features:

— Four bedrooms

— Three full and one half baths

■ A two-story Foyer highlighted by a curved staircase

■ The formal Dining Room has a large front window and decorative columns

■ The Study offers built-in shelves for books and electronic equipment

■ The sumptuous Master Bedroom features a large closet, Sitting Area and entertainment center

■ This home is designed with a slab foundation

FIRST FLOOR — 2,655 SQ. FT.
SECOND FLOOR — 1,090 SQ. FT.

TOTAL LIVING AREA:
3,745 SQ. FT.

FIRST FLOOR

WIDTH 76'-0"
DEPTH 60'-0"

SECOND FLOOR

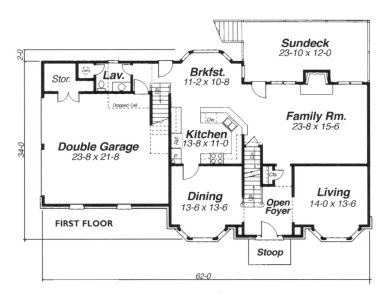

Photography by John Ehrenclou

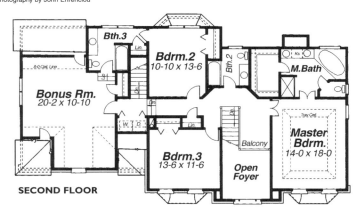

SECOND FLOOR

Bth.3

Bdrm.2
10-10 x 13-6

Bth.2

M.Bath

8-0 Ceil. Line

Bonus Rm.
20-2 x 10-10

Master
Bdrm.
14-0 x 18-0

Balcony

Bdrm.3
13-6 x 11-6

Open
Foyer

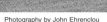

Stor.

Lav.

Brkfst.
11-2 x 10-8

Sundeck
23-10 x 12-0

Dropped Ceil.

Double Garage
23-8 x 21-8

Kitchen
13-8 x 11-0

Family Rm.
23-8 x 15-6

Dining
13-6 x 13-6

Open
Foyer

Living
14-0 x 13-6

Stoop

FIRST FLOOR

62-0

34-0

2-0

Rewards of Success

Price Code: F

■ This plan features:

— Three bedrooms

— Three full and one half baths

■ Formal areas, the Living Room and Dining Room, located in the front of the house, each enhanced by a bay window

■ An expansive Family Room, including a fireplace flanked by windows

■ An open layout between the Family Room, Breakfast Bay and the Kitchen

■ A lavish Master Bedroom crowned by a decorative ceiling and pampered by a private Master Bath

■ This home is designed with basement, slab, and crawlspace foundation options

FIRST FLOOR — 1,282 SQ. FT.
SECOND FLOOR — 1,227 SQ. FT.
BONUS ROOM — 314 SQ. FT.
GARAGE — 528 SQ. FT.
BASEMENT — 1,154 SQ. FT.

TOTAL LIVING AREA:
2,509 SQ. FT.

French Country Styling

Price Code: F

- **This plan features:**
- — Four bedrooms
- — Two full, one three quarter, and one half baths

■ A bay window with a copper roof, a large eyebrow dormer, and an arched covered Entry add to the Country flavor of this home

■ The convenient Kitchen has its own Dining Area for informal occasions

■ The Master Bedroom is located on the first floor and has a large Bath

■ Three Bedrooms and a Future Room are located on the second floor

■ This home is designed with basement and slab foundation options

FIRST FLOOR — 1,765 SQ. FT.
SECOND FLOOR — 802 SQ. FT.
BONUS ROOM — 275 SQ. FT.
GARAGE — 462 SQ. FT.

TOTAL LIVING AREA:
2,567 SQ. FT.

WIDTH 55'-0"
DEPTH 48'-10"

FIRST FLOOR

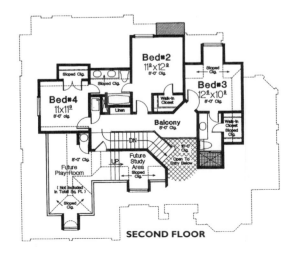

SECOND FLOOR

To order your Blueprints, call 1-800-235-5700

Angled Study
with Built-ins

Price Code: K

■ This plan features:
— Four bedrooms
— Three full and one half baths

■ Brick pavers and a curved staircase enhance the Entry

■ A Playroom and a Bonus Room join two secondary
Bedrooms on the second floor

■ This home is designed with basement and slab
foundation options

FIRST FLOOR — 2,985 SQ. FT.
SECOND FLOOR — 938 SQ. FT.
BONUS ROOM — 170 SQ. FT.
GARAGE — 623 SQ. FT.

TOTAL LIVING AREA:
3,923 SQ. FT.

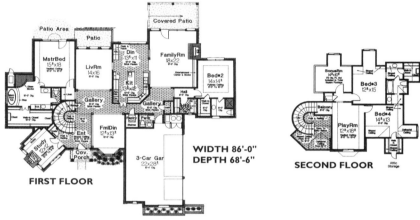

WIDTH 86'-0"
DEPTH 68'-6"

FIRST FLOOR

SECOND FLOOR

All About Windows,
Doors, and Ceilings

Price Code: L

Photography supplied by Frank Betz Associates, Inc.

■ This plan features:
— Five bedrooms
— Four full and one half baths

■ The two-story Foyer offers a grand
welcome to family and friends

■ A niche and arch openings in the Dining Room
presents a formal atmosphere

■ The Master Suite features a tray ceiling, French doors, a
vaulted Bath, a room-sized walk-in closet, a three-sided
fireplace, a Sitting Area, and a private Covered Porch

■ All Bedrooms have direct access to a full Bath

■ An second floor Playroom gives kids and adults
a way to enjoy themselves away from the center
of family activity

■ This home is designed with basement and
crawlspace foundation options

FIRST FLOOR — 2,092 SQ. FT.
SECOND FLOOR — 2,372 SQ. FT.
BASEMENT — 2,092 SQ. FT.
GARAGE — 674 SQ. FT.

TOTAL LIVING AREA:
4,464 SQ. FT.

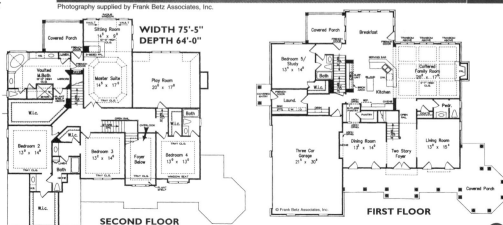

WIDTH 75'-5"
DEPTH 64'-0"

SECOND FLOOR

FIRST FLOOR

© Frank Betz Associates, Inc.

Quaint Dormers and Columned Porch

Price Code: F

■ This plan features:

— Three bedrooms

— Two full and one half baths

■ The Foyer leads into a formal Dining room topped by a decorative ceiling

■ The cooktop island Kitchen is directly accessed from both Dining Areas

■ The Family Room with a fireplace has doors that open to the Deck

■ The Master Bedroom has a bay window and a decorative ceiling

■ This home is designed with a basement foundation

MAIN FLOOR — 2,614 SQ. FT.
BONUS ROOM — 1,681 SQ. FT.
BASEMENT — 2,563 SQ. FT.
GARAGE — 596 SQ. FT.

TOTAL LIVING AREA:
2,614 SQ. FT

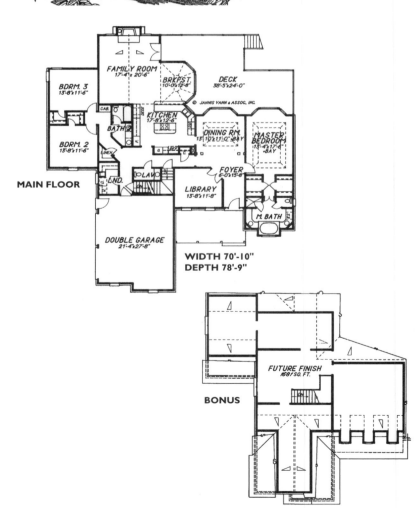

PLAN NO. 99109

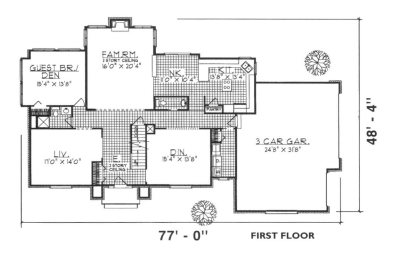

FIRST FLOOR

77' - 0"

48' - 4"

SECOND FLOOR

Brick Home of Distinction

Price Code: H

■ This plan features:
— Four bedrooms
— Three full and one half baths

■ Perfectly sized Living Room and Dining Room allow for comfortably entertaining large groups

■ Voluminous two-story Family Room has a fireplace centered along the back wall with the Nook and Kitchen in close proximity

■ Master Bedroom has a private Bath and a big walk-in closet

■ Two additional Bedrooms upstairs feature ample closet space and share a full Bath

■ This home is designed with a basement foundation

FIRST FLOOR — 1,873 SQ. FT.
SECOND FLOOR — 1,150 SQ. FT.

TOTAL LIVING AREA:
3,023 SQ. FT.

To order your Blueprints, call 1-800-235-5700

221

Lots of Extras

Price Code: J

- This plan features:
— Four bedrooms
— Three full and one half baths
- Enter the Master Bedroom through French doors with niches on either side offering a view
- Access the Bonus Room over the three-car Garage from the upstairs hallway
- The bayed Family Room has a fireplace and built-in cabinets
- The Kitchen has ample counter space, a Pantry, and a center island
- This home is designed with a basement foundation

FIRST FLOOR — 1,931 SQ. FT.
SECOND FLOOR — 1,580 SQ. FT.
BONUS ROOM — 439 SQ. FT.
BASEMENT — 1,931 SQ. FT.

TOTAL LIVING AREA:
3,511 SQ. FT.

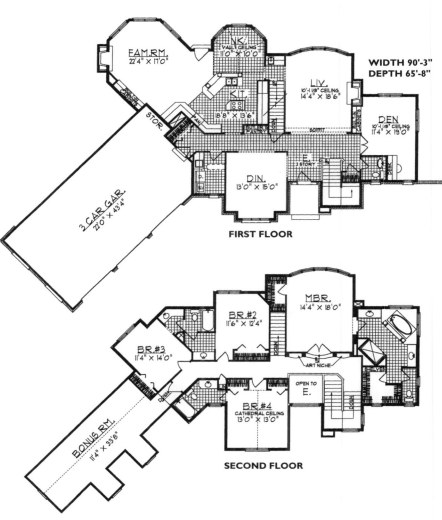

WIDTH 90'-3"
DEPTH 65'-8"

FIRST FLOOR

SECOND FLOOR

To order your Blueprints, call 1-800-235-5700

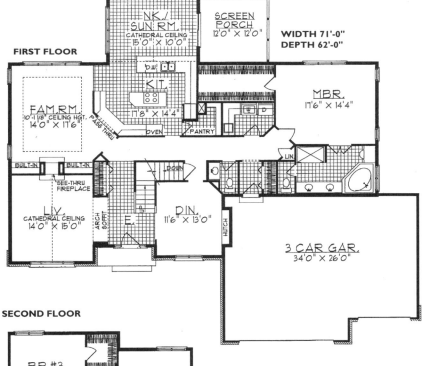

FIRST FLOOR

WIDTH 71'-0"
DEPTH 62'-0"

NK./SUN RM.
CATHEDRAL CEILING
15'0" X 10'0"

SCREEN PORCH
12'0" X 12'0"

KIT.
17'8" X 14'4"

FAM. RM.
10'-1 1/8" CEILING HGT.
14'0" X 17'6"

MBR.
17'6" X 14'4"

OVEN
PANTRY

BUILT-IN   BUILT-IN

SEE-THRU FIREPLACE

LIN

DOWN

LIV.
CATHEDRAL CEILING
14'0" X 15'0"

DIN.
11'6" X 13'0"

ARCH SOFFIT

HUTCH

3 CAR GAR.
34'0" X 26'0"

SECOND FLOOR

BR. #3
13'0" X 13'0"

BR. #2
12'6" X 13'6"

LOFT

DOWN

LINEN

LIN.

PLANT LEDGE

OPEN TO E.

BR. #4
11'4" X 15'0"

Picture Perfect

Price Code: H

- This plan features:
  — Four bedrooms
  — Two full and one half baths
- The Living Room has a vaulted ceiling and a see-through fireplace
- The large Kitchen is highlighted by an abundant Pantry Area, lots of work space and a Breakfast Bar
- The Family Room provides a warm gathering place with built-in cabinetry and a see-through fireplace
- The Master Bedroom has a deep walk-in closet and a Bath with a spa tub
- This home is designed with a basement foundation

FIRST FLOOR — 2,157 SQ. FT.
SECOND FLOOR — 956 SQ. FT.
BASEMENT — 2,157 SQ. FT.

TOTAL LIVING AREA:
3,113 SQ. FT.

Refinement with Brilliancy

Price Code: F

- This plan features:
  — Four bedrooms
  — Three full baths
- Two-story foyer dominated by an open rail staircase
- Two-story Family Room enhanced by a fireplace
- Walk-in Pantry and ample counter space highlighting the Breakfast Room
- Secluded Study easily becoming an additional Bedroom with a private Bath
- Second floor Master Suite with tray ceiling, bayed Sitting Area and a vaulted ceiling over the private Bath
- This home is designed with basement, slab, and crawlspace foundation options

FIRST FLOOR — 1,548 SQ. FT.
SECOND FLOOR — 1,164 SQ. FT.
BONUS ROOM — 198 SQ. FT.
BASEMENT — 1,548 SQ. FT.
GARAGE — 542 SQ. FT.

TOTAL LIVING AREA: 2,712 SQ. FT.

FIRST FLOOR

SECOND FLOOR

Dual Staircases

Price Code: L

- This plan features:
  — Four bedrooms
  — Three full, two three-quarter, and one half baths
- The Master Suite and Bedroom 4 provide Sitting Areas
- An arched opening divides the Breakfast Nook and Great Room
- This home is designed with a basement foundation

FIRST FLOOR — 3,523 SQ. FT.
SECOND FLOOR — 1,690 SQ. FT.
BONUS — 546 SQ. FT.
BASEMENT — 3,523 SQ. FT.

TOTAL LIVING AREA: 5,213 SQ. FT.

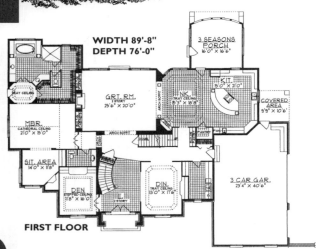

FIRST FLOOR

SECOND FLOOR

To order your Blueprints, call 1-800-235-5700

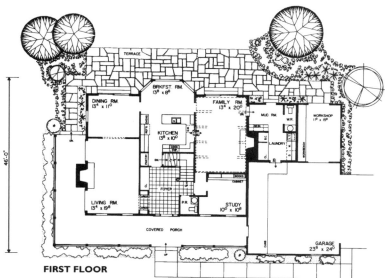

FIRST FLOOR

46'-0"

74'-0"

SECOND FLOOR

Farmhouse Feeling, Family–Style

Price Code: G

■ This plan features:

— Four bedrooms

— Two full and two half baths

■ A sunny Breakfast bay with easy access to the efficient Kitchen

■ A large and spacious Family Room with a fireplace and a pass-through to the Kitchen

■ Sliders that link the Family and Dining Rooms with the rear terrace

■ A private Master Suite with his and her walk-in closets, a Dressing Room with built-in vanity and convenient step-in shower

■ This home is designed with a basement foundation

FIRST FLOOR — 1,590 SQ. FT.
SECOND FLOOR — 1,344 SQ. FT.

TOTAL LIVING AREA:
2,934 SQ. FT.

A Classic Design

Price Code: F

- ■ This plan features:
- — Four bedrooms
- — Two full and one half baths
- ■ An elegant arched opening graces the Entrance of this classic design
- ■ The dramatic arch detail is repeated at the Dining Room entrance
- ■ The Kitchen, Breakfast Room and Family Room are open to one another
- ■ The Kitchen has such amenities as a walk-in Pantry, double ovens and an eating bar
- ■ The Master Suite is designed apart from the other Bedrooms for privacy
- ■ Two Bedrooms share a Bath and have walk-in closets
- ■ This home is designed with crawlspace and slab foundation options

MAIN FLOOR — 2,678 SQ. FT.
GARAGE — 474 SQ. FT.

TOTAL LIVING AREA:
   2,678 SQ. FT.

To order your Blueprints, call 1-800-235-5700

In-Home Office Space

Price Code: H

- This plan features:
  — Four bedrooms
  — Three full and one half baths
- Friendly front Porch adds Country charm to practical design
- Open Foyer with lovely landing staircase is flanked by Study and Living Room
- Hub Kitchen with built-in Pantry, peninsula eating bar, eating Nook, and adjoining Dining Room
- Comfortable Family Room with beamed ceiling, large fireplace, and access to the rear yard, Laundry and Office/Guest space
- Corner Master Bedroom with Dressing Area and his and her walk-in closets
- Two additional Bedrooms with double closets, share a double-vanity Bath
- This home is designhed with a basement foundation

FIRST FLOOR — 1,762 SQ. FT.
SECOND FLOOR — 1,311 SQ. FT.
GARAGE — 561 SQ. FT.

TOTAL LIVING AREA: 3,073 SQ. FT.

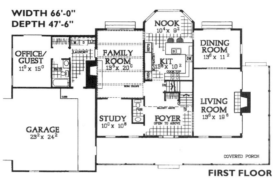

WIDTH 66'-0"
DEPTH 47'-6"

FIRST FLOOR

SECOND FLOOR

Sophisticated Southern Styling

Price Code: G

- This plan features:
  — Five bedrooms
  — Three full and one half baths
- Covered front and rear Porches expanding the living space to the outdoors
- A Den has a large fireplace and built-in cabinets and shelves
- A cooktop island, built-in desk, and eating bar complete the Kitchen
- The Master Suite has two walk-in closets and a luxurious Bath
- Four additional Bedrooms, two on the first floor and two on the second floor, all have easy access to a full Bath
- This home is designed with crawlspace and slab foundation options

FIRST FLOOR — 2,256 SQ. FT.
SECOND FLOOR — 602 SQ. FT.
BONUS ROOM— 264 SQ. FT.
GARAGE — 484 SQ. FT.

TOTAL LIVING AREA: 2,858 SQ. FT.

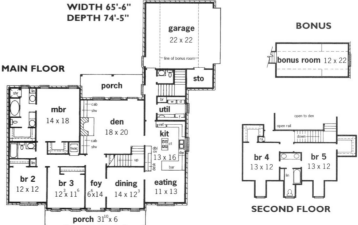

WIDTH 65'-6"
DEPTH 74'-5"

MAIN FLOOR

BONUS

SECOND FLOOR

Full-Length Covered Porch

Price Code: K

■ This plan features:

— Five bedrooms

— Three full and one half baths

■ Natural light floods the Foyer through the dramatic palladium-style window

■ A grand Family Room with a fireplace and a full length covered entrance Porch

■ The first floor Master Suite features a large walk-in closet and a Bath with a separate bath tub and stall shower

■ This home is designed with a basement foundation

FIRST FLOOR — 2,538 SQ. FT.
SECOND FLOOR — 1,295 SQ. FT.
GARAGE — 900 SQ. FT.

TOTAL LIVING AREA:
3,833 SQ. FT.

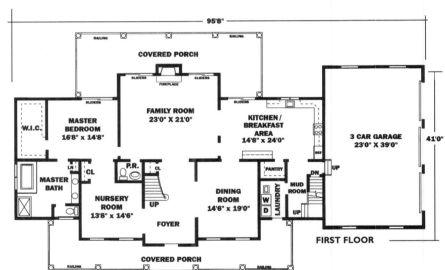

95'8"

COVERED PORCH

FAMILY ROOM
23'0" X 21'0"

KITCHEN / BREAKFAST AREA
14'8" x 24'0"

3 CAR GARAGE
23'0" X 39'0"

41'0"

MASTER BEDROOM
16'8" x 14'8"

W.I.C.

MASTER BATH

NURSERY ROOM
13'8" x 14'6"

UP

FOYER

DINING ROOM
14'6" x 19'0"

PANTRY

LAUNDRY

MUD ROOM

FIRST FLOOR

COVERED PORCH

BEDROOM 2
13'4" x 14'8"

OPEN TO BELOW

GUEST ROOM
13'4" x 10'10"

STORAGE
14'4" x 25'4"

BATH

BEDROOM 3
14'6" x 15'0"

OPEN TO BELOW

BEDROOM 4
14'6" x 15'0"

BATH

STORAGE
11'0" x 8'8"

SECOND FLOOR

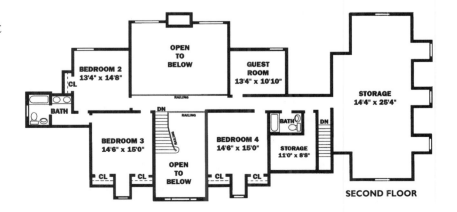

Western Farmhouse with Many Comforts

Price Code: L

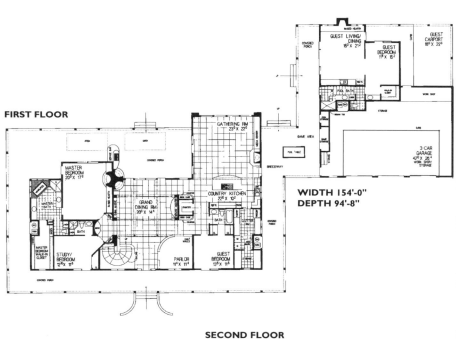

FIRST FLOOR

SECOND FLOOR

WIDTH 154'-0"
DEPTH 94'-8"

■ This plan features:

— Six bedrooms

— Four full and one three-quarter baths

■ A Covered Porch surrounds the home and shades access to many indoor areas

■ Formal Dining Room offers a built-in china alcove, service counter and fireplace

■ Master Bedroom highlighted by a raised hearth fireplace, Porch access and a plush Bath

■ This home is designed with a slab foundation

FIRST FLOOR — 3,166 SQ. FT.
SECOND FLOOR — 950 SQ. FT.

TOTAL LIVING AREA;
4,116 SQ. FT.

Symmetrical, Simple and Stunning

Price Code: F

- This plan features:
  — Three bedrooms
  — Two full and one half baths
- Deep eaves create Covered Porch on three sides
- Entry/Art Gallery is highlighted by second-story windows and plant shelves
- Central two-story Family/Great Room, with a raised hearth fireplace framed by media center and plant shelves, opens to Courtyard and Covered Pergola
- Spacious Kitchen with island snack bar and built-in Pantry accesses Laundry/Garage Entry, formal Dining Room and Family Room
- Private Master Suite pampered by Sitting Area, walk-in closet, and lavish Master Bath
- Two additional Bedrooms with ample closets and access to a full Bath
- Corner Office/Den offers multiple uses
- This home is designed with a crawlspace foundation

MAIN FLOOR — 2,626 SQ. FT.

TOTAL LIVING AREA:
2,626 SQ. FT.

MAIN FLOOR

WIDTH 75'-10"
DEPTH 69'-4"

BONUS OPTION

Enjoyable Living

Price Code: F

- This plan features:
  — Four bedrooms
  — Two full, one three-quarter, and one half baths
- The Master Bedroom is complete with a tray ceiling, two walk-in closets, and a large Bath
- The Family Room has a beamed ceiling and a fireplace
- This home is designed with basement and slab foundation options
- Alternate foundation options available at an additional charge. Please call 1-800-235-5700 for more information.

FIRST FLOOR — 1,400 SQ. FT.
SECOND FLOOR — 1,315 SQ. FT.
BASEMENT — 1,400 SQ. FT.
GARAGE — 631 SQ. FT.

TOTAL LIVING AREA:
2,715 SQ. FT.

FIRST FLOOR

SECOND FLOOR

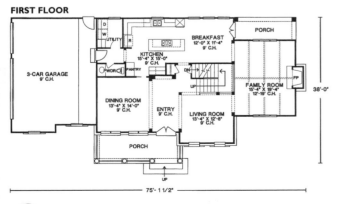

© Carmichael & Dame

To order your Blueprints, call 1-800-235-5700

Unique Angles and Lots of Light

Price Code: G

- This plan features:
  - Three bedrooms
  - Two full and one half baths
- Arched Portico creates impressive entrance into Foyer, which leads to all areas of gracious home
- Unusual angles and windows highlight formal Living and Dining Rooms
- Expansive Family Room with angled fireplace opens to Covered Lanai, Kitchen and Breakfast Nook
- Dream Kitchen offers every option an owner could want—Breakfast Bar/work island, walk-in Pantry, recipe corner, and Breakfast Lanai
- Master Bedroom opens to private Lanai with a Spa and a plush Master Bath with a whirlpool window tub
- Large Den/Study offers many uses, even doubling as another Bedroom
- Two Bedrooms share a reading alcove and full Bath on second floor
- This home is designed with a slab foundation

FIRST FLOOR — 2,137 SQ. FT.
SECOND FLOOR — 671 SQ. FT.

TOTAL LIVING AREA:
2,808 SQ. FT.

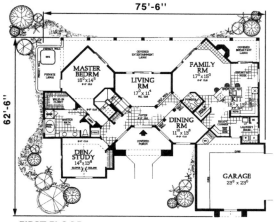

FIRST FLOOR

SECOND FLOOR

A Sense of Stature

Price Code: H

- This plan features:
  - Four bedrooms
  - Three full and one half baths
- A turret and bold double doors add stature to this home
- A bay shaped Study is located in the front of the home
- The impressive Dining Room features a front window
- The unique Living Room has a fireplace and windows that overlook the rear Porch
- The Family Room, Breakfast Nook, and Kitchen are arranged in an open manner
- The first floor Master Bedroom has a decorative ceiling plus his and her closets
- This home is designed with basement and slab foundation options
- Alternate foundation options available at an additional charge. Please call 1-800-235-5700 for more information.

FIRST FLOOR — 2,112 SQ. FT.
SECOND FLOOR — 982 SQ. FT.
BASEMENT — 2,112 SQ. FT.
GARAGE — 650 SQ. FT.

TOTAL LIVING AREA:
3,094 SQ. FT.

WIDTH 67'-1"
DEPTH 65'-10.1"

FIRST FLOOR

SECOND FLOOR

"English Manor" House

Price Code: K

- This plan features:
- — Four bedrooms
- — Two full, one three quarter, and one half baths
- Quarried stone facade enhances Covered Stoop and impressive Entry with a curved staircase
- Private Master Bedroom includes a charming Sitting Area, decorative ceiling, two walk-in closets, and a luxurious Bath
- This home is designed with a basement foundation
- Alternate foundation options available at an additional charge. Please call 1-800-235-5700 for more information.

FIRST FLOOR — 2,813 SQ. FT.
SECOND FLOOR — 1,091 SQ. FT.
GARAGE — 1,028 SQ. FT.

TOTAL LIVING AREA:
3,904 SQ. FT.

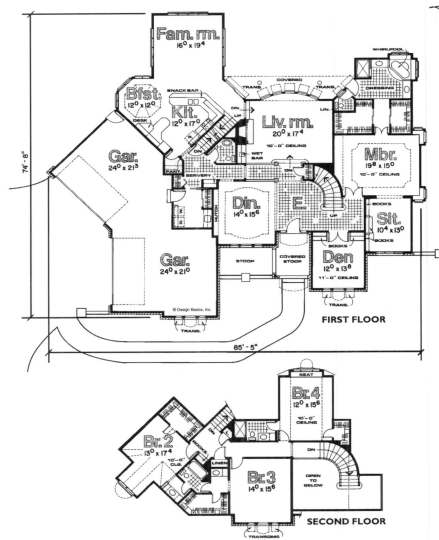

232

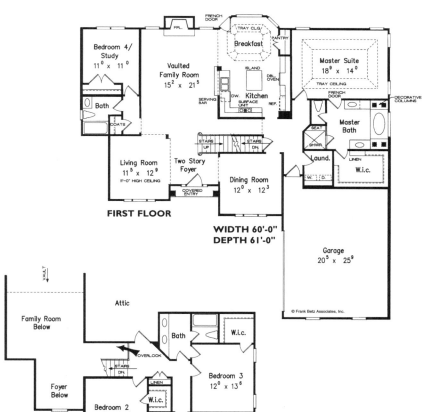

Bedroom 4/ Study 11⁰ x 11⁰

Breakfast

TRAY CLG.

PANTRY

FRENCH DOOR

FPL

Vaulted Family Room 15² x 21⁵

ISLAND

DBL. OVEN

DW. **Kitchen**

SERVING BAR

SURFACE UNIT

REF.

Master Suite 18⁹ x 14⁰

TRAY CEILING

FRENCH DOOR

DECORATIVE COLUMNS

Bath

COATS

SEAT

SHWR.

Master Bath

Living Room 11⁵ x 12⁹ 11'-0" HIGH CEILING

Two Story Foyer

STAIRS UP

STAIRS DN.

Dining Room 12⁰ x 12³

Laund.

W. D.

LINEN

W.i.c.

COVERED ENTRY

FIRST FLOOR

WIDTH 60'-0"
DEPTH 61'-0"

Garage 20⁵ x 25⁹

© Frank Betz Associates, Inc.

VAULT

Family Room Below

Attic

Bath

W.i.c.

OVERLOOK

STAIRS DN.

LINEN

W.i.c.

Bedroom 3 12⁰ x 13⁶

Foyer Below

Bedroom 2 12⁰ x 12³

SECOND FLOOR

Opt. Bonus Room 12⁶ x 19⁵ 10'-0" HIGH CLG.

WINDOW SEAT

WINDOW SEAT

Notable Exterior
Price Code: F

■ This plan features:

— Four bedrooms

— Three full baths

■ Two-story Foyer adds a feeling of volume

■ Family Room topped by vaulted ceiling and accented by a fireplace

■ Private Master Suite with a five-piece Bath and a large walk-in closet

■ Rear Bedroom/Study located close to a full Bath

■ This home is designed with basement, slab, and crawlspace foundation options

FIRST FLOOR — 2,003 SQ. FT.
SECOND FLOOR — 598 SQ. FT.
BONUS ROOM— 321 SQ. FT.
BASEMENT — 2,003 SQ. FT.
GARAGE — 546 SQ. FT.

TOTAL LIVING AREA:
2,601 SQ. FT.

Spectacular Views

Price Code: F

- This plan features:
  — Four bedrooms
  — Two full and one three-quarter baths
- Creates an indoor/outdoor relationship with terrific decks and large glass expanses
- Family Room and Living Room enjoy glassed walls taking in the vistas
- Living Room enhanced by a cathedral ceiling and a warm fireplace
- Dining Room and Kitchen are in an open layout and highlighted by a center cooktop island/snack bar in the Kitchen and large window in the Dining Room
- Master Bedroom enhanced by floor to ceiling windowed area allowing natural light to filter in
- Two additional downstairs Bedrooms, a three-quarter Bath and a Family Room complete the lower floor
- This home is designed with a basement foundation

MAIN FLOOR — 1,707 SQ. FT.
LOWER FLOOR — 901 SQ. FT.

TOTAL LIVING AREA:
2,608 SQ. FT.

MAIN FLOOR

61'-0"

Util. 13-6 x 7-2
Br #2 14 x 9-6
M.Bath
Dining 11-6 x 15
CATH. CLG.
DN.
Kit.
Living 18 x 20
Entry
M. Br 12-6 x 14-6
34'-6"
Deck
Deck
DN.

LOWER FLOOR

Shop 18 x 9
Br #3 11-6 x 10-6
STOR.
UP
Garage 23-6 x 25
WH F
Family 18 x 20
Br #4 11 x 11-2
DECK LINE ABOVE

Magnificent Presence

Price Code: L

- This plan features:
  — Four bedrooms
  — Three full, one three quarter, and one half baths
- Curved staircase leads to elevated two-story Study and Master Suite
- Dining Room is connected to the Kitchen by a Butler's Pantry
- Two-story Living Room has a fireplace and distinctive windows
- Three Bedrooms, a Game Room, and two full Baths on the second floor
- This home is designed with basement and slab foundation options
- Alternate foundation options available at an additional charge. Please call 1-800-235-5700 for more information.

FIRST FLOOR — 2,897 SQ. FT.
SECOND FLOOR — 1,603 SQ. FT.
BASEMENT — 2,897 SQ. FT.
GARAGE — 793 SQ. FT.

TOTAL LIVING AREA:
4,500 SQ. FT.

WIDTH 74'-7"
DEPTH 77'-3"

FIRST FLOOR

SECOND FLOOR

OPTIONAL BASEMENT STAIR LOCATION

234

To order your Blueprints, call 1-800-235-5700

FIRST FLOOR

PORCH

BUILT-IN

FAMILY ROOM
14'-0" X 16'-0"
10'-11" CH

LIVING ROOM
15'-8" X 19'-6"
19'-20" CH

MASTER
BEDROOM
14'-0" X 18'-0"
10' CH

W.I.C.

WHIRLPOOL

BREAKFAST
9'-0" X 12'-0"
10' CH

BUILT-IN

FP

PWDR

MASTER
BATH

HALL

CLO.

DRSG

KITCHEN
15'-6" X 13'-0"

BUTLER'S

GALLERY
10' CH

W.I.C.

10' CH

DINING ROOM
12'-0" X 15'-0"
10' CH

2-STORY
ENTRY
19' CH

PANTRY

UTILITY

UP

PORCH

© Carmichael & Dame

3-CAR GARAGE
21'-4" X 31'-4"
10' CH

76'-7"

64'-11"

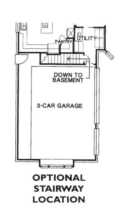

**OPTIONAL
STAIRWAY
LOCATION**

UTILITY

PANTRY

DOWN TO
BASEMENT

3-CAR GARAGE

A Picturesque Setting

Price Code: I

■ This plan features:

— Three bedrooms

— Three full and one half baths

■ The two-story Entry expands into the
Living and Dining Rooms

■ The informal space includes the open
Family Room and Breakfast Nook

■ The Master Bedroom is located on the
main floor

■ The rooms upstairs include a Game
Room, a Study and two secondary
Bedrooms

■ This home is designed with basement
and slab foundation options

■ Alternate foundation options available at
an additional charge. Please call
1-800-235-5700 for more information.

FIRST FLOOR — 2,144 SQ. FT.
SECOND FLOOR — 1,253 SQ. FT.

*TOTAL LIVING AREA:
3,397 SQ. FT.*

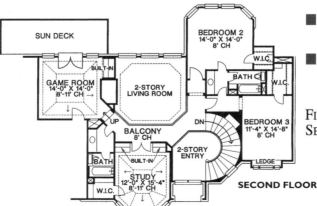

SUN DECK

BUILT-IN

GAME ROOM
14'-0" X 14'-0"
8'-11" CH

2-STORY
LIVING ROOM

BEDROOM 2
14'-0" X 14'-0"
8' CH

W.I.C.

BATH

W.I.C.

UP

BALCONY
8' CH

DN

BEDROOM 3
11'-4" X 14'-8"
8' CH

2-STORY
ENTRY

LEDGE

BATH

BUILT-IN

STUDY
12'-0" X 15'-4"
8'-11" CH

W.I.C.

SECOND FLOOR

Luxury that You Deserve

Price Code: H

- This plan features:
- — Four bedrooms
- — Two full and one three quarter and one half baths
- The Living Room has a see-through fireplace and a wall of windows overlooking the backyard
- French doors lead into a Master Suite which features a private Den and Bath with a whirlpool tub and a glass block shower
- This home is designed with a basement foundation
- Alternate foundation options available at an additional charge. Please call 1-800-235-5700 for more information.

FIRST FLOOR — 2,235 SQ. FT.
SECOND FLOOR — 1,003 SQ. FT.
GARAGE — 740 SQ. FT.
BASEMENT — 2,235 SQ. FT.

TOTAL LIVING AREA:
3,238 SQ. FT.

FIRST FLOOR

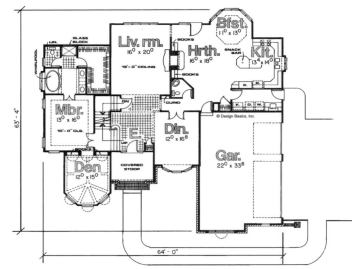

SECOND FLOOR

To order your Blueprints, call 1-800-235-5700

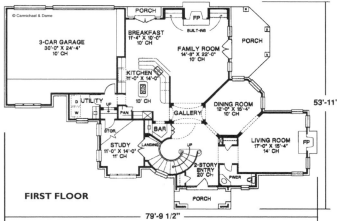

© Carmichael & Dame

3-CAR GARAGE
30'-0" X 24'-4"
10' CH

PORCH

BREAKFAST
11'-4" X 10'-0"
10' CH

FP
BUILT-INS

FAMILY ROOM
14'-8" X 22'-0"
10' CH

PORCH

KITCHEN
11'-0" X 14'-0"
10' CH

UTILITY

PAN

STOR.

BAR

GALLERY

DINING ROOM
12'-0" X 15'-4"
10' CH

53'-11'

STUDY
11'-0" X 14'-0"
11' CH

LANDING

UP

2-STORY
ENTRY
20' CH

LIVING ROOM
17'-0" X 15'-4"
14' CH

FP

PWDR

FIRST FLOOR

PORCH

79'-9 1/2"

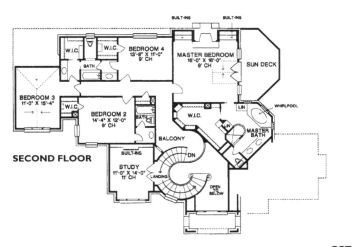

BUILT-INS BUILT-INS

W.I.C. W.I.C.

BATH

BEDROOM 4
13'-8" X 11'-0"
9' CH

MASTER BEDROOM
16'-0" X 16'-0"
9' CH

SUN DECK

BEDROOM 3
11'-0" X 15'-4"

W.I.C.

BEDROOM 2
14'-4" X 12'-0"
9' CH

BATH

LIN

WHIRLPOOL

W.I.C.

LIN

MASTER
BATH

BALCONY

BUILT-INS

SECOND FLOOR

STUDY
11'-0" X 14'-0"
11' CH

LANDING

DN

OPEN
BELOW

DOWN
BASEMENT

**OPTIONAL BASEMENT
ACCESS**

Arches Enhance Style

Price Code: I

■ This plan features:

— Four bedrooms

— Three full and one half baths

■ Living Room is graced by a fireplace and adjoins the Dining Room

■ Family Room has a second fireplace and is open to the Breakfast Nook and Kitchen

■ This plan has four huge Bedrooms and three full Baths upstairs

■ This home is designed with basement and slab foundation options

■ Alternate foundation options available at an additional charge. Please call 1-800-235-5700 for more information.

FIRST FLOOR — 1,786 SQ. FT.
SECOND FLOOR — 1,607 SQ. FT
GARAGE — 682 SQ. FT.

TOTAL LIVING AREA:
3,393 SQ. FT.

Classical Details

Price Code: G

■ This plan features:

— Four bedrooms

— Two full and one half baths

■ Decorative windows and dignified brick exterior combine with classical details to create sophisticated curb appeal

■ The sensible Kitchen provides a large Pantry, two lazy Susans and a large center work island

■ This home is designed with a basement foundation

■ Alternate foundation options available at an additional charge. Please call 1-800-235-5700 for more information.

FIRST FLOOR — 1,469 SQ. FT.
SECOND FLOOR — 1,306 SQ. FT.
BASEMENT — 1,469 SQ. FT.
GARAGE — 814 SQ. FT.

TOTAL LIVING AREA:
2,775 SQ. FT.

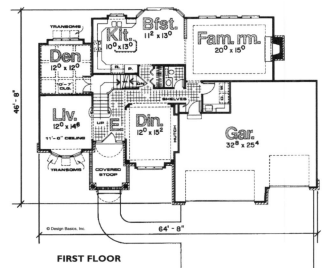

FIRST FLOOR

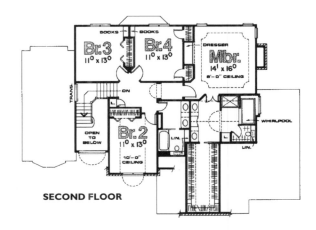

SECOND FLOOR

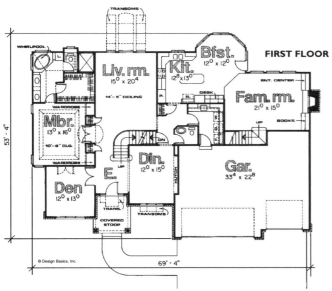

FIRST FLOOR

WHIRLPOOL

TRANSOMS

Liv. rm.
15⁰ x 20⁴

14'-5" CEILING

Bfst.
12⁰ x 12⁰

Kit.
12⁸ x 13⁰

DESK

ENT. CENTER

Fam. rm.
21⁰ x 15⁰

BOOKS

UP

WARDROBE

Mbr.
13⁰ x 16⁰

10'-8" CLG.

WARDROBE

Din.
12⁰ x 15⁰

Gar.
33⁴ x 22⁸

HUTCH

Den
12⁰ x 13⁰

DEN

UP

TRANS.

TRANSOMS

COVERED STOOP

© Design Basics, Inc.

53' - 4"

69' - 4"

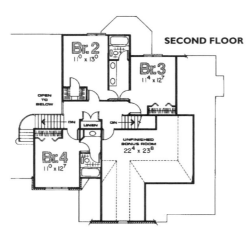

SECOND FLOOR

Br. 2
11⁰ x 13⁰

Br. 3
11⁴ x 12⁷

OPEN TO BELOW

LINEN

DN

DN

UNFINISHED BONUS ROOM
22⁴ x 23⁸

Br. 4
11⁰ x 12⁷

Spacious Living Room
Price Code: H

■ This plan features:

— Four bedrooms

— Three full and one half baths

■ The spacious Living Room has a 14-foot, five-inch ceiling and is accented by large windows

■ The Kitchen/Dinette Area boasts an island, a Pantry and a planning desk

■ The Master Suite includes his and her wardrobes and is topped by a vaulted ceiling

■ This home is designed with a basement foundation

■ Alternate foundation options available at an additional charge. Please call 1-800-235-5700 for more information.

FIRST FLOOR — 2,179 SQ. FT.
SECOND FLOOR — 838 SQ. FT.
BASEMENT — 2,179 SQ. FT.

TOTAL LIVING AREA:
3,017 SQ. FT.

Magnificent Grandeur

Price Code: G

■ This plan features:

— Four bedrooms

— Two full, one three-quarter, and one half baths

■ Decorative ceilings and built-ins enhance the Living Room and the Dining Room

■ The island Kitchen serves the Dining Room and the Breakfast Area with equal ease

■ The Master Bedroom includes a decorative ceiling, a whirlpool tub with a separate shower and a walk-in closet

■ This home is designed with a basement foundation

■ Alternate foundation options available at an additional charge. Please call 1-800-235-5700 for more information.

FIRST FLOOR — 1,972 SQ. FT.
SECOND FLOOR — 893 SQ. FT.

TOTAL LIVING AREA:
2,865 SQ. FT.

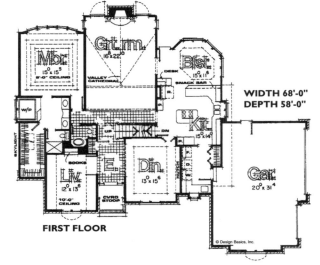

WIDTH 68'-0"
DEPTH 58'-0"

FIRST FLOOR

© Design Basics, Inc.

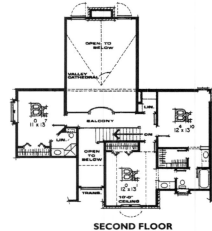

SECOND FLOOR

240

Luxurious Appointments

Price Code: H

- This plan features:
— Five bedrooms
— Four full and one half baths
- Formal areas located conveniently to promote elegant entertaining and family interaction
- Arched openings from the Foyer into the formal Dining Room and the Living Room
- Decorative columns highlighting the entrance to the Breakfast Room
- Two-Story ceiling topping the Family Room, highlighted by a fireplace
- Efficiency emphasized in the island Kitchen with a walk-in Pantry and abundant counter space
- Master Suite with a lavish Bath topped by a vaulted ceiling
- This home is designed with basement and crawlspace foundation options

FIRST FLOOR — 1,527 SQ. FT.
SECOND FLOOR — 1,495 SQ. FT.
BASEMENT — 1,527 SQ. FT.
GARAGE — 440 SQ. FT.

TOTAL LIVING AREA:
3,022 SQ. FT.

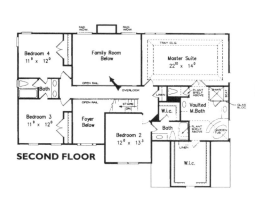

SECOND FLOOR

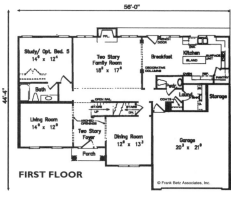

FIRST FLOOR

© Frank Betz Associates, Inc.

Luxurious Master Bedroom

Price Code: L

- This plan features:
— Five bedrooms
— Four full and one half baths
- Master Suite highlights include a fireplace flanked by built-in bookshelves, his and her walk-in closets, a garden tub with decorative columns and a private Covered Porch
- Formal living and dining spaces are defined by pillars and distinctive window designs
- This home is designed with basement and crawlspace foundation options

FIRST FLOOR — 2,095 SQ. FT.
SECOND FLOOR — 1,954 SQ. FT.
GARAGE — 681 SQ. FT.

TOTAL LIVING AREA:
4,049 SQ. FT.

WIDTH 56'-0"
DEPTH 63'-0"

FIRST FLOOR

SECOND FLOOR

© Frank Betz Associates, Inc.

Photography supplied by Carmichael & Dame

Brick Traditional

Price Code: J

- This plan features:
- — Five bedrooms
- — Three full and one half baths
- The stunning exterior of this home is created with brick and large windows
- Inside, the Entry soars to 16 feet
- Both the Living and Family Rooms have rear window walls
- The Kitchen is open to the informal areas of the home
- Upstairs find four Bedrooms and a Study
- This home is designed with basement and slab foundation options
- Alternate foundation options available at an additional charge. Please call 1-800-235-5700 for more information.

FIRST FLOOR — 2,050 SQ. FT.
SECOND FLOOR — 1,467 SQ. FT.
BASEMENT — 2,050 SQ. FT.
GARAGE — 698 SQ. FT.

TOTAL LIVING AREA:
3,517 SQ. FT.

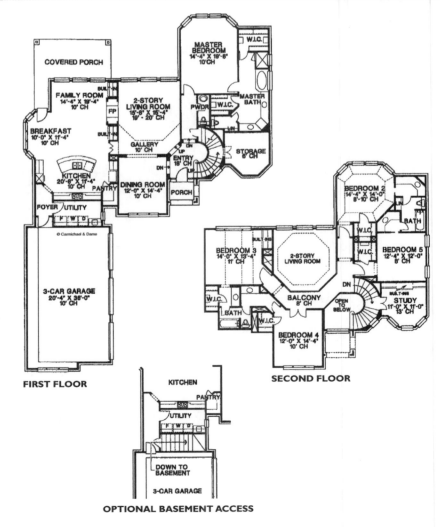

242

WIDTH 66'-0"
DEPTH 66'-0"

Garage
21'-4" x 23'-4"

Wd. Deck
33' x 8'

Cov. Porch
33' x 6'

Util.

Brkfst.
14' x 9'

Great Room
19'-4" x 18'

Ma. Suite
14' x 18'

Hall

Ma. Ba.

Kit.
12' x 12'

Dining
14'-10" x 11'-3"

Ba. 3

Stdy./Gst.Bdrm.
11'-4" x 11'-4"

Foyer

Porch
32' x 6'

FIRST FLOOR

Ba. 2

Dr.

Dr.

Bdrm. 2
11'-6" x 12'

open to below

Bdrm. 3
11'-6" x 12'

SECOND FLOOR

Cottage Influence

Price Code: F

■ This plan features:

— Four bedrooms

— Three full and one half baths

■ Expansive Great Room with focal point fireplace and access to Covered Porch and Deck

■ Cooktop island in Kitchen easily serves Breakfast Bay and formal Dining Room

■ Large Master Suite with access to Covered Porch, walk-in closet, and double-vanity Bath

■ This home is designed with crawlspace and slab foundation options

FIRST FLOOR — 1,916 SQ. FT.
SECOND FLOOR — 617 SQ. FT.
GARAGE — 516 SQ. FT.

TOTAL LIVING AREA:
2,533 SQ. FT.

Statuesque in Appearance

Price Code: F

- ■ This plan features:
  - — Four bedrooms
  - — Two full, one three-quarter, and one half baths
- ■ The formal rooms flank the Entry and provide views to the front
- ■ An angled snack bar in the Kitchen serves the Breakfast Area
- ■ Bedroom 2 is the perfect Guest Suite with its own three-quarter Bath
- ■ His and her walk-in closets and an extravagant bayed whirlpool tub under a cathedral ceiling set the tone in the indulging Master Suite
- ■ A large Bonus Room has the potential to meet the preferences of many
- ■ This home is designed with basement and crawlspace foundation options
- ■ Alternate foundation options available at an additional charge. Please call 1-800-235-5700 for more information.

FIRST FLOOR — 1,333 SQ. FT.
SECOND FLOOR — 1,280 SQ. FT.
BASEMENT — 1,333 SQ. FT.
GARAGE — 687 SQ. FT.

TOTAL LIVING AREA:
2,613 SQ. FT.

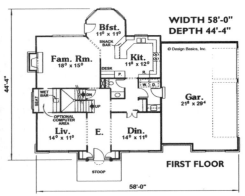

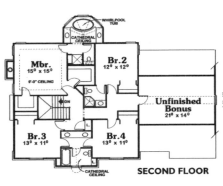

Multiple Gables

Price Code: J

- ■ This plan features:
  - — Three bedrooms
  - — Three full and one half baths
- ■ Impressive Foyer offers dramatic view past the Dining Room and open stairs through the Great Room to the rear yard
- ■ Exquisite columns and detailed ceiling treatments decorate the Dining Room and Great Room
- ■ Gourmet Kitchen with island and snack bar combines with the spacious Breakfast Room and the Hearth Room to create a warm atmosphere
- ■ The Master Suite has a fireplace complemented by a deluxe Dressing Room with whirlpool tub, shower and dual vanity
- ■ This home is designed with a basement foundation

MAIN FLOOR — 3,570 SQ. FT.
LOWER FLOOR — 1,203 SQ. FT.
BONUS — 2,367 SQ. FT.

TOTAL LIVING AREA:
3,570 SQ. FT.

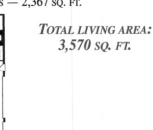

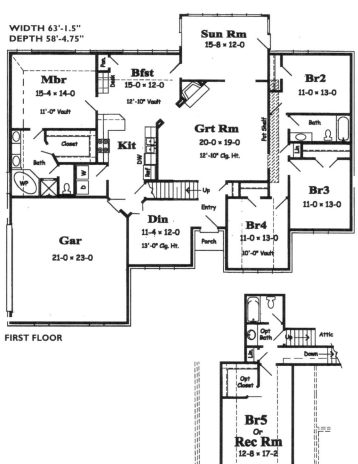

WIDTH 63'-1.5"
DEPTH 58'-4.75"

FIRST FLOOR

Sun Rm
15-8 × 12-0

Mbr
15-4 × 14-0
11'-0" Vault

Bfst
15-0 × 12-0
12'-10" Vault

Br2
11-0 × 13-0

Bath

Pan.
Desk

Closet

Bath

Kit

Grt Rm
20-0 × 19-0
12'-10" Clg. Ht.

DW

Pet Shelf

WP

Ref

Up

Br3
11-0 × 13-0

Entry

Din
11-4 × 12-0
13'-0" Clg. Ht.

Porch

Br4
11-0 × 13-0
10'-0" Vault

Gar
21-0 × 23-0

SECOND FLOOR

Opt
Bath

Up

Attic

Down

Opt
Closet

Br5
Or
Rec Rm
12-8 × 17-2
8' Vault

Family Matters

Price Code: F

■ This plan features:

— Five bedrooms

— Three full baths

■ A beautiful brick exterior is accentuated by double transoms over double windows

■ Big Bedrooms and an oversized Great Room, are designed for a large family

■ Volume ceilings in the Master Suite, Great Room, Dining Room, Breakfast Nook, and Bedroom 4 and 5

■ Three Bathrooms, including a plush Master Bath, with a double vanity

■ This home is designed with a slab foundation

FIRST FLOOR — 2,307 SQ. FT.
SECOND FLOOR — 440 SQ. FT.
GARAGE — 517 SQ. FT.

TOTAL LIVING AREA:
2,747 SQ. FT.

Mansion Mystique

Price Code: K

- **This plan features:**
  — Four bedrooms
  — Four full and one half baths
- A beautiful exterior includes multiple rooflines and a covered Porch
- The Entry includes a curved staircase
- Multi-purpose rooms include a Guest Room/Study and an upstairs Office
- Both the Family Room and the Great Room have fireplaces
- The L-shaped Kitchen opens to the Breakfast Nook
- Upstairs find multiple Bedrooms, Baths, and a bonus space
- This home is designed with a basement foundation

FIRST FLOOR — 2,727 SQ. FT.
SECOND FLOOR — 1,168 SQ. FT.
BONUS — 213 SQ. FT.
BASEMENT — 2,250 SQ. FT.
GARAGE — 984 SQ. FT.

TOTAL LIVING AREA:
3,895 SQ. FT.

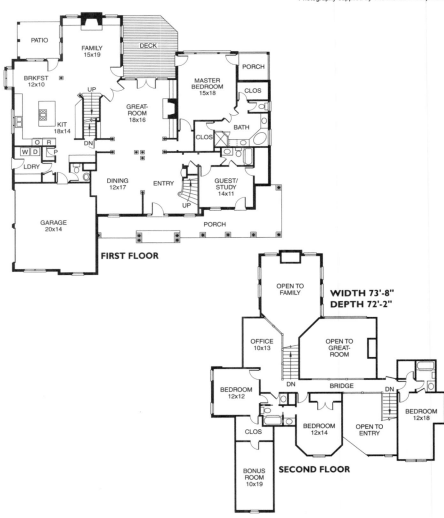

WIDTH 73'-8"
DEPTH 72'-2"

246

To order your Blueprints, call 1-800-235-5700

Everything you need...to Make Your Dream Come True!

Exterior Elevations

Scaled drawings of the front, rear, sides of the home. Information pertaining to the exterior finish materials, roof pitches and exterior height dimensions.

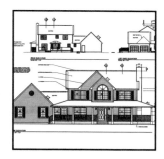

Cabinet Plans

These plans, or in some cases elevations, will detail the layout of the kitchen and bathroom cabinets at a larger scale. Available for most plans.

Typical Wall Section

This section will address insulation, roof components and interior and exterior wall finishes. Your plans will be designed with either 2x4 or 2x6 exterior walls, but most professional contractors can easily adapt the plans to the wall thickness you require.

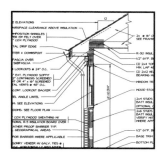

Fireplace Details

If the home you have chosen includes a fireplace, the fireplace detail will show typical methods to construct the firebox, hearth and flue chase for masonry units, or a wood frame chase for a zero-clearance unit. Available for most plans.

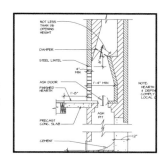

Foundation Plan

These plans will accurately dimension the footprint of your home including load bearing points and beam placement if applicable. The foundation style will vary from plan to plan.

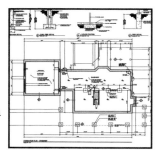

Roof Plan

The information necessary to construct the roof will be included with your home plans. Some plans will reference roof trusses, while many others contain schematic framing plans. These framing plans will indicate the lumber sizes necessary for the rafters and ridgeboards based on the designated roof loads.

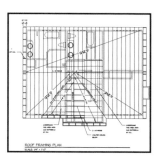

Typical Cross-Section

A cut-away cross-section through the entire home shows your building contractor the exact correlation of construction components at all levels of the house. It will help to clarify the load bearing points from the roof all the way down to the basement. Available for most plans.

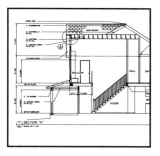

Detailed Floor Plans

The floor plans of your home accurately dimension the positioning of all walls, doors, windows, stairs and permanent fixtures. They will show you the relationship and dimensions of rooms, closets and traffic patterns. The schematic of the electrical layout may be included in the plan.

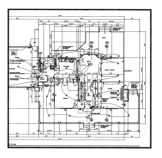

Stair Details

If stairs are an element of the design you have chosen, the plans will show the necessary information to build these, either through a stair cross-section or on the floor plans.

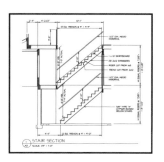

Garlinghouse Options & Extras

Reversed Plans Can Make Your Dream Home Just Right!

You could have exactly the home you want by flipping it end-for-end. Simply order your plans "reversed." We'll send you one full set of mirror-image plans (with the writing backwards) as a master guide for you and your builder.

The remaining sets of your order will come as shown in this book so the dimensions and specifications are easily read on the job site...but most plans in our collection come stamped "reversed" so there is no confusion.

As Shown   Reversed

We can only send reversed plans with multiple-set orders. There is a $50 charge for this service.

Some plans in our collection are available in Right Reading Reverse. Right Reading Reverse plans will show your home in reverse, with the writing on the plan being readable. This easy-to-read format will save you valuable time and money. Please contact our Customer Service Department to check for Right Reading Reverse availability. There is a $135 charge for Right Reading Reverse. **RRR**

Remember To Order Your Materials List

Available at a modest additional charge, the Materials List gives the quantity, dimensions, and specifications for the major materials needed to build your home. You will get faster, more accurate bids from your contractors and building suppliers — and avoid paying for unused materials and waste. Materials Lists are available for all home plans except as otherwise indicated, but can only be ordered with a set of home plans. Due to differences in regional requirements and homeowner or builder preferences... electrical, plumbing and heating/air conditioning equipment specifications are not designed specifically for each plan. **ML**

What Garlinghouse Offers

Home Plan Blueprint Package

By purchasing a multiple set package of blueprints or a vellum from Garlinghouse, you not only receive the physical blueprint documents necessary for construction, but you are also granted a license to build one, and only one, home. You can also make simple modifications, including minor non-structural changes and material substitutions to our design, as long as these changes are made directly on the blueprints purchased from Garlinghouse and no additional copies are made.

Home Plan Vellums

By purchasing vellums for one of our home plans, you receive the same construction drawings found in the blueprints, but printed on vellum paper. Vellums can be erased and are perfect for making design changes. They are also semi-transparent making them easy to duplicate. But most importantly, the purchase of home plan vellums comes with a broader license that allows you to make changes to the design (ie, create a hand drawn or CAD derivative work), to make copies of the plan and to build one home from the plan.

License To Build Additional Homes

With the purchase of a blueprint package or vellums you automatically receive a license to build one home and only one home, respectively. If you want to build more homes than you are licensed to build through your purchase of a plan, then additional licenses may be purchased at reasonable costs from Garlinghouse. Inquire for more information.

Modify Your Favorite Design, Made Easy

#1 Modifying Your Garlinghouse Home Plan

Simple modifications to your dream home, including minor non-structural changes and material substitutions, can be made between you and your builder by marking the changes directly on your blueprints. However, if you are considering making significant changes to your chosen design, we recommend that you use the services of The Garlinghouse Design Staff. We will help take your ideas and turn them into a reality, just the way you want. Here's our procedure!

When you place your Vellum order, you may also request a free Garlinghouse Modification Kit. In this kit, you will receive a red marking pencil, furniture cut-out sheet, ruler, a self addressed mailing label and a form for specifying any additional notes or drawings that will help us understand your design ideas. Mark your desired changes directly on the Vellum drawings. NOTE: Please use only a **red pencil** to mark your desired changes on the Vellum. Then, return the redlined Vellum set in the original box to us.

Important: Please roll the Vellums for shipping, **do not fold.**

We also offer modification estimates. We will provide you with an estimate to draft your changes based on your specific modifications before you purchase the vellums, for a $50 fee. After you receive your estimate, if you decide to have us do the changes, the $50 estimate fee will be deducted from the cost of your modifications. If, however, you choose to use a different service, the $50 estimate fee is non-refundable. (Note: Personal checks cannot be accepted for the estimate.)

Within 5 days of receipt of your plans, you will be contacted by a member of the design staff with an estimate for the design services to draw those changes. A 50% deposit is required before we begin making the actual modifications to your plans.

Once the design changes have been completed to your vellum plan, a representative will call to inform you that your modified Vellum plan is complete and will be shipped as soon as the final payment has been made. For additional information call us at 1-860-659-5667. Please refer to the Modification Pricing Guide for estimated modification costs.

#2 Reproducible Vellums for Local Modification Ease

If you decide not to use Garlinghouse for your modifications, we recommend that you follow our same procedure of purchasing Vellums. You then have the option of using the services of the original designer of the plan, a local professional designer, or architect to make the modifications.

With a Vellum copy of our plans, a design professional can alter the drawings just the way you want, then you can print as many copies of the modified plans as you need to build your house. And, since you have already started with our complete detailed plans, the cost of those expensive professional services will be significantly less than starting from scratch. Refer to the price schedule for Vellum costs.

"How to obtain a construction cost calculation based on labor rates and building material costs in your Zip Code area!"

Why? Do you wish you could quickly find out the building cost for your new home without waiting for a contractor to compile hundreds of bids? Would you like to have a benchmark to compare your contractor(s) bids against? Well, Now You Can!, with Zip-Quote Home Cost Calculator. Zip-Quote is only available for zip code areas within the United States.

How? Our Zip-Quote Home Cost Calculator will enable you to obtain the calculated building cost to construct your new home, based on labor rates and building material costs within your zip code area without the normal delays or hassles usually associated with the bidding process. Zip-Quote can be purchased in two separate formats, an itemized or a bottom line format.

"How does Zip-Quote actually work?" When you call to order, you must choose from the options available for your specific home, in order for us to process your order. Once we receive your Zip-Quote order, we process your specific home plan building materials list through our Home Cost Calculator which contains up-to-date rates for all residential labor trades and building material costs in your zip code area. "The result?" A calculated cost to build your dream home in your zip code area. This calculation will help you (as a consumer or a builder) evaluate your building budget.

All database information for our calculations is furnished by Marshall & Swift L.P. For over 60 years, Marshall & Swift L.P. has been a leading provider of cost data to professionals in all aspects of the construction and remodeling industries.

Option 1- The **Itemized Zip-Quote** is a detailed building material list. Each building material list line item will separately state the labor cost, material cost and equipment cost (if applicable) for the use of that building material in the construction process. This building materials list will be summarized by the individual building categories and will have additional columns where you can enter data from your contractor's estimates for a cost comparison between the different suppliers and contractors who will actually quote you their products and services.

Option 2- The **Bottom Line Zip-Quote** is a one line summarized total cost for the home plan of your choice. This cost calculation is also based on the labor cost, material cost and equipment cost (if applicable) within your local zip code area. Bottom Line Zip-Quote is available for most plans. Please call for availability.

Cost The price of your Itemized Zip-Quote is based upon the pricing schedule of the plan you have selected, in addition to the price of the materials list. Please refer to the pricing schedule on our order form. The price of your initial Bottom Line Zip-Quote is $29.95. Each additional Bottom Line Zip-Quote ordered in conjunction with the initial order is only $14.95. Bottom Line Zip-Quote may be purchased separately and does NOT have to be purchased in conjunction with a home plan order.

FYI An Itemized Zip-Quote Home Cost Calculation can ONLY be purchased in conjunction with a Home Plan order. The Itemized Zip-Quote can not be purchased separately. If you find within 60 days of your order date that you will be unable to build this home, you may then exchange the plans and the materials list towards the price of a new set of plans (see order info pages for plan exchange policy). The Itemized Zip-Quote and the Bottom Line Zip-Quote are NOT returnable. The price of the initial Bottom Line Zip-Quote order can be credited towards the purchase of an Itemized Zip-Quote order, only if available. Additional Bottom Line Zip-Quote orders, within the same order can not be credited. Please call our Customer Service Department for more information. **ZIP**

An Itemized Zip-Quote is available for plans where you see this symbol. **BL**

A Bottom-line Zip-Quote is available for all plans under 4,000 sq. ft. or where you see this symbol.

Please call for current availability.

Some More Information The Itemized and Bottom Line Zip-Quotes give you approximated costs for constructing the particular house in your area. These costs are not exact and are only intended to be used as a preliminary estimate to help determine the affordability of a new home and/or as a guide to evaluate the general competitiveness of actual price quotes obtained through local suppliers and contractors. However, Zip-Quote cost figures should never be relied upon as the only source of information in either case. **Land, landscaping, sewer systems, site work, contractor overhead and profit and other expenses are not included in our building cost figures. Excluding land and landscaping, you may incur an additional 20% to 40% in costs from the original estimate.** Garlinghouse and Marshall & Swift L.P. can not guarantee any level of data accuracy or correctness in a Zip-Quote and disclaim all liability for loss with respect to the same, in excess of the original purchase price of the Zip-Quote product. All Zip-Quote calculations are based upon the actual blueprints and do not reflect any differences or options that may be shown on the published house renderings, floor plans or photographs.

the Garlinghouse company

Order Code No. H2LX6

BEST PLAN VALUE IN THE INDUSTRY!

Order Form

Plan prices guaranteed until 5/1/03 After this date call for updated pricing

_____ foundation

_____ set(s) of blueprints for plan #_____ $_____

_____ Vellum & Modification kit for plan #_____ $_____

_____ Additional set(s) @ $50 each for plan #_____ $_____

_____ Mirror Image Reverse @ $50 each $_____

_____ Right Reading Reverse @ $135 each $_____

_____ Materials list for plan #_____ $_____

_____ Detail Plans @ $19.95 each

     ❏ Construction ❏ Plumbing ❏ Electrical $_____

_____ Bottom line ZIP Quote@$29.95 for plan #_____ $_____

_____ Additional Bottom Line Zip Quote

     @ $14.95 for plan(s) #_____ $_____

     Zip Code where building _____

_____ Itemized ZIP Quote for plan(s) #_____ $_____

Shipping $_____

Subtotal $_____

Sales Tax *(CT residents add 6% sales tax)* $_____

TOTAL AMOUNT ENCLOSED $_____

Send your check, money order or credit card information to:
(No C.O.D.'s Please)

Please submit all United States & Other Nations orders to:
Garlinghouse Company
174 Oakwood Drive
Glastonbury, CT. 06033
CALL: (800) 235-5700 FAX: (860) 659-5692

Please Submit all Canadian plan orders to:
Garlinghouse Company
102 Ellis Street
Penticton, BC V2A 4L5
CALL: (800) 361-7526 FAX: (250) 493-7526

ADDRESS INFORMATION:

NAME: _____

STREET: _____

CITY: _____

STATE: _____ **ZIP:** _____

DAYTIME PHONE: _____

EMAIL ADDRESS: _____

Credit Card Information		
Charge To:	❏ Visa	❏ Mastercard

Card # | | | | | | | | | | | | | | | | |

Signature _____ Exp. _____ / _____

Privacy Statement (please read)

Dear Valued Garlinghouse Customer,

Your privacy is extremely important to us. We'd like to take a little of your time to explain our privacy policy.

As a service to you, we would like to provide your name to companies such as the following:

- Building material manufacturers that we are affiliated with. Who would like to keep you current with their product line and specials.
- Building material retailers who would like to offer you competitive prices to help you save money.
- Financing companies who would like to offer you competitive mortgage rates.

In addition, as our valued customer, we would like to send you newsletters to assist your building experience. *We* would appreciate your feedback with a customer service survey to improve our operations.

You have total control over the use of your contact information. You can let us know exactly how you want to be contacted. Please check all boxes that apply. Thank you.

    ❏ Don't mail
    ❏ Don't call
    ❏ Don't email
    ❏ Only send Garlinghouse newsletters and customer
    ❏ service surveys

In closing, Garlinghouse is committed to providing superior customer service and protection of your privacy. We thank you for your time and consideration.

Sincerely,

James D. McNair III
CEO

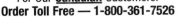

For Our <u>USA</u> Customers:
Order Toll Free — 1-800-235-5700
Monday-Friday 8:00 a.m. to 8:00 p.m. Eastern Time
or FAX your Credit Card order to 1-860-659-5692
All foreign residents call 1-860-659-5667

For Our <u>Canadian</u> Customers:
Order Toll Free — 1-800-361-7526
Monday-Friday 8:00 a.m. to 5:00 p.m. Pacific Time
or FAX your Credit Card order to 1-250-493-7526
Customer Service: 1-250-493-0942

Please have ready: 1. Your credit card number   2. The plan number   3. The order code number ➡ H2LX6

Garlinghouse 2002 Blueprint Price Code Schedule

	1 Set	4 Sets	8 Sets	Vellums	ML	Itemized ZIP Quote
A	$345	$385	$435	$525	$60	$50
B	$375	$415	$465	$555	$60	$50
C	$410	$450	$500	$590	$60	$50
D	$450	$490	$540	$630	$60	$50
E	$495	$535	$585	$675	$70	$60
F	$545	$585	$635	$725	$70	$60
G	$595	$635	$685	$775	$70	$60
H	$640	$680	$730	$820	$70	$60
I	$685	$725	$775	$865	$80	$70
J	$725	$765	$815	$905	$80	$70
K	$765	$805	$855	$945	$80	$70
L	$800	$840	$890	$980	$80	$70

Shipping — (Plans 1-59999)

	1-3 Sets	4-6 Sets	7+ & Vellums
Standard Delivery (UPS 2-Day)	$25.00	$30.00	$35.00
Overnight Delivery	$35.00	$40.00	$45.00

Shipping — (Plans 60000-99999)

	1-3 Sets	4-6 Sets	7+ & Vellums
Ground Delivery (7-10 Days)	$15.00	$20.00	$25.00
Express Delivery (3-5 Days)	$20.00	$25.00	$30.00

International Shipping & Handling

	1-3 Sets	4-6 Sets	7+ & Vellums
Regular Delivery Canada (7-10 Days)	$25.00	$30.00	$35.00
Express Delivery Canada (5-6 Days)	$40.00	$45.00	$50.00
Overseas Delivery Airmail (2-3 Weeks)	$50.00	$60.00	$65.00

Additional sets with original order $50

IMPORTANT INFORMATION TO READ BEFORE YOU PLACE YOUR ORDER

How Many Sets Of Plans Will You Need?

The Standard 8-Set Construction Package

Our experience shows that you'll speed every step of construction and avoid costly building errors by ordering enough sets to go around. Each tradesperson wants a set — the general contractor and all subcontractors; foundation, electrical, plumbing, heating/air conditioning and framers. Don't forget your lending institution, building department and, of course, a set for yourself. * Recommended For Construction *

The Minimum 4-Set Construction Package

If you're comfortable with arduous follow-up, this package can save you a few dollars by giving you the option of passing down plan sets as work progresses. You might have enough copies to go around if work goes exactly as scheduled and no plans are lost or damaged by subcontractors. But for only $60 more, the 8-set package eliminates these worries. *Recommended For Bidding *

The Single Study Set

We offer this set so you can study the blueprints to plan your dream home in detail. They are stamped "study set only-not for construction", and you cannot build a home from them. In pursuant to copyright laws, it is <u>illegal</u> to reproduce any blueprint.

Our Reorder and Exchange Policies:

If you find after your initial purchase that you require additional sets of plans you may purchase them from us at special reorder prices (please call for pricing details) provided that you reorder within 6 months of your original order date. There is a $28 reorder processing fee that is charged on all reorders. For more information on reordering plans please contact our Customer Service Department. Your plans are custom printed especially for you once you place your order. For that reason we cannot accept any returns. If for some reason you find that the plan you have purchased from us does not meet your needs, then you may exchange that plan for any other plan in our collection. We allow you sixty days from your original invoice date to make an exchange. At the time of the exchange you will be charged a processing fee of 20% of the total amount of your original order plus the difference in price between the plans (if applicable) plus the cost to ship the new plans to you. Call our Customer Service Department for more information. Please Note: Reproducible vellums can only be exchanged if they are unopened.

Important Shipping Information

Please refer to the shipping charts on the order form for service availability for your specific plan number. Our delivery service must have a street address or Rural Route Box number — never a post office box. (PLEASE NOTE: Supplying a P.O. Box number <u>only</u> will delay the shipping of your order.) Use a work address if no one is home during the day. Orders being shipped to APO or FPO must go via First Class Mail. Please include the proper postage.

For our International Customers, only Certified bank checks and money orders are accepted and must be payable in U.S. currency. For speed, we ship international orders Air Parcel Post. Please refer to the chart for the correct shipping cost.

Important Canadian Shipping Information

To our friends in Canada, we have a plan design affiliate in Penticton, BC. This relationship will help you avoid the delays and charges associated with shipments from the United States. Moreover, our affiliate is familiar with the building requirements in your community and country. We prefer payments in U.S. Currency. If you, however, are sending Canadian funds please add 45% to the prices of the plans and shipping fees.

An Important Note About Building Code Requirements:

All plans are drawn to conform to one or more of the industry's major national building standards. However, due to the variety of local building regulations, your plan may need to be modified to comply with local requirements — snow loads, energy loads, seismic zones, etc. Do check them fully and consult your local building officials.

A few states require that all building plans used be drawn by an architect registered in that state. While having your plans reviewed and stamped by such an architect may be prudent, laws requiring non-conforming plans like ours to be completely redrawn forces you to unnecessarily pay very large fees. If your state has such a law, we strongly recommend you contact your state representative to protest.

The rendering, floor plans and technical information contained within this publication are not guaranteed to be totally accurate. Consequently, no information from this publication should be used either as a guide to constructing a home or for estimating the cost of building a home. Complete blueprints must be purchased for such purposes.

Index

Option Key

BL Bottom-line Zip Quote **ML** Materials List Available **ZIP** Itemized Zip Quote **RRR** Right Reading Reverse **DUP** Duplex Plan

T O P S E L L I N G
GARAGE PLANS

Save money by Doing-It-Yourself using our Easy-To-Follow plans. Whether you intend to build your own garage or contract it out to a building professional, the Garlinghouse garage plans provide you with everything you need to price out your project and get started. Put our 90+ years of experience to work for you. Order now!!

No. 06016C $86.00

Apartment Garage With One Bedroom

28'

18'

Dining 7-3 x 8-0 | Kit. 11-0 x 8-0 | WH Furn | Bath
DN
Living Rm 14-7 x 9-10 | Bedroom 9-8 x 9-10

- 24' x 28' Overall Dimensions
- 544 Square Foot Apartment
- 12/12 Gable Roof with Dormers
- Slab or Stem Wall Foundation Options

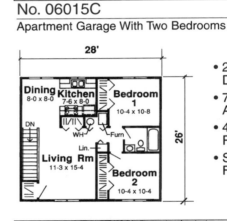

No. 06015C $86.00

Apartment Garage With Two Bedrooms

28'

Dining 8-0 x 8-0 | Kitchen 7-6 x 8-0 | Bedroom 1 10-4 x 10-8
DN
WH
Lin.
Living Rm 11-3 x 15-4 | Furn | Bedroom 2 10-4 x 10-4

26'

- 26' x 28' Overall Dimensions
- 728 Square Foot Apartment
- 4/12 Pitch Gable Roof
- Slab or Stem Wall Foundation Options

No. 06012C $54.00

30' Deep Gable &/or Eave Jumbo Garages

- 4/12 Pitch Gable Roof
- Available Options for Extra Tall Walls, Garage & Personnel Doors, Foundation, Window, & Sidings
- Package contains 4 Different Sizes
- 30' x 28' • 30' x 32' • 30' x 36' • 30' x 40'

No. 06013C $68.00

Two-Car Garage With Mudroom/Breezeway

- Attaches to Any House
- 24' x 24' Eave Entry
- Available Options for Utility Room with Bath, Mudroom, Screened-In Breezeway, Roof, Foundation, Garage & Personnel Doors, Window, & Sidings

No. 06001C $48.00

12', 14' & 16' Wide-Gable 1-Car Garages
- Available Options for Roof, Foundation, Window, Door, & Sidings
- Package contains 8 Different Sizes
- 12' x 20' Mini-Garage   • 14' x 22'   • 16' x 20'   • 16' x 24'
- 14' x 20'   • 14' x 24'   • 16' x 22'   • 16' x 26'

No. 06003C $48.00

24' Wide-Gable 2-Car Garages
- Available Options for Side Shed, Roof, Foundation, Garage & Personnel Doors, Window, & Sidings
- Package contains 5 Different Sizes
- 24' x 22'   • 24' x 24'   • 24' x 26'
- 24' x 28'   • 24' x 32'

No. 06007C $60.00

Gable 2-Car Gambrel Roof Garages
- Interior Rear Stairs to Loft Workshop
- Front Loft Cargo Door With Pulley Lift
- Available Options for Foundation, Garage & Personnel Doors, Window, & Sidings
- Package contains 5 Different Sizes
- 22' x 26' • 22' x 28' • 24' x 28' • 24' x 30' • 24' x 32'

No. 06006C $48.00

22' & 24' Deep Eave 2 & 3-Car Garages
- Can Be Built Stand-Alone or Attached to House
- Available Options for Roof, Foundation, Garage & Personnel Doors, Window, & Sidings
- Package contains 6 Different Sizes
- 22' x 28'   • 22' x 32'   • 24' x 32'
- 22' x 30'   • 24' x 30'   • 24' x 36'

No. 06002C $48.00

20' & 22' Wide-Gable 2-Car Garages
- Available Options for Roof, Foundation, Garage & Personnel Doors, Window, & Sidings
- Package contains 7 Different Sizes
- 20' x 20'   • 20' x 24'   • 22' x 22'   • 22' x 28'
- 20' x 22'   • 20' x 28'   • 22' x 24'

No. 06008C $60.00

Eave 2 & 3-Car Clerestory Roof Garages
- Interior Side Stairs to Loft Workshop
- Available Options for Engine Lift, Foundation, Garage & Personnel Doors, Window, & Sidings
- Package contains 4 Different Sizes
- 24' x 26'   • 24' x 28'   • 24' x 32'   • 24' x 36'

Order Code No: **H2LX6**

Garage Order Form

Please send me 3 complete sets of the following GARAGE PLAN BLUEPRINTS:

Item no. & description	Price
	$ _____
Additional Sets	
(@ $10.00 EACH)	$ _____
Garage Vellum	
(@ $200.00 EACH)	$ _____
Shipping Charges: UPS-$3.75, First Class-$4.50	$ _____
Subtotal:	$ _____
Resident sales tax: CT-6% (NOT REQUIRED FOR OTHER STATES)	$ _____

Total Enclosed: $ _____

My Billing Address is:

Name: _____

Address: _____

City: _____

State: _____ Zip: _____

Daytime Phone No. (_____) _____

My Shipping Address is:

Name: _____

Address: _____
(UPS will not ship to P.O. Boxes)

City: _____

State: _____ Zip: _____

For Faster Service...Charge It!
U.S. & Canada Call
1(800)235-5700

All foreign residents call 1(860)659-5667

MASTERCARD, VISA

Card # | | | | | | | | | | | | | | | |

Signature _____ Exp. ___/___

If paying by credit card, to avoid delays:
billing address must be as it appears on credit card statement

or FAX us at (860) 659-5692

Here's What You Get

- Three complete sets of drawings for each plan ordered
- Detailed step-by-step instructions with easy-to-follow diagrams on how to build your garage (not available with apartment garages)
- For each garage style, a variety of size and garage door configuration options
- Variety of roof styles and/or pitch options for most garages
- Complete materials list
- Choice between three foundation options: Monolithic Slab, Concrete Stem Wall or Concrete Block Stem Wall
- Full framing plans, elevations and cross-sectionals for each garage size and configuration

Garage Plan Blueprints

All blueprint garage plan orders contain three complete sets of drawings with instructions and are priced as listed next to the illustration. **These blueprint garage plans can not be modified.** Additional sets of plans may be obtained for $10.00 each with your original order. UPS shipping is used unless otherwise requested. Please include the proper amount for shipping.

Garage Plan Vellums

By purchasing vellums for one of our garage plans, you receive one vellum set of the same construction drawings found in the blueprints, but printed on vellum paper. Vellums can be erased and are perfect for making design changes. They are also semi-transparent making them easy to duplicate. But most importantly, the purchase of garage plan vellums comes with a broader license that allows you to make changes to the design (ie, create a hand drawn or CAD derivative work), to make copies of the plan and to build one garage from the plan.

the Garlinghouse company

Send your order to:
(With check or money order payable in U.S. funds only)

The Garlinghouse Company
174 Oakwood Drive
Glastonbury, CT 06033

No C.O.D. orders accepted; U.S. funds only. UPS will not ship to Post Office boxes, FPO boxes, APO boxes, Alaska or Hawaii. Canadian orders must be shipped First Class.

Prices subject to change without notice.